MORE PRAISE FOR *GOOD MANNERS FOR NICE PEOPLE WHO SOMETIMES SAY F*CK*

"If you're frequently left gasping by the jaw-dropping social ineptitude of your fellow human beings, or you're guilty of being a rude jackass yourself from time to time, this is the book for you. Alkon doesn't suffer fools lightly, but she also has the gentle wisdom to know that each of us plays the role of the fool sometimes. Armed with fascinating science, great humor, and a preternatural bullshit detector for a mind, she shoots from the hip—and you'll be damn glad she does, too."

—Jesse Bering, associate professor of science communication and author of *Perv*

ALSO BY AMY ALKON

I See Rude People: One woman's battle to beat some manners into impolite society

GOOD MANNERS
— for —
NICE PEOPLE
Who Sometimes Say
F*CK

Amy Alkon

ST. MARTIN'S GRIFFIN
NEW YORK

 For information, address St. Martin's Press, 175 Fifth Avenue, New York, N.Y. 10010.

www.stmartins.com

Library of Congress Cataloging-in-Publication Data

Alkon, Amy.
Good manners for nice people who sometimes say f*ck / Amy Alkon.—First Edition.
pp. cm.
ISBN 978-1-250-03071-9 (trade paperback)
ISBN 978-1-250-03072-6 (e-book)
1. Courtesy—United States. 2. Etiquette—United States. I. Title.
BJ1533.C9A445 2014
395—dc23
2014008115

St. Martin's Griffin books may be purchased for educational, business, or promotional use. For information on bulk purchases, please contact Macmillan Corporate and Premium Sales Department at 1-800-221-7945, extension 5442, write specialmarkets@macmillan.com.

10 9 8 7 6 5 4 3

To Gregg Sutter, whom I can always count on—to do the right thing, to make me laugh, and to make me dinner.

CONTENTS

ACKNOWLEDGMENTS

Writing a book is both a solo undertaking and a team affair, and in the latter department, I've really lucked out.

I'm exceptionally grateful to my editor at St. Martin's, Michael Flamini, for his wisdom, taste, and humor, and for believing in me, and to my wonderful agents and ever-wise and kind guides, Cameron McClure and Ken Sherman.

Danielle Fiorella at St. Martin's gave me the sort of cover that authors usually only dream of, and everyone at St. Martin's has been behind me and this book in a way I am wildly grateful for.

Deep thanks go to: my boyfriend, Gregg Sutter, for all his love and support and for seeing that I always had something to eat besides the aging stack of Costco hamburgers in my freezer; Stef Willen, a talented writer who edited my rough manuscript and had the integrity to fight with me when she knew I was wrong; Etel Sverdlov, who gave me really important and helpful comments in the rough stages; Christina Nihira ("The Velvet Whip") for her loyalty, wisdom, and kindness; copy editor David Yontz, the grammar ninja on this book and my syndicated column, who spots errors few others would and is incredibly good-natured when I (frequently) resort to this Elmore Leonard-ism: "When proper usage gets in the way, it may have to go."

I so appreciate the generosity of those who read and gave me notes on my entire manuscript—anthropologist A.J. Figueredo, bioengineer Barbara Oakley, and biographer David Rensin. Thank you also to economist Tamas David-Barrett, who read several chapters that relate to his and Robin Dunbar's research. And thanks to friends and family who read and commented on various chapters: Debbie Levin, Erika, Ruth Waytz, Christina Nihira, DB Cooper, and my incisive, wise, and wacky sister, Caroline Belli.

I'm also extremely grateful to the members of the Human Behavior and Evolution Society, the NorthEastern Evolutionary Psychology Society, and the Applied Evolutionary Psychology Society, who have, for over a decade, been warm, welcoming, and helpful to me in my mission to turn their research into "science news people can use."

This book was helped into being in part by the generosity, friendship, and support of a number of people in my life: Kate Coe; Sandra Tsing-Loh; Patt Morrison; John Phillips; Matthew Pirnazar; Marjorie Braman; Dee Dee DeBartlo; Andrea Grossman; free speech defender Marc J. Randazza; economist Robert H. Frank; Jackie Danicki; my blog commenter regulars; Maret Orliss, Ann Binney, and all the Los Angeles Times Festival of Books peeps; my New York family, the Housers; my Paris family, Mark, Chantal, Pierre, and Emily; and Linda and Linda at 18th Street Coffeehouse, who are wonderful to writers and ban cellboors.

And, finally, thank you to all of you readers who have bought this book and *I See Rude People*, and who do your part to make the world a less rude and more warm, welcoming, and amusing place for all of us.

GOOD MANNERS FOR NICE PEOPLE WHO SOMETIMES SAY F*CK

— 1 —

I DON'T CARE WHERE YOU PUT THE FORK

(as long as you don't stab anybody in the eye with it)

This is not an etiquette book, filled with prissy codes of conduct to help you fit in to upper-class society (or at least passably fake it), and I am nobody's idea of an etiquette auntie. I don't know the correct way to introduce an ambassador or address a wedding invite to a divorcée, and I'm not sure where to put the water glasses, other than "on the table." I kept this to myself when I got a call from a TV producer from one of the national morning shows. She had seen me in a thirty-second bit about civility on the *Today* show, loved that I wasn't the typical fusty etiquette expert, and—wow—wanted me to fly to New York to be the featured expert in a segment on "manners and civility at the holidays."

"We'll start with the table," she said. "How to set it and how to properly serve the turkey."

"Fantastic!" I lied—same as I would've if she'd asked me to come on national TV and stick my head up a horse's ass to look for lost watches.

I do have a grasp on certain table manners basics, like that you shouldn't lick your plate clean unless there's a power outage or you're dining with the blind, but I'm basically about as domestic as a golden retriever. I don't cook; I heat. My dining room table is piled with books and papers. When my boyfriend makes me dinner, we eat balancing our plates on our legs while sitting on my couch. (Some men fantasize about kinky things to do in bed; he just wants to dine on a flat surface before we're fed through tubes at The Home.)

My domestic failings aside, this was national TV, I needed to sell my book, *I See Rude People*, and I had a classy friend I could hit up for remedial table-setting and turkey-serving lessons. Of course, what I wanted to go on TV and say is what I actually think: What really matters isn't how you set the table or serve the turkey but whether you're nice to people while you're doing it.

Two days before I was to board the plane to New York (on a nonrefundable ticket the network asked my publisher to pay for), I called the producer to double-check that I was prepared for my segment. "Uh . . . um . . . I'll call you back in five minutes from my desk," she said, and then she hung up. Two and a half hours later, I got an e-mail:

> Subject: Saturday
> In a message dated 12/8/10 12:22:01 PM,
> Producer@unnamednetworkmorningshow.com writes:
>
> I just spoke to my executive producer who already had someone in mind for the segment. I am so sorry!
>
> And I am really enthused about you and what you have to say, so let's get you on the next time we have an etiquette segment.
>
> Producer at unnamed network

Of course, I never heard from her again. (Out of guilt, people who've done crappy things to you tend to treat you like you've done something crappy to them.) On the bright side, they'd dumped me from the segment while I was still at home in Los Angeles, unlike a California author friend of mine who learned she'd been given the heave-ho when she logged on to her flight's Wi-Fi over the Kansas cornfields.

Now, nobody owes me or anybody a spot on television, but when you've invited somebody to come on your show (especially your show on civility!), I do think you owe it to them to make sure you want them—and ideally, before they've booked a flight across the country on somebody else's dime. At the very least, when these mistakes are made, you could work your way past that "*Eeeuw*, cooties!" feeling we get about somebody we've wronged and do something to make it up to them instead of just saying you will.

This experience got me thinking about how simple it actually is to treat other people well. Life is hardly one long Princess Cruise for any of us, and there are times when you'll have to fire or disappoint somebody. But at the root of manners is empathy. When you're unsure of what to say or do, there's a really easy guideline, and it's asking yourself, *Hey, self! How would I feel if somebody did that to me?*

If everybody lived by this "Do Unto Others" rule—a beautifully simple rule we were supposed to learn in Kindergarten 101—I could probably publish this book as a twenty-page pamphlet. But so many people these days seem to be patterning their behavior on another simple rule, the "Up Yours" rule—"screw you if you don't like it." I lamented this behavioral shift in a *Los Angeles Times* op-ed featuring a mother flying with her toddler and a blasé attitude about his shrieking for over an hour before takeoff—so loudly that the safety announcements couldn't be heard.

> More and more, we're all victims of these many small muggings every day. Our perp doesn't wear a ski mask or carry a gun; he wears Dockers and shouts into his

iPhone in the line behind us at Starbucks, streaming his dull life into our brains, never considering for a moment whether our attention belongs to him. These little acts of social thuggery are inconsequential in and of themselves, but they add up—wearing away at our patience and good nature and making our daily lives feel like one big wrestling smackdown.

The good news is, we *can* dial back the rudeness and change the way we all relate to one another, and we really need to, before rudeness becomes any more of a norm. That's why I've written this book, a manners book for regular people. The term "nice people who sometimes say f*ck" describes people (like me and maybe you) who are well-meaning but imperfect, who sometimes lose their cool but try to be better the next time around, who sometimes swear (and maybe even enjoy it) but take care not to do it around anybody's great-aunt or four-year-old.

In the pages that follow, I lay out my science-based theory that we're experiencing more rudeness than ever because we recently lost the constraints on our behavior that were in place for millions of years of human history. I explain how we can reimpose those constraints and then tell you how not to be one of the rudewads and give you ways to stand up to the people who are.

Much of this surge in rudeness we're experiencing is a consequence of life in The New Wild West, the world that technology made. Technology itself doesn't cause the rudeness. But technological advances have led to sweeping social change, removing some of the consequences of being rude, especially in the past fifteen years, with so many people living states or continents apart from their families and friends, often spending their days in a swarm of strangers, and being both more and less connected than ever through cell phones, Facebook, Twitter, and Skype.

This book helps you take on and stop rudeness in these techno-spheres and other largely unregulated areas of our lives, such as our neighborhoods, where our society's vastness and transience contribute to all sorts of piggy behavior in both public and private space. I use the term "unregulated" because there's no cop you can call when somebody blogs what was supposed to be a private e-mail or when the lady in the apartment over yours spends the entire evening tap-dancing across her hardwood. To help you prevent situations like these and the cascade of miseries that can ensue, I map out ways for you to preemptively restrain the rude and solutions for when they start acting out.

In how I do this and in the advice I include, *Good Manners for Nice People Who Sometimes Say F*ck* sharply departs from the traditional manners advice books. Except for a few "in case you were raised by coyotes" tips on basic table manners, I've omitted picky etiquette stuff I'd only read at gunpoint, such as the correct way for married people to monogram their towels (a question which, per Google, is covered by a mere 19,400,000 web pages). Also, as I note in the "Eating, Drinking, Socializing" chapter, quite a bit of the advice given by traditional etiquette aunties is rather arbitrary, which is why one etiquette auntie advises that a lady may apply lipstick at the dinner table and another considers it an act only somewhat less taboo than squatting and taking a pee in the rosebushes. You're simply supposed to memorize the particular auntie's rules, and if you take issue with any, well, refer back to "Because I'm the mom!"

I don't think that's good enough. So, in every chapter, I've laid out reasons, based in behavioral science, for *why* we should behave in certain ways. The science behind and throughout much of this book not only provides a foundation for the guidelines within but also gives you a framework so you can figure things out for yourself in the moment and answer any questions that aren't addressed here.

And finally, in addition to all the advice in this book, I've included stories and photos to give you that wonderfully satisfying feeling I call "rudenfreude"—the joy of seeing those who abuse the rest of us called out for what tiny sociopathic little tyrants they are. To borrow from Gandhi, who was asked what he thought of Western civilization: "I think it would be a good idea."

— 2 —

WE'RE RUDE BECAUSE WE LIVE IN SOCIETIES TOO BIG FOR OUR BRAINS

The science of stopping the rude

It was around the year 2000 when I started feeling that people were suddenly ruder than ever—and not just in Los Angeles, where I live, but back in the Midwestern decency belt, where I grew up, and all across the USA. By 2008, I noticed that everybody, everywhere, seemed to be grousing about how the world had become a much ruder place and speculating about why. Many pointed the finger at the permissive parenting of kids these days—conveniently forgetting that the last driver who vigorously flipped them the bird was some wizened old man. Pundits, especially, were quick to blame Scapegoat 2.0, technology: "It's all those cell phones" or "It's the Internet; it alienates people." Oh, right—when it isn't functioning as the single most connective force in human history. And sorry, all you cell phone blamers, but iPhones don't leap out of people's pockets and purses, put themselves on speaker, and float around the grocery store barking into the ears of everybody shopping.

To make meaningful headway in stopping rudeness, we need to understand why we're rude. I'd been attending psychology and evolutionary psychology conferences and referencing sex- and mating-related journal articles in my syndicated love advice column. I expanded my focus to topics like reciprocal altruism (you scratch my back, I'll scratch yours-ism) and compared how ancestral humans lived with how we're living today. Eventually, I came to a stunning conclusion:

> We're rude because we live in societies too big for our brains.

RUDENESS IS THE HUMAN CONDITION

Although we're experiencing more rudeness these days, we haven't really changed; our environment has. Evolutionary psychologists Leda Cosmides and John Tooby, in their online primer on evolutionary psychology, explain, "Our modern skulls house a Stone Age mind," meaning that we're living in the twenty-first century with brains largely adapted to solve prehistoric hunter-gatherers' day-to-day mating and survival problems. Their challenges included finding mates, hunting animals, gathering plants to eat, negotiating fair treatment, defending against aggression, raising children, and choosing an optimal habitat. Sometimes the most sensible behavior for ancestral times can be a glaring mismatch in our modern world, but the adaptations guiding all of these tasks are built of what Cosmides and Tooby describe as "complex computational machinery." Because of that complexity and because even relatively simple changes in our brain's circuitry can take tens of thousands of years, it's not like we can just say to our genes, "Hey, it's the twenty-first century; get with the program!" Cosmides and Tooby give the example that "it is easier for us to learn to fear snakes" than electrical sockets, even though sockets pose a larger threat than snakes in most American communities.[1]

We do continue to evolve; the ability to digest lactose (the sugar

---

[1] It actually seems to be a myth that we are born with a fear of snakes, according to research on babies by developmental psychologist Vanessa LoBue and her colleagues. We're just—*eek*!—fast learners.

in cow's milk), an adaptation in some of us since the advent of dairy farming, perhaps 10,000 years ago, is just one example of that. But, most of the psychology guiding how we approach modern life comes from adaptations to far earlier environments. Take our desire for sweets. We evolved a malnutrition-combating lust for sugary food when we couldn't be sure where our next handful of grubs was coming from—back when eating sweets meant nibbling a handful of vitamin-rich berries off a bush. This sugar-lust is still with us—but you can now drive to a warehouse megamart, have them bring twelve cubic feet of chocolate-covered doughnuts out to your car on a forklift, and then mow through them like you can't be sure where your next handful of grubs is coming from.

Our brains are especially unprepared for suburban sprawl. The problem seems to be the size of our neocortex, the brain's reasoning and communication department. British anthropologist Robin Dunbar noticed that in various animals, neocortex size corresponded to the maximum number of others of their species they could associate with without chaos and violence breaking out. Dunbar looked at the human neocortex size and predicted that humans would have the capacity to manage social interaction in societies with a maximum of 150 people (148.7, to be exact).

Looking to test his prediction, Dunbar poked around human history and found the 150-person group size everywhere—in archeological evidence of hunter-gatherer societies and in 21 hunter-gatherer societies still in existence. (The average group size was 148.4.) One hundred fifty was the population size of villages in traditional farming societies and the size of most military units from Roman times on, and it even showed up in a study of the number of people other people have on their Christmas card list (a mean of 154). Dunbar and other researchers who have done studies on social networking also find that people have, on average, about 150 Facebook friends.

Whatever the exact limit of human social relationships, Dunbar notes that sociologists have long recognized that there's something unmanageable about groups of more than 150 to 200. Bill Gore, the founder of the company that makes the waterproof and breathable fabric GORE-TEX, finds that there's a "precipitous drop in cooperation" when everyone in a group no longer "knows" everyone else, so he limits occupancy in his plants to 200 people. When a plant reaches that occupancy limit, he opens another. The Hutterites, a fundamentalist religious sect in the US and Canada, regard 150 as the maximum size of their communities. "They explicitly state that when the number of individuals is larger than 150, it becomes difficult to control their behaviour by means of peer pressure alone," Dunbar writes in *Grooming, Gossip, and the Evolution of Language*. "Rather than create a police force, they prefer to split the community."

Of course, there would have been no need for a police force back in the Stone Age. In a small band of people who all know one another, piggish behavior like grabbing more than one's fair share of a resource would have been extremely risky, possibly leading to being expelled and forced to go it alone in the wilderness—very likely a death sentence back in an ancestral landscape not exactly flush with 7-Elevens and couchsurfing opportunities. This would have been a powerful force for keeping would-be rudesters in line.

It all started to become clear to me: We're experiencing more rudeness because we've lost the constraints on our behavior that we've had in place for millions of years. We didn't evolve to be around strangers and aren't psychologically equipped to live in a world filled with them, yet that's exactly how we're living—in vast strangeropolises, where it's possible to go an entire day or days without running into anybody we know.

You can behave terribly to strangers and have a good chance of getting away with it because you'll probably never see your victims again. If, on the other hand, that's your neighbor driving behind you and you flip him off, you're likely to find a Mount Whitney–sized pile of dog poop on your front walk the next morning.

Being around people you know doesn't just deter rude behavior; it promotes neighborly behavior. In a small, finite community, reputation is a major concern. Even if you aren't exactly fond of Mrs. Jones, you may need her to help you or vouch for you at some point, or vice versa, and strained relations will probably reflect badly on both of you, so you both act neighborly. The motivation may be selfish, but the end result is a community of people who treat one another better.

Living in a world of strangers is a very recent development. In the first half of the twentieth century, it was still common for people to be born and die in the same house, next to houses of others doing the same. The shift to a more transient society got kicked off in the 1950s, with the building of the interstate highways. After airline deregulation in the 70s, relocating thousands of miles away suddenly meant living only a few hours and a few hundred dollars away. The growth of cheap or free long distance and the Internet further shrank the miles, and it became common for people to live great distances from their friends and relatives. At the same time, people's working lives began becoming increasingly unstable. Being employed by one company all the way through retirement—or even having a single career—is now a quaint situation mainly seen in black-and-white movies. These days, a family might stay a year in one house and then move thousands of miles to another, and another. It hardly seems worth it to get to know the neighbors.

GETTING THE RUDE OUT

We can't turn back the clock to a world where we all live in small villages and everybody knows everybody and the blacksmith. What we can do is take steps to re-create some of the constraints and benefits of the small groupings we evolved to live in. This may sound like an enormous undertaking, but it's actually not. In fact, we could dial back a lot of the ME FIRST!/SCREW YOU! meanness permeating our society if we do just three things:

- Stand up to the rude.
- Expose the rude.
- Treat strangers like neighbors.

Most people aren't comfortable standing up to the rude. That's totally understandable. Because humans didn't evolve to be around strangers, when someone we don't know is abusing the rest of us, the course of action suggested by our genes is something along the lines of "Page Not Found." There are some people, however, who can't help but say something on behalf of the group or another person they see being taken advantage of. I'm one of them. In economist-speak, I'm a "costly punisher," someone who gets outraged at injustice they perceive and is compelled to go after wrongdoers, very possibly incurring some serious personal costs in the process.

Say, for example, I ask somebody at the movies to stop yammering on their phone. They're unlikely to thank me warmly or cut me in on their lottery winnings. They may even stab me in the neck with a turkey baster, as did the boyfriend of a phone-yammering woman whom some movie theater patron in Orange County, California, asked to pipe down. (The patron survived; the turkey baster's in an evidence locker; the slasher's doing forty-plus years in the pen.)

Costly punishment has yet to be that costly for me—maybe because I'm a good judge of character or maybe because I'm just lucky and a fast runner. The truth is, I don't speak up to just anyone. If somebody being rude looks armed or crazy, I curse them silently and wish them a bad case of genital itching. But, in general, my ire at the rude blithely taking advantage of the rest of us overwhelms my fear of being gutted with a kitchen implement, and has ever since I started looking at rudeness for what it really is: theft.

If somebody steals your wallet, it's a physical thing that's there and then gone, so you get that you've been robbed. The rude, on the other hand, are stealing valuable intangibles like your attention (in the case of cell phone shouters who privatize public space as their own). When somebody parks straddling the two spaces behind the dry cleaner—forcing you to drive around and hunt for a spot at a meter—they're stealing your time and peace of mind. Rude neighbors who blast music at 2 a.m. are stealing your good night's sleep and maybe even your life and others', should you drowse off behind the wheel and take out a school bus. Letting the rude get away with robbing you emboldens them to keep robbing you—and the rest of us. We all need to start identifying the rude as the thieves they are, which is what it will take for more people to get mad enough to get up on their hind legs and refuse to be victimized.

Exposing rude behavior to a wide audience is particularly important. In the modern strangerhood, when someone's abusing a person or group of people they don't know and won't see again, concerns about what it will do to their reputation are pretty much moot. We can change that through a form of positive shaming that I call "webslapping"—yanking away the anonymity of the rude by discreetly shooting a photo or cell phone video of them in action and uploading it to the Internet. (Yes, ironically, the road back to the civility of the 150-person village goes straight through the Global Village.)

Webslapping is typically the best solution when somebody's egregiously rude—when whatever they're doing reflects such a sense of entitlement that asking them to be more considerate will likely only result in their acting more rudely out of spite. Even if the particular rudester never learns of their ignominious star turn on the Internet, the fear of being similarly exposed should deter other rude people from acting assholishly to the rest of us. We may have lost the built-in peer pressure of a tiny world of people who all know one another, but there's a new sheriff out there, and it's the YouTube video gone viral.

Of course, most people probably aren't going to shoot and post a video, but there is something we all can do, and that's to make a daily effort to treat strangers like neighbors: smile at the guy passing us on the sidewalk, say hello to the cashier, do the small kindnesses that we would for somebody we know.

Once you start, you'll see that this not only makes other people feel good but makes you feel good, too. As I explain in detail in the final chapter, "Trickle-Down Humanity," it turns out that it's actually in our self-interest to do kind acts for others. Research by positive psychologist Sonja Lyubomirsky suggests that being generous to others is one of the main ways (along with expressing gratitude) that we can increase our happiness. Showing another person a little generosity of spirit is also likely to put them in the spirit to "pay it forward" to people they encounter . . . and so on, and so on. The way I see it, a bare minimum of one kind act a day should be our self-imposed cover charge for living in this world. We get the society we create—or the society we let happen to us.

— 3 —

COMMUNICATING

I ran into a guy I hadn't seen for a while, and he told me he'd reunited with a former girlfriend and they'd gotten married. Life was great, he said, except for a few things he needed her to change. Six things, in fact. He opened his wallet and proudly presented me with a business card with some writing in ink on the back. In small, neat print, it said:

1. Quit smoking.
2. I get my Lexus back, and you drive your Jeep.
3. No dogs.
4. Tidy up the kitchen when you make a mess.
5. Get a job instead of just living off your inheritance.

(I can't remember the sixth.)

He said it was a list of demands he'd given his new wife. Handed to her. On that very business card.

Surely, he was kidding.

He wasn't.

"Um . . . how did she take it?" I asked.

"She stopped talking to me for a week."

YAPPING DANGEROUSLY

With a little forethought, we can usually predict the effect that something we say or write will have on another person, yet apparently rational and intelligent adults pull pudding-brained stunts like sticking a business card with a "must don't" list in their wife's face and demanding she comply. Free speech *is* an important right. In the words of that Aristotle of episodic television, Abe Vigoda, guesting on *The Rockford Files*, "Everyone gets to work their mouth; that's the American way." Interpersonally, however, things tend to go better if we recognize that merely having a thought isn't reason enough to release it into the atmosphere and if we apply what I see as the three essentials for getting through to people. The Big Three are:

- Listening
- Empathy
- Dignity

Listening and Empathy: Are you communicating or just pelting somebody with words?

Fran Lebowitz laid bare the reality of many people's approach to conversation: "The opposite of talking isn't listening. The opposite of talking is waiting."[2]

The sorry truth is, even waiting is sometimes too much for us. And by "us," I mean me. Let's just say I was reminded that I had listening issues when my boyfriend was forced to interrupt my interrupting him with "Hello? Gregg now has the talking stick!"

I've improved a lot in the listening department thanks to the thinking of Mark Goulston, an LA–based psychiatrist, business

---

[2] *Social Studies*, by Fran Lebowitz, Random House, 1981. But pretty much all Fran Lebowitz is worth reading.

coach, and hostage-negotiation trainer who had an epiphany about how to get through to people—how much it means to them to be *understood*—which he wrote about in a 2006 *Los Angeles Times* op-ed. Goulston had a session scheduled with a despondent female patient who, before being referred to him, had made multiple suicide attempts and been institutionalized for depression. He feared that he was failing her. In six months of sessions with him, the woman rarely spoke and had yet to even make eye contact with him, instead staring off to his left or right.

By the time he started his session with her, he had been up for thirty-six hours evaluating the mental condition of patients in various LA emergency rooms. He was so blisteringly exhausted that at one point, his office furniture appeared to be melting and everything seemed to go drab and colorless.

He worried that he might be having a stroke or seizure—until he suddenly had the notion that he was seeing the world through the depressed woman's eyes, as filtered by her despair. "I never knew it was so bad," he blurted out to her. "And I can't help you kill yourself, but if you do, I will still think well of you, I'll miss you, and maybe I'll understand why you needed to."

Goulston was horrified that he'd basically given the woman permission to off herself, but for the first time, she met eyes with him, giving him a funny look, smiling slightly. "If you can really understand why I might need to kill myself," she told him, "maybe I won't have to." The woman, in time, went on to recover, get married, have two children, get a degree in psychology, and become a therapist herself, and Goulston came to recognize the value of hearing people "from their inside out" rather than from his "intellectual understanding in."

Of course, we've all heard the advice that we *should* listen a kajillion times before, but Goulston taps into the nuances of *how* to listen—and why. He explains in his book *Just Listen* that almost all communication is an effort to persuade people, whether we want them to give us a job, agree to a date, or just find us witty. We think we persuade people by using reason and facts. But, Goulston explains, they won't hear our reasoning unless we connect with them—ask them about themselves, truly listen to them, and make them feel heard, valued, and *understood*. This breaks down their resistance. They can stop fighting us off and relax, and it's only then that they can hear what we're saying, consider it, and maybe come around to doing what we want them to do.

Empathy is essential to the listening process—putting yourself in the other person's shoes and then making them feel "felt," as Goulston puts it, by letting them know that you get how they feel.[3] For example, when speaking to somebody who seems at the end of their rope, he says things like, "I bet you feel that nobody understands how hard it is when you have to (whatever it is that they have to do)." He got the antagonistic CEO of a company in trouble to open up by saying, "You've been burned before, haven't you?" (These aren't canned responses on Goulston's part; he's paying attention and doing his best to sense what they're feeling.)

Even if you guess wrong about what somebody's going through, by asking yourself *What is it like to be that person right now?* and by attaching an emotion to how you *think* they're feeling, you show them that you care about their feelings and you'll be more likely to get them to open up to you in response. Once they do, you need to put in the effort to *really listen*—in a heartfelt way, with a mind as open as you can make it; you can't just

[3] There's debate among researchers about how to define empathy. In this book, I go with social psychologist Martin Hoffman's 2000 definition: "Psychological processes that make a person have feelings that are more congruent with another's situation than with his own situation." This means you don't have to have *the exact same feeling* as the person you're empathizing with. As the *Stanford Encyclopedia of Philosophy* explains Hoffman's definition, empathizing could just mean "feeling sad when seeing a child who plays joyfully but who does not know that (he) has been diagnosed with a serious illness."

cock an ear in the direction of their moving mouth and ride on your assumptions.

Because our default position is *ME! ME! ME!*, drawing people out and truly listening to them will probably take preplanning—reviewing these steps, resolving to use them, and reminding yourself to do it. I put Goulston's advice into practice in the weeks just before and after I had him on my weekly radio show, and then I mostly reverted to being the unrelenting self-promoter I too often was when meeting new people.

I didn't do this because I have a huge ego. Like many writers, I've seen some tough times. When I was in my twenties and living in New York, things once got so bad that I couldn't afford both rent and a bed, and for about six months, I ended up sleeping on a door laid across two milk crates. (The fond way some people reminisce about their first car, I look back on the first mattress of my adult life.) Out of fear that I'd end up eating cat food at eighty (or fifty), there was always part of me—my inner PR department—that was never off duty; it was always looking to persuade *somebody* to hire me for *something*.

I wanted to change this, so a few years ago, I stuck a Post-it note on my bathroom mirror that said just "Goulston: Listen!" Days later, when heading off to an annual party for LA journalists, bloggers, and authors, I vowed to say as little as possible about myself all evening—to only briefly answer questions when asked. The difference in the sort of time I had, in how I connected with people, and how interesting and fun the evening was, was stark—so stark that it became a turning point. Now I don't have to try to shut up and listen; I *want* to listen and do.

Getting in the habit of listening socially has helped remind me in stressful situations to muster the self-control to listen and communicate instead of just barking out my points. This isn't to say I always succeed, but ultimately, I've found that being a better listener makes me not only more persuasive but a better friend, a better girlfriend, and less likely to give new people I meet the impression that I'm looking to strap them down, put their head in a vise, and force them to hear me talk for days.

Dignity: The value in making people feel valued.

Although I like to joke that I'm not violent, just hostile, I sometimes feel the urge to take a Nerf bat to passing strangers. I'll be walking around my neighborhood, see some person walking toward me, and I smile and say hello. People mostly say hello, smile, or give a little nod. But now and then, somebody will just walk on, stone-faced, saying nothing.

I'm immediately enraged. I continue on my way, but I long to run after the person, get in their face, and jeer, "Oh, was 'hi' too big a word for you to squeeze out?! A little civility too much for you, ASSFACE?!" (I do love combining calls for civility with words like "ASSFACE.")

And yes, I get that my feelings are out of proportion with the actual offense—just some stranger failing to acknowledge my greeting. And who knows—maybe they're deeply introverted or their dog died and they're lost in thought. But such a minor offense bites unexpectedly hard because it's a violation of our dignity—the sense of well-being we have when we're treated as if we have value.

Psychologist Donna Hicks, a Harvard University conflict resolution specialist who has mediated entrenched disputes in the Middle East, Central America, and Northern Ireland, finds that fostering dignity is fundamental to dispute resolution. In *Dignity: Its Essential Role in Resolving Conflict*, she observes that a "missing link in our understanding of conflict" is "our failure to realize how vulnerable humans are to being treated as if they didn't matter."

Respecting people's dignity takes what I think of as applied grace. It involves extending yourself to make people feel they belong. It also involves giving them the benefit of the doubt (using Hicks's suggestion to start from the premise that they are acting with integrity). And it involves treating them like their opinion and feelings mean something.

Hicks believes that a violation of our dignity—having our worth dismissed—probably has such a devastating effect on us because of our evolved drive to protect our reputation. Shame wells up in us, and our frequent default reaction—rage—is what psychologist Daniel Goleman, in *Emotional Intelligence*, calls an "emotional hijacking." Even though the wound from a dignity violation is social, not physical, a signal that we're under attack heads off to the brain, and the amygdala, the brain's emotion center, reacts instantaneously; the brain's reasoning center isn't consulted. The amygdala messages our adrenal glands to mount a defense. Adrenaline and other stress hormones surge, and we're driven to save face in an instinctive fight-or-flight way that's overkill in our world, where we're usually combating slights and insults, not hungry tigers.

Expressions of rage are powerful and can sometimes be the right choice for sending the message "Don't tread on me! (again)" to an unrepentant bully. But with someone who appears to have some conscience, you can compose yourself and tell them (face-to-face or in writing) that their treatment of you was absent dignity—that they could have accomplished the same thing more kindly, charitably, humanely. Getting someone to feel remorse for demeaning you unnecessarily is probably more effective in inspiring them to mend their ways than trying to make them fear you, especially if you aren't a particularly scary person. Perhaps more important, by calling somebody on their rotten treatment of you, you become a person who refuses to take crap from people, bolstering your dignity in your own eyes. You can't always stop people from kicking you when you're down, but you don't have to roll over for them so they can land better blows.

TALK IS CHEAP. EXCEPT WHEN IT'S EXPENSIVE.

My neighbors are lovely people who treat me like part of their family. They always invite my boyfriend and me and an older female friend of theirs to join them and their three kids for cozy Christmas and Thanksgiving dinners. These are meant to be warm family affairs, not debate sessions, so I avoid any discussion of politics and economics, which, in turn, helps me avoid my temptation to go after weak or illogical thinking in these arenas in the way a coyote is tempted to go after a wobbling cow.

At their 2010 Thanksgiving dinner, this sweet but very emotional older friend of theirs, who works part-time at Whole Foods, ranted about the grocery chain's new "wellness"-promoting policy giving employees a discount on their health insurance for meeting certain health benchmarks. "They're like the Nazis!" she bayed. A response billowed in my head and hammered to get out: "Um, sorry, but unless they are shoving their workers in ovens with their tofu bake . . ." My boyfriend gave me the look one gives a dog about to pee on the living-room rug. I smiled and said nothing.

As we've all learned and as we have a tendency to forget or ignore, the brain has yet to prove itself able to outrace the lip. It's essential to make yourself wait for it to catch up before speaking, as you can throw yourself in social purgatory (or claw your way out of it) through what you say or refrain from saying to others. This is why, in addition to becoming accomplished in The Big Three of communicating—listening, empathy, and treating people with dignity—it's important to become versed in The Next Four: the four other brain-engaging essentials that make up a full communication skill set:

- **Request management:** Ensuring that you have full use of the human vocabulary, including the word "no."
- **Honesty management:** How and when to be imperfectly frank.

- **Behavior management:** How to politely and effectively persuade people to mend their ways.
- **Hurt management:** How to respond to inconsiderate clods, what to say when you've been one, and how and when to help a stranger who's hurting.

REQUEST MANAGEMENT

How to say no.

If you're one of those people who just can't squeeze out the word no, chances are you're the slave of just about anyone who asks anything of you. (The world is your chore wheel!)

That used to describe me, by the way. "No" was not a word (or attitude) that came naturally to me. In fact, I think one of my greatest accomplishments was becoming kind of a bitch. Not all the time but when called for. It's a huge improvement over the person-shaped doormat I used to be, thanks to having no friends—not even one—until I was thirteen.

As soon as I was no longer a total outcast, I seized the opportunity to become a total suck-up, which I remained well into my twenties. It was then that I finally realized that I had lots of "friends" but only one real friend and that I couldn't find my opinion with a search party because I was always trying to say whatever I thought people wanted to hear. (This doesn't earn you anyone's respect, but people do sense that you're the one to call when they need help moving.)

The ability to say no comes out of self-respect. For people who have it, standing up for themselves is second nature. Unfortunately, developing self-respect generally takes a good bit of time. Do get to work on that if you're in need. (Nathaniel Branden's book *The Six Pillars of Self-Esteem* is an excellent resource.)

In the meantime, don't just resign yourself to bending over upon request. Instead, try Option B, the guts approach: Squirrel up the courage to say no when it needs to be said—whenever somebody's violating your boundaries (or what you sense should be your boundaries) or even just pressuring you to go to a party you think will be a real drag. You need to *choose* when to do nice things for people instead of allowing them to wring them out of you. The thought of doing this will be terrifying at first, but once you stutter out your first no, the experience should prove revealing: The earth will not open up and a big clawed hand will not pull you in, and you'll find that people actually respect you when you stand up to them. It's also how you'll come to have real friends—the kind who are *interdependent* with you and will come around for you when the chips are down instead of letting all your calls for help go straight to voicemail.

The more you keep saying no the easier it gets, and there's a bonus: *Acting* as if you have self-respect should bring it your way faster and more easily than *thinking* really hard about how you should have it. Decades of research finds that one of the fastest ways to change how you feel is to change how you behave. In one of these studies, from 2010, experimental social psychologist Dana R. Carney found that even your posture seems to matter. Male and female subjects assuming the body language of a high-powered executive for just two minutes experienced empowering psychological, biochemical, and behavioral changes in line with actually *being* a high-powered executive. Those assigned the "power poses" (like sitting, Master of the Universe–style, with their feet up on a desk and their arms crossed behind their head) showed an increase in their level of the dominance hormone, testosterone. They reported feeling significantly more powerful and "in charge" than subjects assigned the "low-power" poses, and their greater willingness to take risks in a subsequent gambling test suggests that they meaningfully increased their confidence. Other studies of power poses have shown similarly positive effects.

What this should tell you, if you're one of the wimps of the world, is that there's really no reason to wait until you're a ballsier person. You can start right now by walking tall—regularly and whenever you particularly need to stand tall. If you're at work, close your office door (or find a big broom closet and lock the door), and then stand up straight, put your hands on your hips, stride around the space and tell your chair or the janitor's mop just how things are going to be. It will probably seem ridiculous, but remember, the research does suggest that your body will lead your head in the direction you need to go. Realistically, you probably aren't going to be George Clooney–smooth right away, but if you've previously resigned yourself to remaining meek, this is your chance for a change of plans. Today could be the first day of the rest of your noes—and maybe even the occasional "absofuckinglutely not."

How to retroactively say no.

It's important to be a person of your word, but there will be times when you have given your word that you'd do some life-sucking favor for someone but realize, as the deadline looms, that you absolutely shouldn't have and maybe can't even deliver. If you're like most people, instead of doing the healthy thing and telling the person you're in over your head (explaining why you overpromised and apologizing), you get mad at them for asking and mad at yourself for saying yes, and you start marinating in dread.

We humans are born overpromisers. Our brains are prone to "optimism bias"—the tendency to think positive instead of considering what's actually realistic. Often, at the moment we're saying yes to doing some favor, empathy for the person in need and enthusiasm to help shove aside practical, rational considerations, like calculating what, exactly, helping will entail. At that moment, time is made of spandex, and our calendar is vast and white like the first big snow.

If you generally keep your word, don't be too harsh on yourself on the occasions you overpromise, but do use the experiences to guide you in predicting more realistically in the future.

Often, bucking up and following through on whatever you offered is the right thing to do, but if you won't cause real harm or hardship by telling the person you made a mistake in saying yes, pulling back can sometimes be okay—assuming you don't make a habit of it.

When you must shed some favor you've agreed to, tell the person as soon as possible. They may be annoyed at you for bailing, but if you pull out in a timely way, explaining that you didn't really understand what was involved, they can probably understand and even forgive you. This also may allow them time to find another patsy, *uh*, helper.

How to avoid having people retroactively say no to you.
When you're asking someone a favor, be mindful of our tendency to breezily say yes without quite processing what it will take for us to follow through. The "retroactive no" often follows the inappropriate request—something unfair or unrealistic to ask of somebody because it exceeds their comfort zone or abilities or because your interactions with them are starting to seem modeled on the parasite/host relationship.

I did my best to explain all this to a doctor friend of mine who vented to me about his "RUDE!" doctor colleague who'd agreed to read an article he'd written. Not an article in a medical journal. An article on modern dance. Maybe his colleague sincerely intended to read it, or maybe it was just easiest to say yes (and kinder than "I'd rather have my toes snipped off with rusty garden shears"), but he will most likely go to his grave in forty or fifty years never having looked at a word of it. And, frankly, it's to be expected.

It's an imposition to ask someone who is not your mom or your grandma to read something you've written, whether it's the community center bulletin or your award-winning short story. (In Los Angeles, a person's greatest fear is not that somebody will pull a gun on them but that somebody will reach in his jacket and pull out a script.) It's likewise out of bounds to expect a friend to give you an assessment of your band's latest CD—beyond "Thanks, really liked it!" People who are not professional critics often have no idea how to read or listen critically or give meaningful criticism, and they're afraid of seeming stupid or hurting your feelings if they say the wrong thing. The whole deal becomes overwhelming—as is the case with many chores we try to stick on friends and acquaintances. If you want to maintain your friendships, it's often best to hire a professional to do your dirty work and ask your friend to go out for a beer with you while you're waiting for that person to finish.

If you do decide to ask someone a favor, consider whether you have enough of a relationship—meaning a reciprocal relationship—or whether you're that "friend" who's always there for them whenever *you* need something. Like lions scanning the veld for the limping gazelle, there are human predators who search out the psychologically wobbly types who will say yes to even the most absurd requests simply because they lack the self-respect to say no. (Will they drive the getaway car? Babysit the feral cat? *Surrre* they will.) The wobblies' inability to stand up for themselves doesn't make it okay to make them your choreslave; it just means it's possible—at least until they crack open that box of Froot Loops that has a map to their spine inside and start plotting against you for all the times you took advantage of them.

It's also important to consider whether what you're asking of someone is less a favor than an insult with a question mark on the end. Some people, for example, think nothing of asking some acquaintance or a neighbor they barely know to drive them to the airport—because, hey, that guy's time has no value and a cab would cost them 60 bucks. If that person asking for the ride stripped away all their insincere hedgings and couchings (like "Wouldja mind?" and the obvious lie "I would normally not ask this, but . . .") and let their swollen sense of entitlement do the talking, their request would come out something like this: "Look, schmucko, I'll give you a choice. You can either drive me to the airport or give me the $60 for a cab."

HONESTY MANAGEMENT

When, why, and how to weasel out of telling people exactly what you think.

Sometimes it's best—less hurtful and more relationship-preserving—to hint, suggest, and dance in the direction of "no" instead of actually saying it. The same goes for variations on no, like "Leave me the hell alone!" and, of course, advice that someone send some idea or object on a brief tour of their rectum. In short, as you'll see in the examples just below, honesty is the best policy—except when lying or euphemizing your ass off is a better policy.

THE BEAUTY OF INDIRECT SPEECH.

(Why horny people invite you up to see their art collection.)

Euphemism—a pleasantly vague word or phrase substituted for a harsher, franker one—is the plastic nose and glasses of civilized speech. It's a silly, cheap-ass disguise but usually just enough of one that both you and the person you're saying the dicey thing to can pretend you really meant something else, which keeps them from getting offended and chewing you out.

For example, we all know that somebody who asks "Wanna come up and see my etchings?" isn't inviting you up for a few hours of art appreciation. But sending their message in disguise cloaks their intent in plausible deniability, eliminating the offense or embarrassment that a direct request—"Wanna come up so we can fuck our brains out?"—might cause if you'd be appalled to think of that particular person thinking of you in those terms.

It seems sort of unbelievable that such a flimsy euphemistic cover works. But psychologist and linguist Steven Pinker, speaking about the etchings weasel-ism and other forms of "indirect speech" at the NorthEastern Evolutionary Psychology Society conference in 2008, explained that we don't seem to need *substantial* plausible deniability. Even the slimmest possibility that the euphemism peddler wants to guide you to something other than their broom closet sex dungeon seems to serve as a conversational air bag—allowing the two of you to pretend that sex wasn't on the person's agenda and to maintain whatever cordial, sexparts-free relationship you had previously.

Having witnesses weaponizes criticism.

A favorite weapon in many a passive-aggressive person's war chest is the cc function in e-mail—the digital version of humiliating remarks dropped on a person while they're in the company of others. This is frequently used in the office:

> From: Bob Backstabbinsky
> To: Joe Co-worker
> cc: Hal Higherup
> Subj: Let's not gross out the clients, mkay?
>
> Luckily, the client only came into the men's room as you were leaving it. You know those sinks they have in there? Hint: They're actually good for more than recovering from hangovers.

Our drive to guard our reputation makes us acutely sensitive about having criticism of us made public, whether the conversation is spoken or digital. Pinker concedes in *The Stuff of Thought* that we are all aware that other people talk trash about us—even our good friends. We may overhear some unflattering remark about us, but if nobody knows we've heard it, we can let it slide, he explains. But when we know that some third party has heard the remark, and when *they know* that *we know* they were witness to our dressing down, if we don't seek redress from the person who made the remark, we can lose face—although by fighting back, we may lose in other ways, like by doing damage to a friendship or relationship we need or by coming off as an argumentative asshole.

Accordingly, when it's your turn to tell somebody they've messed up, be mindful that including witnesses cranks your bitchslap up to turbo and that you're less likely to get through to a person if you're also getting them all ashamed and thus all the more defensive. So, in e-mail, for example, if you must loop in a third party, separately forward that person any scoldmail you've sent (instead of visibly cc'ing them on your original scolding) or otherwise privately relate what went down. Again, in keeping with Pinker's assertions on plausible deniability, the scoldee can believe and even be pretty darn sure you've looped somebody else in. But if you don't tell them so in so many words, you'll leave that much more of their ego unchewed.

The right time to discuss something is sometimes never.

We all know this, right? But when you're speaking with someone who's trotting out obviously idiotic beliefs, it's tempting to yank out all the evidence they're wrong and beat them over the head with it until they give in. So, consider this a reminder: Nailing somebody to the wall with your incisive logic is a good thing if you're trying to win the seventh-grade state debate finals. Socially, it's best to identify people who will never be convinced and who, in fact, are likely to be deeply wounded that you hold different beliefs (and maybe even think you're a bad person for holding them). Talk with those people about shoes, good books, and the weather.

It's also a good idea to consider whether all truths need to be told to all people. I am open with my friends and blog commenters that I see no evidence there's a god. They can handle it. I, however, saw no reason to reveal my nonbelief to my boyfriend's late mother, a sweet little devout Catholic lady who was fond of me and would likely have worried that I'd burn in hell and Gregg would be left alone for all eternity.

Deliver the bad news about a person last.
You catch more flies with a fly swatter.[4] (Honey is messy and hard to throw.) But when speaking critically to someone, you'll catch less hatred and anger if you start on a positive note. Even really bad news about a person's fate is best presented with a flattering startup (assuming you aren't telling them, "You have beautiful eyes, and oh, yeah, you have a month to live"). For example, if you have to tell somebody that they're fired, first give them props for some things they did right. Next, say something like, "But, you messed up, and here's how, and we have to let you go." The positive lead-in doesn't make a person any less fired, but at least you won't clear out all their dignity before you have them clear out their desk.

Bad news is kinder than no news: Breaking up with a friend.
We humans are conflict-avoidant beings. We hate uncomfortable conversations and will put them off endlessly if we can. For example, there may come a time when you need to break up with a friend. The thing you're probably most tempted to do—make like Casper and disappear—is also the cruelest.

Unfortunately, I say this from experience. My best friend of eight years broke up with me without a word. We were very much entwined in each other's lives, and for years, we had been meeting in the mornings at a café and e-mailing multiple times daily. All of a sudden, he wasn't at the café and wasn't responding to e-mail. He's a professor, so I figured he'd just gotten crazy-busy at school. But time passed, and I still heard nothing from him. I worried he was lying hurt somewhere and nobody at school had missed him. I escalated to calling (not how we usually communicated with each other), left desperate voicemail messages, and sent pleading e-mails, "Maybe you're mad at me, but just tell me you're okay."

---

[4] Actually, I do really well with a DustBuster, which eliminates the need to squish the buggers if you just keep the thing running and release them outside.

Probably out of sheer annoyance at the message storm, he sent me a curt e-mail telling me he no longer wanted me in his life, saying I had "gotten angry" in recent months. As he knew, a good friend of mine had died two months prior after a painful and protracted battle with lung cancer, and I was one of a group of her friends caring for her. So, sure, maybe I *was* angry. But we all go through pissy periods in life, and a friend gives you a heads-up—"Hey, I find it hard to be around you these days . . ."—and maybe tells you he has to take a break from you; he doesn't just vanish.

In other words, yes, you actually need to tell your soon-to-be ex-friend that it's over—as briefly and kindly as possible. Getting officially dumped allows them to lick their wounds and move on. As for how to tell them, a friend of mine who got dumped by e-mail by her male best friend and the godparent to her children said, "Only a coward breaks up with a friend by e-mail, phone, or text." Perhaps. But, to me, the point isn't to seem brave but to get the message across in the least humiliating way possible, and a face-to-face firing by a friend is pretty humiliating, which is why I think it's best to do it in a gently worded handwritten note. (Handwriting your message takes more effort than e-mail, possibly eliminating some of the notion in their mind that you just took the easiest way out.)

Whatever your reasons for ending the friendship, it's kindest and most dignity-preserving to stick to vague excuses for your departure, explaining it as a conflict in dynamics, which it almost certainly is. For example, you just have "different approaches" to life, you've "grown apart," or you feel you're just not "clicking" anymore. Be prepared to stick to the reason you choose in case you're called and pressed for more. The important thing isn't telling the whole truth about why you're outta there but telling them the least hurtful thing you can that says "goodbye forever."

BEHAVIOR MANAGEMENT

Criticizing people doesn't make them change; it makes them want to clobber you.

I was inside my house, in my office, with all the windows closed, struggling with a passage I was writing, when my thoughts were suddenly drowned out by some chickie's loud argument. I opened my front door and saw a woman in a blue Volkswagen Bug parked across the street yelling into her cell phone speakerphone—and out her open driver's side window—which meant she was basically loudspeakering her conversation to every house on my block.

I do not live in the countryside with six grazing cows and four acres of land between the street and my front room. It is an urban neighborhood where the houses and apartments and a number of residents' windows are right along the sidewalk—a fact that should be apparent to anyone not taking a stroll while blindfolded.

Thanks to my inability to crack the passage I was trying to write, I'd already gotten a head start on being annoyed when the woman's loud conversation shoved its way into my office. I stomped out onto my porch, glared over my fence at her, and hissed: "I can hear you *inside my house*."

Sure, my annoyance also came from the reasonable presumption that the sounds you hear in your house will be house sounds—the teakettle whistling, bacon frying, your dog snoring—but I usually know better than to go out and hiss at somebody. Criticizing a person's behavior, especially angrily, is not a way to get them to change it. Not for the better, anyway.

In this case, it led to the spitting of angry words between the two of us. But standing there on my porch, yelling to her about how rude she was, I realized that I was being a counterproductive ass and surely causing even more of a disturbance to my neighbors than she had been. I went back inside—at which point the girl marched up to my gate, yelled in the direction of my closed front door for five minutes straight, and then vandalized my mailbox.

On a positive note, this was such an obvious example of how I *shouldn't* behave that I turned it into a benchmark for how I *wouldn't* behave in the future. I realized that I'd forgotten to consider my goal when I stormed out on my porch. Did I just want to go off on the girl, or did I want to get her to pipe down? I'm more likely to get peace and quiet—and avoid flooding my body with the poisons that well up from the biochemistry of fight-or-flight—if I ask in a way that doesn't make somebody long to give me a colonoscopy with that cute VW dashboard bud vase.

As I noted earlier in the chapter, because of the lack of firmware updates to our body's ancient fight-or-flight system, when we're verbally attacked, we launch the same supercharged biochemical ammo we'd need to fend off something sharp-fanged that thinks we'd make a nice dinner. It's criticism and blame—statements that attack and diminish a person—that fire up this defense system, causing people to rationalize and defend their behavior and then attack you for attacking them.

Therapist Carl Alasko, in *Beyond Blame*, suggests you test whether something you're about to say is a blaming statement by considering whether it is likely to provoke "a reaction of anger, resentment, anxiety, pain, fear, or humiliation." Common blaming statements start out with "How come you didn't," "Didn't you know that," and "It would help if you'd just." But Alasko says the single most common blame trap is a "why" question, like the accusatory "Why didn't you put the milk away?" Answer: "Because I'm too stupid to remember!"

To avoid ugliness and maybe even motivate change, forgo accusation and criticism for a request—"Hey, honey . . . please remember to put the milk away"—or offer a calmly uttered statement of fact: "Hey, just wanted to let you know: The milk was still out on the counter when I came home. It smelled funny, and I had to throw it away."

Calm fact-stating was the tactic I started using on bar-going loudsters who park in my neighborhood. One night, at midnight, right outside my house, four guys were sitting in an SUV with most of the windows down, playing their radio at a wake-the-dead volume and repeatedly yelling, "Woo-hoo!"

My first impulse was to vaporize them and their vehicle with an alien ray gun. Instead, I channeled—I dunno—Desmond Tutu, the Dalai Lama, and somebody who's had way too much electroshock therapy and went outside in my robe. I knocked on the driver's-side window. Entirely without animus. Cool as chalk.

Looking surprised, the guy rolled it down.

I said in a calm, matter-of-fact tone, "Hey, just wanted to let you know, we're real close to the street here in these houses, and we hear pretty much everything."

Despite my restrained approach, I had low hopes for their response, since the *woo-hooing* made them sound plastered. I waited for the drunken "Fuck you, bitch!"

"Oops, sorry," one of the guys said. "We'll be quiet."

"Sorry!" "We're sorry!" others singsonged.

"Hey, thanks," I said and went back in the house—with nary a *woo* or a *hoo* in my wake.

Awful truths and uncomfortable requests are often best expressed in ink—sometimes anonymously.

Say somebody has bounced a check to you or a friend has gotten in the habit of taking advantage of you in some ugly way. Trying to straighten things out face-to-face will be icky and uncomfortable for you and for them. As I advised about how to dump a friend, telling them in writing—perhaps in a gently worded e-mail—allows them to get the message offstage, minimizing the embarrassment both of you would feel if you were there to see their reaction.

Other merits of sending a note include adding time and distance, giving the person you've sent it to the chance to cool down and respond in a more reasoned way. It also allows you to support any solutions you propose with reference material, if needed (such as an article about no-bark collars for a neighbor with a persistently yapping dog).

The gentle anonymous note is particularly helpful in alerting co-workers to their failures in hygiene or other personal care issues. (What's even more embarrassing than learning that you stink? Knowing who knows you stink.)

Take a common problem, especially in the workplace—cologne wearers who seem to confuse "spray-on" with "hose-on." If you're like many of those suffering from the regularly overscented, you may find it too uncomfortable to say something to them. Even if you *are* comfortable speaking up, if you don't have a solid working relationship with the person—and if they're a little unstable—they could turn your working life into working hell.

Still, many people would argue against sending an anonymous note, as it allows the recipient no opportunity to reply. This may seem unfair—and even rude. Well, it's also unfair that you're being gassed, and the point isn't to start a conversation about it but to have the stench purveyor realize that they need to stop.

You could also speak to your supervisor or drag the problem up to human resources and ask them to do the talking for you (and to keep mum that you're the one who's complained). In an ideal situation, HR would put out a memo telling everyone to be mindful that some co-workers have allergies and chemical sensitivities and asking them to cut back on (or cut out) the Napalm No. 5. In a less-than-ideal situation, they'd yank the offender in for a talking-to, which could be very embarrassing for that person and potentially very bad for you should the HR people drop any clues as to who made the complaint.

That's why an anonymous note is sometimes the best solution—or at least the best first attempt—to solve the problem of an overly-perfumed co-worker, providing your workplace is large enough that they won't easily guess the sender. Be prepared to have no clue as to what the hell they're talking about, in case they ask. Cover your tracks by printing the note at home (because workplace printers may have distinctive imprints or quirks that make it easier to narrow down which computer a particular printout came from). Fold it (so nobody popping into their office can read it without going into snoop mode), and sneak it onto their desk or chair.

In your message, tell the offender (usually a she) that her fragrance is lovely (even if it's anything but) but that you have chemical sensitivities and/or terrible allergies and perfume makes your nose and eyes itch and your throat swell and gives you these terrible headaches. Could she kindly wait until she leaves work to put it on? This tactic makes the issue a medical problem on your part, and your request that she take a compassionate approach to it should go down far easier than the truth: She smells like she narrowly escaped being killed in an explosion at a ladies' bathroom deodorizer factory, in turn causing anyone who works in the same zip code to feel as if a scented railroad spike is being hammered up their right nostril and into their brain.

The best way to bend people to your will is to avoid trying to bend people to your will.

I'm an advice columnist who defies her job description, which is supposed to be telling people what to do. I instead use humor to try to show people the absurdity of their behavior, both because it's more fun to read than finger-wagging advice and because research in psychology and addiction treatment suggests that leading them to their own conclusions is more effective than hammering them with mine.

Addiction treatment specialist Stanton Peele explains that telling people what to do just makes them defensive, leading them to cling to whatever they were doing instead of being open to giving it up. "People change their behavior when they sort it out in their own mind that what they're doing violates what they care most about and what they want most for themselves," Peele told me.

Peele, in *7 Tools to Beat Addiction*, writes about motivational interviewing, a technique used to stimulate positive change in addicts, which can also be useful with any person stubbornly clinging to a damaging behavior. First, you draw out the person's thoughts, feelings, values, and goals by asking them what they want for themselves. You listen empathetically and without judgment. And then—the kicker—after they've laid out how they'd like their life or some situation to play out, you gently ask them how their current course of action dovetails with that (or doesn't). This is the point at which they are most able to see the discrepancy between what they want and what they're doing.

Peele, in *7 Tools*, cautions: "The aim in this kind of questioning is never to place yourself in direct conflict with the target. Whenever you sense resistance, back up. The key to this approach is to push the ball back to the other person (generally by asking questions), even when you feel you know what the truth of the matter is."

It's unrealistic to expect that person to do an immediate U-turn in their thinking and behavior, but by eliminating the element of defensiveness and getting them to more open-mindedly consider what they're doing, you at least help them plant some seeds that may lead to change.

I've often seen this approach be more successful than direct advice. In addition to readers I've given advice to who've written me to report on the progress they've made, a cop friend who worked a domestic violence beat for the LAPD told me she had the best success getting victims to pull themselves out of abusive situations by persuading them to attend discussion groups with other victims. They'd hear other victims' stories and see bits of their own situation in them. Because nobody was directly challenging them, they didn't feel compelled to defend their behavior or their abuser's, and they were more likely to recognize how crazy and dangerous it was for them to keep going back to their abuser.

HURT MANAGEMENT

When your mouth becomes a storage area for your foot.

I was at a friend's dinner party, and a few of the twelve or so guests were really pretentious Hollywood types I hated instantly. About 9 p.m., when we sat down to eat, one guy kept his sunglasses on. *Oh, come on,* I thought. *Glare of the salad dressing too much for you, dude?*

For some inexplicable reason, I decided to share this thought. "Sunglasses indoors? What are you, blind?"

"As a matter of fact, I am," he said.

Time to crawl under the table and die!

I can't remember my response, but the temptation when hoof goes into mouth is to let your embarrassment run the show. This leads you to get all rambly in apologizing, drawing the incident out and making it more embarrassing for everyone. You should instead get in and out with a quick, neat apology—"Oops, I bungled that one. Really sorry!"—and then change the subject so everyone can move on.

How to respond to well-intentioned idiots.

Sometimes people with the best of intentions say or do hurtful things. Someone may offer a bus or a subway seat to a woman they believe is pregnant. This happened to a friend of mine—several months *after* she'd had her baby, just when she was feeling good about starting to get her pre-pregnancy body back. She was wearing an outfit she'd chosen specifically for what she called its "doesn't-make-me-look-pregnant quality." So, in the span of five minutes, on a single subway ride, when the third person offered her their seat, she had a mini-meltdown—dropping her bags and making a loud announcement to the entire subway car: "I AM NOT PREGNANT!"

I've always found public meltdowns fascinating—second in entertainment value only to televised slow-speed police chases. But when people who surely mean well do something hurtful to you, it's best to respond to their intentions instead of their actions. A woman in my friend's situation, for example, should thank the person offering her the seat and sit down—because it's nice to take a load off and because when people are just trying to be considerate, it's kindest to avoid embarrassing the hell out of them by doing as my friend did: screaming, ". . . ACTUALLY, I'M JUST FAT!"

Fighting ugly with pity: An all-purpose comeback for cutting remarks. You're in some social situation when somebody says something seriously rude about your looks or maybe your intelligence, right to your face. Of course, you come up with the perfect comeback—two days later while sitting on the toilet.

The truth is, even professional comedians can find it hard to have a good comeback in a social situation. They're ready for the occasional heckler when they're onstage (and often have a fistful of preplanned comebacks, since how they'll be heckled is pretty predictable). But when they're standing in a group of people at a party and somebody puts them down, shock and anger can take hold, shutting down the smartass remark-building parts of the brain. (It's that "emotional hijacking" Daniel Goleman talks about in response to dignity violations.)

Sure, when you're loose from a few beers, maybe your wit will sometimes come through for you, but it's safest to assume that it will instead scurry off and hide behind a large piece of furniture. In other words, you should dispense with the notion that a winning reply to a rude remark involves a response so witty that it incinerates the rudester right where they're standing. Rather, keep in mind that there's a reason somebody is being so ugly and cutting. Happy people tend to be kind or, at least, uninterested in tearing other people down. Miserable people often want to lash out at the world—and there you are, so conveniently located as a target for their hate.

When one of these spitebags hurls a put-down at you, they expect that you'll either try to fight back or just stand there blinking and wishing you could disappear. Instead, you should do the last thing they'd expect: Look straight at them for a moment, and coolly call them on their rottenness with a remark like "Clearly, you must have had a pretty bad day to feel the need to say something so nasty to me. I hope you feel better." (Sincerity is not required here—just believability—so say it devoid of anger, and sound like you mean it.) By expressing sympathy for them, you've accomplished three things:

1. You've refused to accept their turning you into their victim.
2. You've come off classy and bigger than they are.
3. You still managed to stick it to them, sending the message, "Sorry your life is such a suckhole that your lone path to happiness is trying to make other people feel like shit."

How to shut down prying questions.

Conversational bullies—especially those who share your DNA—will feel free to ask you prying personal questions, such as "When are you two lovebirds having kids?" No matter how obnoxious the intrusion, getting ugly will only reflect badly on you. This isn't to say you should feel compelled to give any sort of direct answer, both because you'll surely feel victimized (if in a minor way) and because answering encourages the prying person to keep trying (which, if they're old and related to you, they'll probably do anyway). You may be tempted to respond with something jokey, like "Actually, we'll go upstairs right now and get cracking," but that's still an answer of sorts. Your best bet is refusing to engage. This takes only five words: "Time to change the subject!" Say only those words, in a singsong tone (more "just joshin'" than spittle-flecked with annoyance), and keep saying them until your interrogator gives up.

Public crying: When to butt in.

One day, around lunchtime, for about ten minutes straight, I heard what I thought were the loud, persistent howls of a child coming from the city parking lot by my house. I kept thinking a parent would calm the kid down, but the howls persisted. I went out to see what the deal was and found that it wasn't a child at all but a woman in the driver's seat of a parked car, wailing at the top of her lungs.

"Are you okay? Did something bad happen to you?" I asked her.

"My father died," she sobbed.

"I'm so sorry," I responded. And never really knowing what to say in death situations, I blurted out, "Can I get you a bottle of water?" She nodded. I announced, "I'm going to go get you a bottle of water," and I ran back to my house. How a bottle of water relates to a father dying, I don't know, but I said I was going to get her one, so I did. I took it back across the street and handed it to her through her open car window.

With that, she stopped wailing and, through sniffles, thanked me.

In retrospect, I don't think what I gave her mattered. What she needed was to have another human being reach out and show her some kindness.

This got me thinking about public crying. Some people believe that when you come upon a stranger crying, you should just leave them be. I think that's true—when they're crying quietly and doing their best to hide it from passersby. In that case, you probably help them most by pretending not to notice.

But a person sobbing their guts out in public is different. It's the emotional version of running down the street naked—a sign that something has gone so drastically wrong for them that normal social conventions have gone out the window. They are not just upset; their world has been yanked out from under them in some awful way. That's a terribly lonely feeling. Maybe the loneliest feeling. So, even if they end up declining your offer to help, chances are it will mean a lot to them that you, a total stranger, noticed their pain and made an effort to comfort them.

WHY I ALWAYS TALK TO STRANGERS

I know, "the gift that keeps on giving" sounds like something you get from eating a bad clam, but on a more positive note, it describes what you can get—or give—when you strike up a conversation with a stranger. To me, it's like an Easter egg hunt without the plastic eggs. You'll never know whom you'll meet, what you might become to each other, or what fascinating, funny, or useful things a person can tell you until you crack them open.

I'm a chatter. I chat with the skycap, with the parking lot cashier (briefly if somebody's behind me), with the lady who checks me in for my mammogram and with the lady who administers it, and with probably a good third of the people who sit next to me in coffee shops. I'll pretty much talk to anyone who doesn't seem to be putting out vibes of "Sure, people *could* talk to me, but I'd rather they throw hot coffee in my face." The point is just to connect—if briefly—and make people feel good, which usually makes me feel good right back.

My longtime boyfriend, an introvert whose favorite kind of social event is one that's been canceled, finds my love of talking to strangers bizarre. Of course, if I weren't this way, he'd just be some guy who was once in the Apple computer store at the same time as some redheaded woman and I'd have a number of blank spaces in my life where some very good friends are.

Beyond the practical benefits from connecting, life just seems warmer and more livable when you have friendly interactions between all the transactions. Also, with most of us living in these vast strangerhoods where we can sometimes go days without running into a single person we know, striking up conversations with strangers seems even more of a necessity—which isn't to say it's always easy. A friend remarked to me, "Unlike you, I'm afraid to just go up and talk to people."

"Actually," I said, "I'm often afraid to go talk to people, but that doesn't seem a good enough reason to avoid doing it." This is sometimes underscored when I see how reaching out to people can help change the world in small but meaningful ways. One Saturday at my favorite coffeehouse, I remarked to the woman in the next booth about an ornate book on her table with hundreds of linen-y looking pages and a beautiful, obviously handmade collaged cover. It was all she had left of her blog, she said. A good friend of hers had printed out all the entries and created the book for her shortly before her blog had fallen, suddenly and irretrievably, off the Internet.

A few hours later, a guy sat down at the booth where she'd been. Out of the corner of my eye, I saw him pushing some item aside. It was her book. I was horrified. The café is closed on Sundays, and I imagined her, Saturday night, realizing her book was missing and having to wait for the coffeehouse to open on Monday to see whether they'd found it.

I got on the Internet, using clues from talking to her to try to track her down. I sent a tweet to some professor who might've been her teacher and messaged a woman on Facebook who I thought might be her. (Her profile picture showed only a close-up of an eye, so I couldn't be sure.) But minutes before closing, she dashed back into the coffeehouse, hugged her book, hugged me, and tearfully told me how wonderful I was. I thanked her but said I thought it was just what a person should do.

The following Saturday, Gina, who works at the coffeehouse, told me that the woman had put $20 on account for me. I thought that was really great of her, but I also felt a little icky about getting $20 simply for acting like a decent person. And then a homeless man whom a few of us regulars buy coffee and breakfast for came in and sat down. I went over and said hello and told him I'd love to buy him lunch. I put the turkey and cheese croissant and Coke he wanted on my "account," telling Gina she could use the money still left to feed him when he came in in the future. I hopped on Facebook and messaged the woman, thanking her and telling her about the lunch she'd bought: "Your gift has done a little good in the world—thought you might like to know."

Now, this is a man who sleeps in alleys around Santa Monica and seems schizophrenic or otherwise not all there. Obviously, a turkey and cheese croissant isn't the answer to all his problems, but it's something—lunch for a guy who surely doesn't always get lunch. That and reuniting a woman with an irreplaceable item that meant a lot to her came out of a little friendly busybodying. People will tell you that opportunity knocks. I've never even heard it tap a little, but I've found time and time again that it chats.

—4—

THE NEIGHBORHOOD

I opened my front door onto a beautiful, balmy Southern California night, only to see a guy in the city parking lot across the street looking straight at me as he peed on the chain-link fence.

My boyfriend had given me a powerful flashlight—the kind night watchmen use to patrol aircraft factories for intruders. I grabbed it. Whaddya know, the beam carried all the way across the street.

"Hey, blond dude . . . urinating on the fence!" I called to the guy in my spotlight. "It makes my neighborhood smell like a giant men's bathroom when it rains."

He ducked down and hurried along the fence. "I'm not urinating!"

From my porch, I followed him with the flashlight beam, calling after him, "Let's see, pants unzipped . . . small, fleshy object in your hand. Whaddya doing, checking for genital warts?"

Luckily for him, I was too far away to take his picture, as I sometimes do when I come upon visitors to my neighborhood who think of the Great Outdoors as their Great Big Potty. I use these shots on little posters I put up on telephone poles, suggesting ideal and un-ideal places to leave urine and fecal matter when you're hitting bars and restaurants in my neighborhood.

Of course, my community pee-licing approach is not one the traditional manners experts support. *New York Times* reporter Douglas Quenqua asked some descendant of Emily Post for her thoughts on my vigilante tactics against the unrepentantly rude. "Two rudes don't make a polite!" she clucked. Well, no . . . not if we're talking about snapping at your great-uncle for slurping his soup, but showing that there's a price to be paid for using my neighborhood as your toilet does seem to help those of us who prefer to stop and smell the flowers instead of the urinal cake.

HELL IS OTHER PEOPLE

If your neighbor finally loses it over how your tree keeps maliciously dropping leaves onto his driveway and he starts chasing you around the cul-de-sac with an ax, the legal system's got your back. Armed police officers will be dispatched to your location—and possibly before one of your arms ends up as somebody's mailbox ornament.

The neighborhood disputes that are the hardest to resolve

involve unregulated piggy behaviors in shared public space, like the sidewalk or the street, and on private property. Sure, there are laws against some of these violations, like 4 a.m. stereo blasting and persistently yapping dogs, but just try getting them enforced. As I learned when my car was stolen and saw again as the victim of identify theft, police officers have about seven million more pressing concerns than solving nonviolent crimes, starting with watering the ficus tree in the police department's lobby.[5]

I don't mean to police-bash. They lay their lives on the line to protect the rest of us, and I truly appreciate that. But how often do you encounter ax-wielding killers? It's the lesser bad behaviors by neighbors and passing strangers that can make your life a daily living hell. This isn't to say that it should be the job of the police to intervene, and it doesn't have to be if we just understand and accept an essential fact about human nature:

We're all jerks.

Come on, admit it. We all want what we want, when we want it, and we'd like other people to shut up and scurry out of our way so we can get it already. As depressing as it may seem to see ourselves this way, being honest about our jerkitude is the best way to personally dispense less of it and to decrease others' emissions—and maybe even prevent them.

When *Homo Barbarus* moves in next door: How to stop rudeness before it happens.

Contrary to what the snippy next-door neighbor says in a Robert Frost poem, "good fences" do *not* make good neighbors, just some-

[5] They aren't lying when they say somebody will look at your complaint, but they probably mean archaeologists digging up the police station in 2121. You can improve your chances of getting their attention in the present by mentioning that there's also a body lying bleeding on your kitchen floor. (Ideally, to avoid penalties for filing a false police report, this should be true.)

what more contained neighbors. And frankly, if you get off on the wrong foot with one of yours, a good fence will be patterned on the Great Wall of China and will include Chinese soldiers with shoulder-fired missile launchers patrolling the top.

Many people make the mistake of keeping to themselves until their neighbors do something annoying. Bad idea. Even if you use the gentlest tone and pussyfooty language, if your first contact with the guy next door is letting him know how wrong he is, how rude he is, and how his mother must have been off with the sailors instead of teaching him manners, you encourage him to achieve his natural human potential for assholishness. (Did you mention that your car takes its gas black, no sugar?)

Better neighbor relations start with canny strategizing and proactive neighborliness:

- *Machiavellian altruism*

  Various biographers say sixteenth-century political theorist Niccolò Machiavelli is misunderstood as a bad guy for writing *The Prince*, a self-help book on how to be a royal scheming user. The truth is, scheming doesn't have to play out with somebody's getting screwed over. In fact, you can manipulate your neighbors for the greater good while manipulating them for your own good.

  A little calculated generosity—I like to call it "boomerang altruism"[6] because it's likely to come back to you—can help you deter all sorts of ugliness from the people who live around you. When new neighbors move in, bring over a plate of

[6] Anthropologist Robert Trivers came up with the term "reciprocal altruism" to describe showing generosity to another person at cost to yourself in hopes that they'll repay you in kind at some point in the future. Absolute altruism is giving with no expectation of getting anything in return. But, as Trivers has pointed out, there's likely no such thing as baseless altruism. If you're sacrificing for somebody related to you, it benefits your genetic line, and if you're sacrificing for somebody unrelated, you get a reputational bump out of the deal if others see what you're doing and probably at least a self-respect bump if they don't.

cookies or a bottle of wine. Wait—shell out for total strangers? Absolutely. And don't forget to look out for the neighbors who've been living around you for a while. Text them when they've forgotten to move their car on street cleaning day. Bring the package to their door that the delivery guy chucked in your bushes. Replace the bulb in their porch light when it goes out while they're out of town (and leave a little smiley note telling them so).

It's not only nice to be nice but also in your psychological self-interest. There's a growing body of research that suggests that doing kind acts for others gives you a helper's high (a little neurochemical *yabbadabbadoo!* in the brain's pleasure centers) and makes you feel happier and more satisfied with your own life. (More on this in the final chapter, "Trickle-Down Humanity.") Plus, for the price of some wine or the time spent baking cookies for the new person next door, you're putting a lot of positivity into the world: making them feel welcomed, creating community, and generating or reinforcing a social norm for neighborliness. Meanwhile, you're also inoculating yourself against that person's suddenly going all lifelong blood feud on you because your sprinklers killed their nap. (Doing this is particularly important if you can't just walk away from some neighbor's pointless but life-sucking daily hate-fests without also walking away from your heavily mortgaged dream house.)

• *How the nice-neighbor sausages are made*

A little preemptive neighborly gift giving can have such a transformative effect thanks to our powerful drive to reciprocate. As I've noted, a couple of million years ago, in the harsh environment in which we evolved, being seen as a freeloader or a mooch could mean getting booted from one's band—a likely death sentence. Being an easy mark would have posed other survival and mating issues. To keep our giving and taking in balance, humans developed a built-in social bookkeeping department. Basically, there's some little old lady in a green eyeshade inside each of us who pokes us—"Wake up, idiot!"—when somebody's mooching off us so we'll get mad and try to even the score. When somebody does something nice for us, our inner accountant cranks up feelings of obligation, and we get itchy to pay the person back.

A fascinating modern example of reciprocity in action is a 1971 study by psychology professor Dennis Regan. Participants were told it was research on art appreciation. The actual study—on the psychological effects of having a favor done—took place during the breaks between the series of questions about art. Regan's research assistant, posing as a study participant, left the room during the break. He'd either come back with two Cokes—one for himself and one he gave to the other participant—or come back empty-handed (the control group condition).

After all the art questions were completed, the research assistant posing as a participant asked the other participant a favor, explaining that he was selling raffle tickets and that he'd win a much-needed $50 prize if he sold the most. He added that any purchase "would help" but "the more the better." Well, "the more" and "the better" is exactly what he got from the subjects he'd given the Coke, who ended up buying *twice as many tickets* as those who'd gotten nothing from him.

Regan's results have been replicated many times since, in the lab and out, by Hare Krishnas, who saw a marked increase in donations when they gave out a flower, book, or magazine before asking for money; by organizations whose fund-raising letters pull in far more money when they include a small gift, like personalized address labels; and by me after I did something nice for a bad neighbor.

A TV soap actress moved in next door and started

throwing all-night backyard parties. (Sure, chickiepoo, have your hipster friends over for campfire-style guitar sing-alongs, but not at 3 a.m. in a backyard that's five feet or less from four other houses.) Asking her to be more considerate was useless. The way she saw it, why should her neighbors' silly sleeping hobby take precedence over her drunken friends' need to belt out "This land is your land . . ." in the wee hours?

What finally changed this was my e-mail to my more neighborly neighbors, warning them about a spate of break-ins in the neighborhood. I didn't have Soap Snot's e-mail address, so I printed the e-mail and slipped it under her gate, with a note scrawled at the bottom: "You aren't very considerate of those of us who live around you, but I don't think you should be robbed because of it, so FYI." If memory serves me correctly, I think I added that my other neighbor and I would keep an eye out (for anybody who might be trying to break in to her house during the day, when she's away).

Amazingly, from that day on, there were no more wee-hours guitar-apaloozas. A few weeks after leaving her the note, I ran into her at her gate, and she said, "Hey . . . just wanted to let you know I'm having some friends over tonight, but just for a dinner party, and we'll come inside at 10 p.m." As soon as I could rehinge my jaw, what was there to say but "Uh . . . thanks"?

• *A Neighborhood Watch program that doesn't require an actual human to be watching*

Sitting out in a lawn chair by your mailbox with your twin Rottweilers and a shotgun is a highly effective way to keep passing dog walkers and litterbugs from violating your lawn. Should you find this impractical, you might take advantage of our evolved concern for preserving our reputation and post a picture of human eyes on your mailbox, tricking potentially rude passersby into feeling that they're being watched and improving their behavior accordingly.

Yes, it seems even a *picture* of a pair of eyes triggers that feeling, according to research by UCLA anthropologist Daniel M.T. Fessler and his then grad student Kevin J. Haley. The picture they used was just a stylized drawing of a pair of eyes, not a photograph. But, in a computer game they designed to measure generosity, when the stylized eyes were displayed on a computer's desktop, participants gave over 55 percent more money to other players than when the logo for the lab was positioned in the place of the eyes. These findings were echoed in a later study, by Newcastle University ethologist Melissa Bateson and psychologist Daniel Nettle, in which people put nearly three times more money into a university coffee room "honesty box" on the weeks when a photograph of a pair of eyes was posted above the box.

These findings seem to have a lot of application beyond the ivory tower—like on coffeehouse tip jars everywhere. In neighborhood terms, shit happens, but tape a picture of eyes to your mailbox and that Great Dane's leavings just might get shoveled up and carried home in a baggie instead of being left in a big steaming pile for you.

Where there's land, there's room for land mines: Whether to approach a problem neighbor.

In a neighborhood spat, when you feel strongly that you're on the side of what's good and right, it's tempting to let that drive your approach to conflict resolution. Keep in mind that it takes surprisingly little for even the pettiest neighborhood squabble to escalate to DEFCON Boiling Your Cat And Feeding It To The Squirrels. As entertaining as it can be to watch two housewives cage-fighting in the homeowners association gazebo, if you prefer that your life be consumed by living rather than revenge seeking, there are a number of things you should take into account when trying to resolve some issue with a neighbor.

- *Proximity*
  In neighborhood dispute resolution, as in real estate, location is everything. The closer a neighbor lives the more forbearance you need to show. For example, a next-door douchenozzle who often plays loud music with all his windows open is to be communicated with using the utmost in polite restraint. Not because he is in the right but because he is in the right place to replace your sleep and maybe your every waking moment with music that makes your soul break out in hives.

- *Protection from the elements*
  Is your house surrounded by a moat? If not, do you at least have a tall fence with a locking gate? How about a locking mailbox? Private, locking garage parking? And, when you leave the house, are you in the habit of carrying bear-repelling pepper spray?
  Factor in how exposed you and your property are when you're about to go after an abusive neighbor or a rude person passing through your neighborhood. Even if you approach them with great maturity and civility, your house may be vandalized or your car keyed, and you may find a little present in your mailbox—one that didn't come out of the housewares section at Bloomingdale's.

- *Batshittery. (Is your neighbor seeing voices?)*
  When I was at the University of Michigan, living in an off-campus apartment in an old house, I was getting my mail, when the wild-eyed creepy guy from an apartment upstairs stuck his face right in mine and hissed, "Redheads are witches and should be burned at the stake!"

Because the guy always seemed unhinged, I thought it was possible he wasn't just messing with me. I talked to the neighborhood beat cop, and he said, "Unfortunately, we can't do anything until he lights a fire." Wonderful. Especially since I translated this as "till he lights *you* on fire."

This is often the case. Still, if you're living next to some crazycakes who seems dangerous, you can call your local police station and ask to make an appointment with somebody there so you can find out what the parameters are for dealing with him or her. In Los Angeles, we have "community policing" officers, whose job, in part, involves proactively mediating neighborhood problems, including "quality-of-life issues." Go to the station accompanied by other neighbors, if possible, so the police don't wonder whether you're just fussy, and bring a written record with times, dates, and details of the crazy neighbor's scariness. Ask the police to keep from letting on to the neighbor that it's you who's complained to them.

If police can't do anything and if you're renting and the landlord can't or won't take action, consider the likelihood that the crazy neighbor will actually follow through on whatever they're alluding to. Because there's no reasoning with crazy, moving away from it as fast as you can may ultimately be your least costly option.

- *The bar fighter next door*

There are born lovers, and there are born fighters—people who see any interaction as a potential opportunity to break a bottle over someone's head. While these fight-pickers will claim they just want respect, they actually live to be disrespected. Even the tiniest unintended slight by a clerk or a waitress gives them an excuse to launch into revenge mode: Wrong change delivered? What else is there to say but "My name is Inigo Montoya. You killed my father. Prepare to die"?

Practice identifying the fight-pickers you encounter in business and elsewhere so you can avoid directly engaging with those living around you, and seek alternate, evasive ways to solve whatever problem they're causing you. (Maybe get a homeowners association board member to propose some new rule to prohibit whatever's tormenting you.) Remember, no matter how reasonable the request you make of a fight-picker, the slightest challenge to what they perceive as their supremacy and correctness in all matters just provides them ammunition to escalate things between the two of you. If they could, they'd invent a time machine so they could go back and slaughter all your ancestors.

Murder-suicide and other forms of diplomacy: Ways to defuse a problem neighbor.

"Who do you think takes that mattress downstairs? Magical fairies?" Toronto-based blogger Josh Bowman spat that out—not to the neighbors he despises for leaving garbage in the hallways of his apartment building but to readers of the blog *The Good Men Project*. Because many people understand how tricky confronting a neighbor can be, blogs have become huge as a forum for venting about neighbor-on-neighbor rudeness. This is understandable but ultimately pointless.

If you'd like to change more than some website's traffic count, you need to engage—but judiciously, using strategic thinking and tactics like these below to defuse anger and make your problem neighbors feel understood. "Feel understood"? I know—oh, hurl. Then again, in Sun Tzu's words from *The Art of War*, "the supreme art of war is to subdue the enemy without fighting."

- *Empathy, the great panty-unwadder of humanity*

  In many conflicts, like when your neighbor leaves his trash cans in front of your property, the injury we feel is largely symbolic. As I've written in my advice column, we're all basically large, easily wounded children. More than anything, we want to be treated like we matter.

I suspected that this was the bottom line in the dispute "Christine in San Juan Capistrano" called in about when I was a guest on Patt Morrison's show on Southern California public radio on the subject of rude and annoying neighbors.

Christine explained that from time to time, the balls her kids played with in the backyard would fly over the fence into a neighboring backyard. The first time, she and the kids went over and knocked on the neighbors' door. "The lady seemed to appear very friendly," Christine said, "and she let us into the backyard to get the balls." But, the next three or four times, the balls got tossed back over the fence, slashed.

Eek.

Creepy. And really mean.

But, in trying to resolve conflicts—even with neighbors acting horror-movie ugly to your kids—it helps to try to consider where they're coming from: Do the kids' balls maybe bounce against the windows and startle the lady? Are the couple in poor health, and do they have a hard time getting into their backyard? It's possible they're just awful people, but by trying to call up some empathy for bad neighbors or anyone behaving badly, you'll deflate some of your anger—improving your ability to approach the offending party in a calm, solution-oriented way.

I explained this to Christine and suggested she write a note along the lines of "Dear Neighbors, I just want to let you know, we're so sorry about the balls going into your yard. I'm sure this is annoying. And I just want to let you know we're really trying to not do this. I'm having the kids play at the other end of the yard," etc.

In retrospect, I realize that I should have suggested that Christine tuck a $10 Starbucks gift card in with her apology. Beyond gift giving's power to ramp up goodwill, research suggests that an apology is more likely to dissolve anger and lead to forgiveness if it's accompanied by some sort of payout or gift. (More on this in "The Apology" chapter.)

Yes, I'm actually suggesting she not only write this kowtowing letter but actually spend money on these horrible people, and yes, this probably seems like suck-up overkill on top of suck-up overkill. But, when you've got a bunch of children separated by only some fence slats from some knife-wielding, toy-slashing neighbors, sucking up seems just the thing to do.

- *Talk is expensive: Why a handwritten note is often the best approach to problem neighbors.*

There's that silly saying, "The pen is mightier than the sword." Maybe it is—if you can write like Thomas Jefferson. Otherwise, the next time somebody challenges you to a knife fight, see how far that Pilot gel-point gets you. But when you're trying to resolve a beef with a neighbor—one you're reasonably sure will come to the door armed with nothing more dangerous than a spatula—the pen tends to be far more effective than the face-to-face conversation.

Again, we humans aren't the most mature creatures. We have the ability to reason, but we're apparently terrified of wearing it out. We also have these fantastic evolved adaptations, like our fight-or-flight response, which makes us perfectly prepared to have some chance of escaping from a bear and rather imperfectly prepared to respond in a reasonable manner to a neighbor telling us our leaky hose is flooding his posies. Even the most valid criticism gets us defensive before we can give a moment's thought to whether the person criticizing us might be, you know, an itsy-bitsy, teeny-weeny bit . . . um . . . right?

A handwritten note about an issue (like the one I gave to my hootenanny-having neighbor) puts time and distance between you, your criticism, and the criticized person, giving them the chance to cool down and respond in a more reasoned way. In fact, if you've written a diplomatic, empathetic message like the one I suggested to Christine, a neighbor might even concede that you have a point. Or concede that it might behoove them to act like you have a point.

And yes, you actually do need to hand-write your message, not put it in an e-mail. E-mail makes it just too easy for you to dash off something rash and for your neighbor to dash back an irate reply, and before you know it, missile silos will be sprouting in two suburban backyards.

- *In neighborhood disagreements, honesty is the worst policy.*

In my advice to Christine, I warned her to make no mention of the neighbors' ball-slashing, explaining, "It is a normal part of life for kids' balls to go over fences, and these people are a little psycho." The truth is, calling somebody on their bad behavior in anything but a roundabout way tends to provoke denials, which are basically angry attempts to save face. A less provoking approach is presenting an issue by appearing to give your neighbor the benefit of the doubt—even when you both know they don't deserve it for a minute.

Say, for example, that the lady next door has been letting her unleashed dog run over and poop on your lawn. And say you know that this is not a secret to her (because you've seen her on her porch in her bathrobe with a cup of coffee, shouting, "Muffin, go shit in the neighbors' bushes!"). You still need to pretend otherwise and write her a note that leads off with "You probably don't know this . . ."

This approach allows the two of you to maintain a polite fiction in which you and she both pretend that you don't find her about as genteel as an ass boil. This, in turn, keeps the conflict from escalating, giving you some chance of having your lawn just be your lawn instead of her dog's giant free-range litter box.

- *When you're the problem neighbor: Listen to criticism instead of clobbering the critic.*

Selfish, self-absorbed little beasties that we are, listening does not come naturally to us. And because we tend to fly off the handle when criticized, listening when somebody's putting us in the hot seat takes preplanning: being mindful of our bratty tendencies and resolving that we'll take some deep breaths and hear a critic out.

Considering things from a complaining neighbor's point of view may sometimes require a field trip, as I advised "Michael from Brea," who also called in to Patt Morrison's show. His neighbors kept complaining about the thumping bass line from the music he listens to on weekends, he explained. I told him that he should say something like "Listen, I want to solve this; I don't want to torture you" and then ask to go over to their place when his music's playing so he can hear what they hear. (Just letting them know that you're willing to investigate means a lot.)

If he *is* rocking not only his world but theirs, he needs to correct that: listen through headphones, figure out what the volume has to be to stop the thumping, or look into ways to sound-mask his place. Whatever you do in and around your home or apartment—smoking, playing music, cooking stinky food, racing Shetland ponies across your hardwood floors—being a considerate neighbor means not letting it leak into the lives of those living around you.

Revenge is the best revenge: If you can't stop the rude, maybe you can globally shame them.

The rudesters in your neighborhood whose craptastic behavior you will have the least control over are visiting strangers and neighbors who don't live near you. Total strangers know they're unlikely to see you again, and a rude neighbor whose car, house, and peace and quiet are five blocks away gets that it'll be hard for you to do much more than shoot them the occasional hate glare. ("Ooh, that smarts!")

These people's obnoxious behaviors may call for multimedia measures. An increasingly common one is what I call "PooTube"—shooting and uploading video to YouTube of one of those dog walkers who always manage to spot something absolutely riveting going on up in a tree as their mutt's taking a crap on the sidewalk or somebody's lawn.

You can shoot the video on your smartphone (taking care to avoid being caught in the act) or use security cam video from your house or a neighbor's. To improve its chances of going viral (as a number of these videos have), in addition to posting it on social media, e-mail the link to local bloggers and traditional media. Pull screenshots from the video and post fliers around your block—"Hey, Dog Poo Leaver . . ."—with a photo of the perp with the dog doing its business and maybe a close-up of the poo left behind.[7]

One rude neighborhood dog walker did pick up after his dog but hung on to the poobag, waiting to dump it until he reached the manicured shrubbery of Palm Beach Gardens, Florida, resident Steve Miller. After Miller found a whole pile of poobags in his bushes, he bought a video surveillance system and caught his neighbor in the act—day after day for a month—once even capturing the guy doing an artful swinging windup and toss of the day's poobag.

---

[7] Be sure you do have video of them in action in case they try to go after you for "defamation," because truth is the defense against that.

Miller wasn't sure what to do. He has daughters and worried that the poo-flinger might be a crazy. He finally called the head of security for his community and showed him the video. The security guy talked to the neighbor and gave him three tickets—one for improper pet waste disposal, one for leash law violations, and one for littering. Best of all, he ordered the guy to come pick up the dog droppings, which he did.

Miller's video, "Dog Crap Booby Trap," went viral, and the story was covered on numerous TV stations and in *The New York Times*. But, even if your perp never sees your video or signs, others spotting them are likely to be deterred from behaving jerkoffishly in your neighborhood in the future—not because you've transformed them into better human beings but because you've reminded them that every nosy neighbor peering over their fence has a smartphone.

For rudesters you only hear in the act, I suggest posted signage—or, as I like to think of it, the "Hey, asshole!" flier.[8] In my neighborhood, for example, some self-important Hollywood

[8] For best results, no, don't actually call them that in your note.

bigwhoop started walking his dog at 5 a.m.—while shouting showbiz lingo into his phone at colleagues in a different time zone. He stopped after I typed a note in big letters, printed it on hot-pink paper, and posted it on my fence before going to bed:

> Hey, guy on cell phone at 5 a.m. The houses on this block are actually not a Hollywood set but real homes with real people trying to sleep in the bedrooms.
> Thank you.

The Tragedy of the Asshole in the Commons

There are homeowners who'd start the second Hundred Years' War to defend the sanctity of their property, but a half-block from their property line, everything changes. In fact, some stranger could come by their block in a truck, release a half-dozen feral cats, and then toss a stack of old mattresses onto the street, dump out several drums of used motor oil, and light the whole mess on fire. In response, these fierce defenders of private property would busy themselves with their petunias.

This "Ain't *my* land!" response to the trashing of public spaces illustrates what biology professor Garrett Hardin referred to as "the tragedy of the commons" in his 1968 essay on overpopulation. In a space owned by nobody and shared by many, the piggy can take advantage by grabbing more than their fair share of resources or by slopping up the space, ruining it for everyone.

One solution to the tragedy of the commons is private property ownership, but that doesn't solve the problem of the neighborhood corner used as a dumping ground. What does is *acting* like we have shared ownership of public spaces and getting as indignant about people's polluting them as we would if they were redirecting traffic across our front lawn.

That sentiment—feeling like part owner of my neighborhood—prompts me to speak up when I see people trashing it. When I manage to photograph them in the act, I sometimes create what I think of as low-tech blog items (phone-pole "blog posts" like the one at the start of this chapter, which I staple to the poles on both street corners by my house). In some of these, I include a few words encouraging my neighbors to feel a sense of ownership for our neighborhood and to say something to those uglying it up.

One day, I was disgusted to come home to bags and boxes of garbage dumped on the grassy strip lining my cute street.

To my surprise, the trash pile included a calling card of sorts: a name and address on a UPS label on a box of window treatments ordered by a woman Google told me is the wife of a top foreign surgeon. Facebook said she and her husband live abroad, but she'd had the window treatments shipped to somebody's ritzy address in Pacific Palisades—a $2.6 million house overlooking the ocean, in a neighborhood where they surely have trash pickup.

That address label, flaunting itself on the box, suggested that the dumpers may have been stupid enough to leave other identifying information. I put on gloves and rifled through the boxes and bags and found an invoice for the curtain order in the wife's full name, as well as a boarding pass with the surgeon husband's name, flight, and seat number. Other items I dug out suggested that they were spending the Christmas holiday in Los Angeles (with a day trip to the Cabazon outlet mall and stops at fast-food outlets along the way). Upon further googling, I surmised that the Palisades address belongs to friends of theirs to whom they'd had the window treatments shipped, probably to avoid paying the postage to their home country.

I messaged both the surgeon and his wife on Facebook and told them to come get their refuse.

Of course, this could have been their opportunity to say they weren't the dumpers but victims themselves. You never know; there could be a gang of garbage robbers operating in Richville, hauling shopping bags and boxes of trash miles and miles away to my neighborhood in hopes of tarnishing an innocent couple's reputation.

No response.

Grr.

Double *grr.*

I posted the story and photos on my blog and on social media, naming names (hoping the blog item would be picked up by bloggers in their country).

Still no response.

Well, surely, their trash had to miss them. I boxed up a sampling of it with a photo of the dumping and, for a very well-spent $3.69, mailed it to them at the ritzy address where the window treatments had been sent.

Note reads: "Our street is not your personal trash dump. What kind of upbringing did you have that you think this is okay?"

No, they never did come get their trash, and I never heard either a word of denial or an apology from them. The garbage is long-gone from my street, but the piles remain on the Internet, where, as of September 15, 2013, when you google the wife's name, the first entry that comes up is my blog item.

Although I didn't get the resolution I'd asked for, the experience underscored something I learned while I was tracking down my stolen pink 1960 Rambler (which I eventually recovered): Even if you never get your perp to return what they took or otherwise make amends, one of the best ways to stop feeling victimized is to refuse to roll over and take it like a good little victim. And I have to say, it's hard to keep feeling victimized when you're walking out of the post office snickering to yourself after mailing a trash sampler and a scoldy letter to some tony Pacific Palisades address and imagining somebody's fancy friends calling them up to ask them whether they maybe littered in Venice.

Mailing them that package—along with going after them like a gnat with web privileges—also sent them (and any would-be litterbugs who saw my blog item) a couple of important messages: Sometimes, the "easy way out" isn't so easy on your reputation. Also, because people are strangers doesn't mean you get to turn their lives into your personal trash dump—both because it's not nice and because you never know when you'll dump trash on the street of some nutbag who has not only a problem with that but rubber gloves, a broadband connection, and a penchant for going all Nancy Drew on your ass.

Turning the strangerhood into a neighborhood: How to create community.

I get that most people don't have it in them to go all medieval schoolmarm on the rude as I do, but anyone can do the little things that bring neighborhood residents together, making them people to one another instead of people who speed past one another in their cars.

- *Create a neighborhood lending library.*
  Dollhouse-like book hutches are popping up in neighborhoods across the country, thanks to the Little Free Library movement (littlefreelibrary.org), started in Wisconsin by Todd Bol in memory of his late book-loving schoolteacher mother. Sherman Oaks, California, resident Jonathan Beggs built and stocked one of these book hutches outside his house, where anyone is free to take a book or leave one. "It has evolved into much more than a book exchange," reported Martha Groves in the *Los Angeles Times*. "It has turned strangers into friends and a sometimes impersonal neighborhood into a community. It has become a mini-town square, where

people gather to discuss Sherlock Holmes, sustainability and genealogy."

Here's the Little Free Library I patronize in Venice, California, created from a vintage beer case and put out by Susan and David Dworski. (That's Mojo, the librarian, on the top left.)

- *Charity begins at the home next door.*
  Enlist neighbors to help an elderly resident with faraway relatives or somebody who's going through something really difficult, like chemo.

- *Start a neighborhood association.*
  Ask neighbors to join a neighborhood e-newsletter mailing list. Some of these just announce the occasional crime alert, but I love the neighborhood bulletin board feel of the *Venice Walk Streets Neighborhood Association* e-newsletter, with items like this one (complete with the hurried spelling):

Neighborhood Carwash
Willie is a nice responisble teenager in our neighborhood who is looking to keep your cars clean. I checked him out; he does a really good job.

Having your neighbors' e-mail addresses also allows you to stand together as an organized group. This is helpful should you need to take action against somebody who repeatedly goes all 800-pound assholezilla on your neighborhood (like by illegally doing construction at 6 a.m. on Sundays, and never mind the noise laws because the police are too short-staffed to come out and ticket violators).

- *Invite, invite, invite.*
  Throw neighborhood potlucks, block parties, movie nights (showing a classic movie on a garage door covered with a king-size bedsheet). Have an all-block yard sale, a neighborhood cleanup, a twice-a-year wine and cheese gathering at somebody's house. Start a neighborhood playgroup—for kids, that is. The adult sort with the bowl of keys brings the community closer in ways some may end up regretting.

- *Band together and take over for lame-ass government.*
  When government is failing you, don't sit on your collective hands. Consider doing as a bunch of people did in Hawaii. When Hawaii's Department of Land and Natural Resources didn't have the $4 million it estimated it would take to fix an access road to Kauai's Polihale State Park, local businesses and residents banded together and fixed it themselves. Mallory Simon reported on CNN.com that Ivan Slack of Napali Kayak, who needs the park open to keep his company's doors open, donated resources. Other businesses and residents rounded up

machinery and manpower, and together they completed $4 million in roadwork for free in eight days.

Don't be geographically snobby about whom you treat like a neighbor. As I noted in the beginning of this book, being around strangers all the time can be really cold and alienating unless we regularly take steps to remedy this with some generosity of spirit. The way I see it, a neighbor is anybody you treat like a neighbor.

Say a stranger's car breaks down on your block. Go out and offer them a glass of lemonade or a bottle of water and ask whether they need to borrow anything—a flashlight, your phone, a wrench. I've actually never had anybody take me up on these offers; these days, everybody has cell phones and auto club memberships, but they always look and sound really grateful—even moved—that a total stranger cared about what they were going through.

It's also nice to do as they do in Paris, where passing strangers are likely to greet each other. You'll walk through a courtyard of a building and cross paths with a woman you for sure will never see again, and she'll say, "Bonjour, madame," and you say it back to her. It's really nice. It's this little moment in which you're connected to somebody. They've saluted your existence.

After experiencing this in France, I started greeting people everywhere—saying hi to coffee shop and takeout cashiers instead of just giving my order, and smiling and saying good morning to passersby. In time, I came to realize that a stranger is just someone you have yet to treat like a neighbor and that a friendly hello is shorthand for the French phrase, *Ne seriez-vous pas mon voisin?* Or, as Mr. Rogers used to put it, "Won't you be my neighbor?"

— 5 —

THE TELEPHONE

Sometimes I have this fantasy in which I march into a quiet restaurant, the drugstore, or a coffeehouse, stand on a chair and launch into a long, loud monologue on Me, Myself, and My Day:

> *Yoo-hoo! Yooooo-hooo!* Helloo, people of Earth! My name is Amy Alkon, and I really need a tampon . . .

Fortunately, each of these businesses has numerous visual cues that remind me to restrain myself. The interior of Starbucks, for example, pretty much screams "Starbucks!" and not "church basement AA meeting" or "open mic night at the community theater." Bizarrely, many other patrons of Starbucks and these other venues think it's okay to belt out the sordidly boring minutiae of their lives to the rest of us simply because they are holding a small electronic device to their ear.

ALEXANDER GRAHAM HELL: PHONE MANNERS IN THE TWENTY-FIRST CENTURY

When Alexander Graham Bell first got on the phone and said "Mr. Watson, come here. I want to see you!" Mr. Watson, of course, came running. These days, Mr. Watson might grudgingly answer the phone when it rings—or just let the call go to voicemail and never pick up the message.

Modern telephone technology has transformed our lives in incredible ways and in some pretty sucky ones. The average American thirteen-year-old now has a small gadget in his pocket with more computing power than NASA used to put the first man on the moon.[9] But with such power comes responsibility, or *should* come responsibility, any sense of which is absent from all those bank-line cell phone shouters making the rest of us long to take out our eardrums with one of those pens-on-a-chain.

Many are quick to blame cell phones for the decline of civilization, just as grumblers in ages past probably pointed the finger at those big stone tablets lugged around town by a nobleman's eunuch. But the real problem isn't the particular message delivery system; it's the narcissistic asswad using it.

Even if you are among the considerate, you may want to rethink how you use the telephone. There have been a few changes in what's considered polite telephone behavior—most strikingly that, in many cases, one of the rudest things you can now do with your phone is to use it to call somebody.

Especially for people under forty, the spontaneous phone call has largely become rude.

Unless you are employed by a police state as a roving interrogator, you probably wouldn't storm into somebody's office, sweep their work off their desk, and bark, "Tell me what I want to know right this second!" But, that's pretty much what you're doing if you engage in promiscuous phoning—ringing somebody simply because the urge to know *right now* happens to strike you and *right now* happens to be convenient for you.

[9] *Physics of the Future*, by Michio Kaku, Doubleday, 2011.

In general, if you are not on fire, having a heart attack, or in some sort of business where your phone calls are expected and appreciated, the default position on phoning people should be what I have deemed the "Do Not Ever Call" rule.

There are now more demands on our time than ever, along with more ways than ever to reach people that do not require their immediate attention. In addition to the classics—the U.S. mail, a message in a bottle, and telepathy[10]—it is now possible to text, tweet, e-mail, or Facebook-message one's quarry. If you *must* have a phone conversation with somebody, err on the side of using one of the above options to arrange a mutually convenient time for it.

If that sounds overly picky to you, think about how it feels to get into what psychologist Mihaly Csikszentmihalyi deemed "flow"—that super-engaged state where you lose yourself in some activity—and then . . . *BRINNNNG!* Sure, a person could put his ringer on silent to avoid all calls—and then interrupt his work time by fretting that he might be missing an urgent call.

To keep people from phoning you, tell those you meet who want your phone number that you're "not really a phone person," and if you give out business cards, see that they include only an e-mail address, no phone number. Naturally, there will surely be some in your life not subject to the "Do Not Ever Call" rule: very good friends, your spouse, your lover, your parents, or other close relatives. Presumably, they will be familiar with thc okay times to phone you, although some may occasionally use the telephone as a weapon: "I woke you? How crazy that you'd be sleeping at 6:22 a.m. on a Sunday!" (If this sounds like your mother, snail-mail her a card with your weekend waking hours. Scrawl a smiley on the bottom to take the edge off.)

Before you willy-nilly call those you're close with, make extra sure you know *their* phone preferences. For an increasing number

[10] Your telepathy plan may or may not come with thought-waiting.

of people, the optimal time to reach them by telephone is never. My nerdywriterfriend Andrea Kuszewski tweeted:

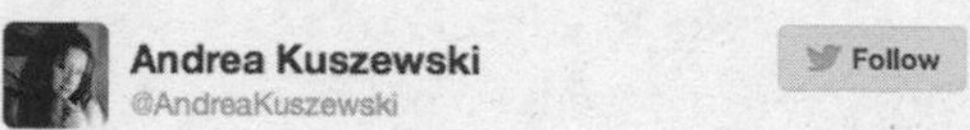

Dear person calling me on the phone: Don't do that. Thanks! Love, Person-Who-Doesn't-Answer-Her-Phone-Ever

Leave a hang-up at the beep.

Voicemail should not be treated as a content delivery system. A voicemail kidnaps the recipient's time for as long as it takes to hear that rambling message you left, assuming they don't rebel and delete it halfway through. (My friend Jackie Danicki refuses to listen to any voicemail longer than a minute and often deletes them in the first ten seconds if they lack promise.) If you must speak your piece—like when your doctor's office needs your insurance card number and your call goes to her receptionist's voicemail—do your best to keep it snappy. But, otherwise, unless somebody's told you that they like or prefer voicemail, consider hanging up and texting or e-mailing them instead of rambling on: "Hi, it's Amy. I was just sitting here having Jell-O, petting my dog, and watching Ultimate Fight Club and thought of you . . ." In general, modern voicemail manners boil down to this: Don't leave voicemail.

Polite enjoyment of one's phone features

- *Call blocking*

  Having your call appear on caller ID as "private caller" or "blocked number" can be helpful in getting pus-bags who owe you money to accidentally pick up. But now that we're all used to getting a caller preview from caller ID, mystery callers creep out a lot of people. If you have call blocking, take that extra three-quarters of a second to dial *82 to disable it before calling friends and family, lest they wonder whether they'll be picking up to heavy breathing from the pay phone in cellblock D.

- *Call waiting*

Call waiting is the rudest feature in telephoning, the phone version of The Hollywood Conversation, where some Hollyweasel is talking to you but staring over your shoulder to monitor whether somebody more important has come into the room.

When somebody with call waiting leaves you on protracted hold, don't let them make you their phone bitch; hang up. If they complain, don't engage; just restate the obvious: "You were gone for a while, so I hung up." Next time, they will likely do better.

If you use this feature, be mindful that it's called "call waiting" and not "call waiting and waiting." Also, before clicking through to another call, show consideration for the person you've been speaking with by using interrupter-dissing language like "Hold on. Gotta *get rid of* this person beeping in." If you must dump the caller who was there first, make it sound like an emergency. (Remember: Honesty is always the best policy, except when lying your ass off will preserve somebody's feelings.)

- *Your outgoing message*

Record your own brief phone message[11] for callers to your cell phone instead of using the phone company's prerecorded one if that means enabling their rude bill-padding. Certain greedy companies jack up people's phone minutes usage with their

[11] The briefer the better, like my friend Max Ferguson's "Machine, beep, etcetera."

filibuster of a default message, explaining in minute detail what one must do to leave a voicemail. There are still people on earth who don't know how to do that, but most are members of Amazon tribes whose "phone packages" include an unlimited number of smoke signals.[12]

- *Your cell phone's ringer*
  Telephones carried into public places should be put on vibrate or, better still, on silent—silent like the repeating "g" in "enough is e-fucking-nough" (which is what we've all had of "happy hardcore" ring tones and every other ring tone there is).

A public cell phone call is an invasion of mental privacy.

Imagine somebody drilling a big hole in your skull and then grabbing their fast-food trash from lunch and jamming it all in. Welcome to somebody else's public cell phone call. It's mental littering. Brain-invasion robbery. You can become a victim simply by going out for pancakes, which, these days, often come with both maple syrup and a big unordered scoop of some cellboor's *BLAHBLAHBLAH*.

Yes, I'm aware of the saying, "There is no right not to be offended." And I get that lots of people offend in lots of ways, like by pairing a ginormous, jiggling, hairy belly with a midriff shirt and marching back and forth past where you're eating. But you can look the other way. You can't hear the other way.

Cellboors in restaurants and coffeehouses will often justify shoving their conversations on us by sneering, "What's the difference whether two people are sitting at a table talking or one person's talking to somebody on the other end of the country?" There *is* a

[12] Amazon tribes actually communicate by drumbeats, which I find rather inconsiderate, since "smoke signals" ends this paragraph funnier.

difference. Research by University of York psychologist Andrew Monk and colleagues showed that a one-sided conversation commandeers the brain in a way a two-sided conversation does not, apparently because your brain tries to fill in the side of the conversation you can't hear. (It doesn't help that people tend to bark into their cell phones in the way white men in cowboy movies talked to Indians.)

A team at Cornell led by then grad student Lauren Emberson deemed these one-sided conversations "halfalogues" and reinforced Monk's findings when they tested halfalogues made up of gibberish words against those with words that could be understood. They found that when the words spoken were incomprehensible, the brain drain was removed; there were no costs imposed on bystanders' attention. So, although many see public cell phone yakking as a noise issue, which it often is, it's the words being spoken that are the real problem. Basically, even if somebody on a cell phone is trying to keep their voice down, they're probably giving many around them an irritating case of neural itching.

This mind-jacking is an annoying side effect of the very useful human capacity to predict what others are thinking and feeling and use that information to predict how they'll behave. This is called "mental state attribution" or "theory of mind" (as in, the theory you come up with about what's going on in somebody else's mind). When you see a man looking deep into a woman's eyes, smiling tenderly and then getting down on one knee, your understanding and experience of what this usually means helps you guess that he's about to ask "Will you marry me?" and not "Would you mind lending me a pen?"

Unfortunately, this mind-reading ability isn't something we can turn on and off at will. "It's . . . pretty much automatic," blogged University of Pennsylvania linguist Mark Liberman. "You can't stop yourself from reading [others'] minds any more than you can stop yourself from noticing the color of their clothes." But when you're only getting half the cues, like from one side of a stranger's cell phone conversation, your brain has to work a lot harder, and it interferes with your ability to focus your thoughts on other things.

"The world is my phone booth!": Cellboors' hostile takeover of shared space.

As I noted in chapter 2, a cellboor who takes over a public space like a coffee bar or post office line with his yakking—effectively privatizing shared space as his own—is stealing from everyone there. It's important to look at it that way because even people who are seriously annoyed at having their attention colonized by some baboon on his cell are often reluctant to speak up. Understanding that we're being robbed—that the cellboor is hijacking our attention—is the best way to inspire even meeker types to eke out, "*Psst,* Bub—you mind keeping it down?"

Although *any* publicly made cell call is annoying, no matter what the volume, approaching somebody with a request *merely to talk more quietly* is probably the most effective approach, both because giving strangers orders tends to end badly and because it's impossible to briefly communicate the greater annoyance of one-sided versus two-sided conversations to somebody heehawing into their phone. By asking them to cut the decibel level, you're still communicating the essential point: Their cellular overshare is not flying with their captive audience. If they don't look armed or insane, feel free to lay the science on them (à la "You probably didn't know this . . .") after they detach their big donkey lips from their phone.

Pavlov's ring tone: Who's the boss of you, you or your phone?

A cell phone is not a bomb. It will not explode and take your arm off if left unanswered. Yet, not only will many answer business calls on the airport rent-a-car shuttle but if a phone rings at a wedding, a funeral, in the middle of a Broadway play,[13] or during sex, there's a pretty good chance the person it belongs to will pick up.

To understand why, follow the trail of doggy drool back to 1890s Russia, to physiologist Ivan Petrovich Pavlov's famous experiment on conditioned reflexes—learned responses that happen automatically, absent critical thinking. Pavlov would put out bowls of food for his dogs and then ring a bell. Before long, all he had to do was ring the bell and the dogs would salivate.

These days, the drooling animals are two-legged, the bell is the ring tone, and the toll is on the rest of us, thanks to how the cell phone has become the adult pacifier of choice. For some grocery shoppers, it's just too much to bear to walk the ENTIRE beverages aisle while alone with their thoughts. Others are incapable of buying a couple of apples or a jar of peanut butter without a heated phone consultation. Yes, much like an air traffic controller talking an eight-year-old through landing a plane, it is now possible to have one's spouse supervise every inch of one's shopping experience[14] (and never mind how other shoppers feel about being forced to hear a loud recitation of the names of twenty-nine kinds of salad dressing). The worst is when you're trapped behind some cellboor in the checkout line. Wouldn't it be nice if they'd turn around and ask the rest of us, "Hey, anybody mind being bored shitless about my friend's asinine problem with her boss?"

Those who absolutely must take a call in public could at least slink off to an out-of-the-way corner and whisper—and the more they get guff from the rest of us about streaming their loud, dull

[13] Kenneth Terrell and Sara Hammel wrote in *U.S. News & World Report* in 1999: "During a performance last March of the Broadway play *The Lion in Winter*, an audience member's cell phone rang. After putting up with the annoyance for 20 seconds, actor Laurence Fishburne stopped the scene and boomed: 'Will you turn off that f—ing phone, please?' He got a rousing ovation."

[14] Amazingly, when I was growing up in the Midwest, my dad managed to go to the supermarket for my mother without trotting out to the pay phone numerous times.

lives into our brains the more likely they'll be to do that. And let's get real: Most "emergency" calls are anything but—unless we've redefined "emergency" to mean "whatever doesn't inconvenience me in the slightest."[15]

Muzzling the mobile savage: My usual approach.

Unfortunately, interior design for businesses has yet to catch up to cell phone innovation. Businesses provide little closets for their customers so they can leave their human waste without an audience. It would be nice if they'd also provide other little closets (these used to be called phone booths) so their customers could make their calls without polluting everybody else's attention. (Please put in a request for this ambience improver at your favorite eating establishments.)

At my favorite coffeehouse (which has NO CELL PHONES signs posted), some of the employees and many of the other customers have come to depend on me for enforcement when anybody there gets or makes a call.[16] When somebody is glaringly rude, marching into this serene place while barking into their phone, I long to tackle them, stuff dirty tube socks in their mouth, and bounce on them until they beg for air. (I never said I had mature impulses; I just try to avoid giving in to them.) But, along the lines of what I write in the "Communicating" chapter about direct criticisms just making people defensive, an approach to a cellboor that's at all aggressive usually just makes them aggressively rude (or, rather, *more* aggressively rude than they already

---

[15] One night at the supermarket, a guy a few people ahead of me in a long checkout line got up to the cashier. He might've greeted her, but his phone rang, and he flipped it open and barked, "DUUUUDE!" On Sunday night. At 8 p.m. At the 'hood-adjacent supermarket we locals call "The Ghetto Ralphs." (I'll hazard a guess that he wasn't answering because he's the one with the missile launch codes.)

[16] Some regulars have grown so reliant on me for cellboor-muzzling that if I have my headphones on, they'll wave to get my attention and then point to whoever's on their cell so I'll go over and tell them it's against the rules.

were in forcing a play-by-play of their weekend errands on a bunch of strangers).

The truth is, most of the people who get on their phones at this café aren't rule-flouting cellboors; they simply aren't mindful. (This is probably true of many people on phones in many places, with or without NO CELL PHONES signs.) So, the tack I find most productive is to smile a little, crouch down at their table level to keep from coming off "alpha," and stage whisper, "Excuse me, but they have a 'no cell phones' policy here. They like that people take their calls outside." Most just say "I'm sorry; I didn't know" and scurry outdoors.

In establishments lacking a cell phone ban, again, a request that somebody on their phone merely talk more quietly is actually the best way to get them to end their call or take it outdoors. This communicates that those around them are bothered—the essential detail. But merely asking the person to keep it down a bit suggests that you assume that they have good manners and a sense of consideration for others and inadvertently forgot to exercise them. Telling people what to do, on the other hand, tends to turn them into defiant six-year-olds who want nothing more than to do—louder, longer, and harder—whatever it is you're telling them they need to stop.

Two scolds are better than one: Enlisting the power of peer pressure.

You may have graduated from junior high school, but in a lot of ways, none of us ever gets out. Thanks to our evolved concern for protecting our reputation, we can still succumb to peer pressure, even as adults, and even when the peers putting on the pressure are strangers to us.

This works in our favor when there's some cell-blathering socio-turd in the DMV line who refuses to get off her phone. Don't just keep telling her *you're* bothered; round up some reinforcements. Even if you enlist just one other annoyed person and even if they just mutter "Yeah, I was bothered, too," the most amazing thing usually happens: A woman who belligerently insisted that nothing short of a nuclear attack would end her call suddenly finds reason to cut it short. Sure, she'll probably turn around periodically and give you dirty looks. Fortunately, those don't come with a soundtrack.

Other ways to stop cellular rudewads

- *When a person on a phone is multitasking deep into your eyes*
  As I wrote in my advice column, answering the phone while at a restaurant with a date is the digital version of deserting your dining companion and bopping over to sit with friends across the restaurant. Texting? In old-school terms, it's like whipping out a pen and legal pad and saying to your date, "You busy yourself with that pork chop, sweetcheeks. Got a couple letters I gotta mail out first thing."

  When your dining companion gets on the phone or starts texting, don't just sit there pretending to examine your napkin for hidden messages. Allowing disrespect tells people you're okay with it. If the person's a friend, put your foot down: You're not going to share their attention with the sports scores (and that goes for any covert peeks, as well). On a date, if there aren't understandable extenuating circumstances for the interruption, you're within your rights to excuse yourself to the bathroom and crawl out through the window. At the very least, strongly consider making it your last date with them. Their flagrant lack of consideration doesn't bode well for a relationship, nor does any flagrant lack of response from you. In short, you get what you put up with. As I noted in that column, "if you're going to invite somebody to dinner and ignore them, at least have the decency to get married first and build up years of bitterness and resentment."

- *When you discover you've spent $12 or more for tickets to Raging Bullshit*

At the movies, it's tempting to lean over and say something to the cellboors diverting your attention from the movie with their call or the glow of their phone while they text or check their e-mail, but it's usually futile. It's rare that somebody's doing this because they just aren't mindful. They usually know they're being rude, and they don't care. Go get an usher to stop them—somebody with the power to throw them out.

Some theaters are more proactive than others in evicting cellboors. Let's all thank them and beg others to hop on their bandwagon. The Alamo Drafthouse in Austin, Texas, is one of these theaters, starting their movies with a message warning patrons that they don't "tolerate people that talk or text in the theater" and that when somebody doesn't follow the rules, they do, "in fact, kick their asses out."

Some of their moviegoers must think they're bluffing. Here's an excerpt from an awesomely irate voicemail (with fabulously fractured phonetics) that a woman left for the Alamo Drafthouse staff, who turned it into a YouTube video:

> So EXCUSE ME for using MY phone in USA MAGNITED STATES OF AMERICA! where yer-you are FREE to TEXT in a THE-A-TER! . . .
>
> I've texted in ALL the other theaters in Austin, and no one ever gave a fuck. . . . I will never be comin' back to your "Alamo Drafthouse" or whatever. . . . I'm gonna tell EVERYONE about how SHITTY you are . . . . Thanks for takin' my money, ASSHOLE!

The Alamo Drafthouse, in text on-screen in the video, replied:

> You're welcome! Thanks for not coming back to the Alamo, texter!

- *Cell phone rehab for co-workers*
  After I did a presentation at a TV network, two of the younger producers took me aside, asking how they could deal with co-workers who were only partially present in meetings because they were texting, e-mailing, and Facebooking from their phones. The worst offender was an executive who apparently thought she got a manners waiver with the title of VP. She would consistently miss things said in presentations and cause problems because of it. Well, you can't single out your boss, but you can suggest a "productivity-increasing idea" to some higher-up: At the start of the meeting, everybody puts their phone in a basket in the middle of the table. This policy not only makes for more polite and productive meetings but also sends a helpful message: No, bosslady, you actually aren't earning a six-figure salary for checking cakewrecks.com multiple times daily.

- *Cell phone jammers: Reach out and block someone.*
  I've probably had 300 people gleefully e-mail me to inform me about these electronic gizmos, illegal in the United States, that transmit a radio frequency that blocks cell phone signals, cutting off calls. Yes, I've heard of them—and I'm opposed to them. I'm all for boor-silencing, but some people do need to be reachable and aren't rude, and it isn't fair to blot out their signal just because other people are cell-bellowing swine. (Taken to the extreme, it's like sending everybody on a bus to jail because one person on it robbed a bank.) Besides, it turns out that cell phone signals might not be the only ones that are blocked. When Philly's NBC affiliate reported on a guy using a jammer on his daily bus ride, Drexel University criminal justice professor Rob D'Ovidio told them that jammers may also cut off GPS, two-way police radios, and 911 calls.

Focus pocus: Why be in one place at once if you can be in two?

LA public radio doyenne Patt Morrison had me on her show to talk about "distracted walkers"—those so engaged in texting or phoning that they aren't paying attention to their immediate environment. This oblivious walking is, of course, bad—if they're so immersed in their little screen they stroll out into traffic or stop short on the subway steps at rush hour. Yet there are people who get enraged at the mere sight of another person on a cell phone, even if that person is talking outside or is texting and isn't bothering or impeding anyone. To these cellhaters, even discreet, noninvasive cell phone use is a sign of our civilization's slow suicide (along with food items that are deep-fried that shouldn't be and reality shows about New Jersey housewives and the apparently endless supply of Kardashians).

One of these horrified people, "Merle from Woodland Hills," called in to Patt's show. She compared those staring into their cell phones to the pod people from *Invasion of the Body Snatchers*, proclaimed it "antisocial to behave that way in public," and added that she feels sorry for the cellphoners because "they're missing out on their environment." Her time was up before she could accuse them of mass murder and not wiping the toilet seat after they go.

Merle apparently takes for granted that one should always be "present" and be "in the moment"—meaning in the environment that one is physically in. But, who's to say that the environment people are physically occupying is the most important environment for them—or should be? As I pointed out on the radio, maybe some of these people Merle objects to aren't "antisocial" but "multisocial." (Of course, seeing this as a good thing assumes they aren't harassing others in earshot with their call.) Say you're on the West Coast and the person you love is on the East Coast. A hundred and fifty years ago, communicating with them would have meant handing a letter to a guy on a horse and waiting a month or two for a reply. These days, I can be in Los Angeles on a walk exploding with gorgeous flowering trees and vines while I'm on the phone with my boyfriend who's driving down some bleak street in Detroit, where he travels for his work. Sure, I could stop and smell the flowers—but sometimes I'd rather walk past them and focus on telling him how much I love him so I can make him promise to lock his car doors so he won't get jacked.

Like Merle, we're all guilty of assuming we know what's best for other people—especially when whatever that is happens to present a lovely frame for our own moral and intellectual superiority. But unless your cellphoning makes me want to take a shrimp fork to my eardrums or causes me to swerve into oncoming traffic to avoid running you down, it really isn't up to me to dictate whether you text your days away or spend them reading Good Books Approved by the Reviewing Staff of The New Yorker.

That said, I think we could all be a little more mindful of the dangers cell phones can pose when used less than mindfully. Per the research on how a one-sided conversation commandeers the brain, a phone call by the passenger in a car could cause the driver's attention to the road to wane. Also, many who talk on the phone while driving weave down the street like drunks, and every few months, you hear a story about someone who thought she'd just send that one little text while speeding down the highway—and who ends up sending a family of four to the funeral home.

To keep from being one of these people, I have a personal rule (in addition to the California law that so many ignore) that I am never allowed to send a text or even look at my phone while driving.[17] I do sometimes talk with an earbud while behind the wheel, but never in dicey driving situations, and if a phone call gets dropped and the person I'm talking to doesn't call me back, I don't

[17] Look for apps, like DriveSafe.ly, that you can set up to automatically read you texts as they come in and automatically message those texting you to let them know you are driving and will get back to them when you stop.

call them back until I'm stopped. In general, I drive in terror of hurting anyone and with the belief that everyone on the road is simultaneously talking on their phone, applying mascara, getting oral sex, and trying to swerve into my lane and kill me.

Perhaps because of this, I've avoided being physically injured by others, and my own episodes of distracted phoning (outside the car) have merely led to my dying of embarrassment. For example, one afternoon, I was in the middle of a productive writing jag at the coffeehouse, so I dashed off a quick text to my boyfriend:

Honey, we should wait until end of day to book my travel.

Or, rather, I thought I sent it to him.

The woman who edits me texted back:

ok, baby.

Oh, how embarrassing. I resolved to be more careful. And about an hour later, knowing that he was under a lot of pressure to pull research on the Apache Indians, I texted him a little pick-me-up:

Smooches from your squaw. PS honey, I know you're doing great.

Again, my editor texted back:

just hanging here in my wigwam laughing my ass off

Thankfully, having texted from a public place, I'd been unable to take advantage of the mood-enhancing qualities of eight megapixels of bared cleavage.

— 6 —

THE INTERNET

Facebook founder Mark Zuckerberg was nine when I got on AOL in late 1993, probably about five years before I began hearing this complaint: "The Internet alienates people." In 1993, what alienated me was having too little money. I was a struggling writer in New York, the city that never sleeps (because it's too busy dining out at pricey restaurants). My budget limited me to dinners that came in dented cans, but when a group of my gainfully employed friends was dining out, I'd sometimes drop by the restaurant after they'd finished their entrees. The hard part was that moment when the waitress would come over to ask what I was having. I'd make the face of a person thinking (or perhaps constipated) and say "Just a glass of water—for now" as if I couldn't make up my mind which caviar or pricey glass of port to order.

Dreading that exchange, I began to bow out of these dinners altogether. Instead, I'd buy a big bottle of Diet Coke, crank up my dial-up modem, and drop in on an AOL chat room. A lot of these were home to some pretty inane chatter—LOL! ROFLMAO!—but if I found the right one, I'd get in on a fast-paced dinner conversation with no need to hand over my current life savings at the end.

One night, some chat room lout got pretty crass in attacking me. I can defend myself and did, but somebody else came to my defense, too—screen name "The Counte"—in a way that was both chivalrous and hilarious. The Counte was far more interesting than anyone else in the chat room. I instant messaged The Counte to thank him, and we kept talking, writing long e-mails every day and sometimes spending hours in the evening IM'ing each other, sharing ideas about science, human nature, politics and life, and tossing around raunchy humor.

Over about six months of this, we became close friends, telling each other stuff we told no one else. Yet, I had no idea who this person was and felt no need to find out. In fact, it seemed kind of amazing to have this deep friendship without our having each other's dull, job application-y particulars. And no, this wasn't one of those panting Internet affairs. Ours was an intellectual romance. Besides, with it being winter and my being intermittently penniless and renting a "bedroom" that was essentially a heavily trafficked hallway in a drafty loft, if he'd asked "What are you wearing?" my answer would have been "An old snowsuit I got at the Army-Navy surplus."

One day, I informed The Counte that for a few weeks, I might not be on AOL so much because I had to go to Los Angeles for a freelance job. He said he lived in LA, and he wanted to meet me. He told me to call him and gave me his number. I dialed it, and God answered—or at least that's how it sounded when he said his slow, deep, raspy "Hello?" We talked for a long time, and before we hung up, we decided to tell each other our names. It was only then I learned that my friend was Marlon Brando.

Before I flew back to New York, he invited me up to his place on Mulholland, and we hung out for an afternoon. After I moved to Los Angeles, we hung out a lot. He was the first person to believe in me as a writer and thinker and would send me these long, poetic, supportive e-mails when I felt disappointed and lost. He ended up becoming pretty much a second dad to me, as well as a human mountain range to my three-pound Yorkie, Lucy, who liked to prance back and forth across his shoulders and then sit licking the back of his neck when he and I were seated on his living-room couch.

The Marlon I hung out with was the Marlon few people got to know: the inventor who loved literature, poetry, science, logic, and sleight-of-hand magic tricks. He'd call me at 3 a.m. to tell me something fascinating he'd just read about, say, Madame Ching, the Chinese pirate. And most fun of all, there was Marlon my co-prankster. We were like two adult eight-year-olds. I'd come over, and he'd make prank calls in various voices and identities, including that of a British lady's maid, and I'd try to laugh out of my eyes instead of out loud so I wouldn't blow his cover.

Of course, we never would have become friends in "real life." Famous people and regular people generally can't become friends, because the famous are like human wild game to many or most regular people. Even regular people who don't have userish motives can end up acting all weird around famous people, deferring to their fame. And, as I came to learn, even some movie stars treat other movie stars—bigger movie stars—like fame objects. In Marlon's case, it seemed that some other stars thought that if only they could get close to him, some of whatever he had might rub off on them. This made them act creepy around him, which made Marlon itchy and late to some dinner parties (later than he would have been just by being Marlon) so he didn't have to spend so many hours being treated like a thing.

Once, Marlon took me to one of these soirees as a sort of psychic bodyguard, knowing that at least two of those in attendance (all six of whom were movie stars) would be on him like vultures on a downed wildebeest. We were already late to dinner when he got to my dumpy Venice Beach apartment in the back of a hot-pink duplex shack. He wanted to be even later, so he parked his white Lexus in my spot, and we sat on my couch for a half-hour coming up with elaborate excuses for our delay. Storywise, he decided to go for plausibility over flash, settling on the rather dull tale of his supposedly coming to the aid of a stranded motorist on Pacific Coast Highway. When I complained that this story was boring, he said he'd jazz it up by weaving in the big gauze bandage on his shin from some minor injury he'd gotten at home.

I found this funny because it made no sense in the context. How would he have gotten this injury, by borrowing the person's tire iron and cracking himself in the shin? And at what medical facility would he have gotten this bandaged between wherever we supposedly stopped on Pacific Coast Highway and the dinner-hosting star's Malibu home?

I declined to let him introduce me as Dolores del Schwartz, his Jewishizing of Dolores del Rio, a Mexican Hollywood star from the 1920s and 30s he'd probably had the hots for. I instead went as myself, and as I predicted, the only thing the snotty, fawning famous people were less interested in than the commoner taking whole molecules of Marlon's attention away from them was that commoner's name.

Seeing how Marlon was treated, even by people who, famewise, were close to being his peers, made me understand the truth in the cliché "It's lonely at the top." So many "regular" people long to become famous, because out there in ordinary citizen-land, they see only the upsides. But when you're really, really famous—one of the most famous movie stars of the twentieth century—it seems that one of life's joys is finding that you're just "some guy" some girl can't stop writing to on the Internet.

THE MISSING MANUAL

For most of us, the Internet was like a shiny thing that dropped out of the sky. The phone was like that at first, too. But, in 1878, ten months after the first telephone exchange came into existence in

New Haven, Connecticut, the phone company put out the first phone book, which included directions on how to use the thingamajig. Ammon Shea writes in his history of the telephone directory, *The Phone Book*, that "there were admonitions to restrict calls to three minutes at a time and to not use the telephone more than twice in an hour without first getting permission from the central office." The book also advised starting a call with a "firm and cheery" hello (written "Hulloa")—ignoring Alexander Graham Bell's insistence that callers open with "Ahoy!"

It might seem a little late now for Internet guidelines. We've all managed to find our way to Google, and most of us have figured out that Dr. Mubutunde in Nigeria really isn't going to give us a million dollars if we'll just send him our bank account login and password. But because the Internet puts so much power right at our fingertips and it's so much fun to use, we underestimate the tendency for even otherwise responsible adults with serious jobs to devolve into mouth-breathing chimps who've just been handed the button for an info-nuke. As Twitter-lovin' disgraced former congressman Anthony Weiner discovered, disseminating boner shots far and wide is as easy as spreading your legs and clicking your cameraphone.

As in Weiner's case, people who fall back on what's *technically* possible as the standard for their behavior typically give the most thought to how to act online *after* they get in trouble—after they lose their job or a friend or just go medieval on somebody on Facebook in a way they're later ashamed of. To avoid disaster, you need to come up with personal policies *in advance* for how you'll fly online, covering three essential areas:

- Your online identity.
- Privacy: yours and everybody else's.
- How to treat other people online and what to do when they treat you badly.

CRAFTING YOUR ONLINE IDENTITY

You're only anonymous on the Internet because nobody's tried very hard to figure out who you are.

Exactly how public do you want to be? Answering that question takes deciding how closely your online identity should follow your actual identity. I'm one of those open-book types. I'll keep your secrets, but I have a harder time keeping my own. Also, I find that people are more interested in reading what I write about my life if I reveal the idiotic, humiliating, and hypocritical things I've done rather than all the ways I'm smart and together. So it literally pays for me to let it all hang out, or at least a whole lot of it.

Figure out parameters for how much of yourself you want to reveal online in comments, photos, and videos—from your name and occupation to your true politics to your naked parts. Be proactive about articulating these parameters to others in your life so, for example, friends will know that they'll need to ask your permission before tagging you in Facebook photos or perhaps even posting photos that include you. Remember, every picture tells a story, and your name in a caption on somebody's Facebook photo makes that photo appear on your Facebook page[18] and become visible to your Facebook friends. When it does, it's best that the story it tells (*personal best for slamming tequila shots!*) doesn't lay waste to the story you told your boss about tending to your sick auntie instead of staying late to tend to his spreadsheets.

Having a clear sense of your boundaries for exposure will also give you a better chance of keeping hold of them should you find yourself in something of a stupor. Sure, when you've had a few and somebody videotapes you naked and frisky, you can probably sue or maybe even have them prosecuted, but that won't close the barn

[18] There are privacy settings you can activate so you have to approve all photos that go on your Timeline, but remember that Facebook's default settings are generally "Y'all come have a look!"

door after the sex tape of you and Mr. Ed has gone viral on You-Porn.

When considering how much of the real you to share online, err on the side of assuming that whatever you or other people post or e-mail will be speedily copied, pasted, and forwarded to anyone with an Internet connection, because that sometimes happens even when you're sure you've taken stringent precautions. For example, Facebook "privacy" settings are wildly complicated and ever-changing and no guarantee that your private life will be kept private. In 2012, Geoffrey A. Fowler wrote in *The Wall Street Journal* about Bobbi Duncan, a twenty-two-year-old woman from a fundamentalist family "who desperately wanted her father not to know she is a lesbian." Duncan, a student at the University of Texas, had adjusted her Facebook privacy settings to hide any hint of her sexuality from her father after she helped him sign up for Facebook. But one of Duncan's extracurricular activities was singing in a college choir. When its president added Duncan to the choir's Facebook group, it triggered Facebook to notify Duncan's nearly 200 Facebook friends, including her dad, that she was part of the unambiguously named "Queer Chorus." "That night," wrote Fowler, "Ms. Duncan's father left vitriolic messages on her phone, demanding she renounce same-sex relationships . . . and threatening to sever family ties."

On blogs and in other discussion forums, if you think you can guard your identity simply by posting under some made-up name or using some techno-trick to hide who you are, think again. You're sure to get sloppy, as did an employee from the Department of Homeland Security who *almost always* cloaked his IP address (the numerical address of a computer or network a person is posting from) when he was violating numerous Homeland Security policies in pretending to be just an ordinary citizen posting multiple abusive attacks on me on my blog posts criticizing the TSA's violations of our civil liberties. The attacks by this guy, who used the moniker "Knowing" and posted forty-four times from September 2011 to November 2012, were so rude and relentless that I got curious and looked up the IP addresses that he had posted from. I then discovered that he was a (taxpayer-salaried) Homeland Security employee posting from (taxpayer-funded) Homeland Security servers in Washington, DC, during the workday! No sooner did I reveal this on my blog than his tone changed from vicious and abusive to regretful and apologetic. I demanded his identity and swore I'd go after him and expose him. In his final comment on my site, he wrote, "I know you will pursue me." Not surprisingly, his colleagues at Homeland Security are not cooperating with my efforts, so rooting him out may take a while longer—and a Freedom of Information Act request. I'm guessing he's spent at least a few months worrying that he'll lose his job or be demoted or at least be shamed in the eyes of his superiors—that is, if he isn't one of the Homeland Security superiors. As we've seen in numerous government scandals, including Weiner's and head spook General David Petraeus's resignation in the wake of his unencrypted Gmail-conducted affair[19] with his biographer, there's some pretty high-placed stupidity in the reckless use of technology.

In sharing on social media, keep in mind that even your most carefully thought-out boundaries can wither when you have a strong emotion and the smartphone technology to vent it to the universe in seconds. If there's a lot at stake for you in emotionally driven

---

[19] As Jim Emerson writes on RogerEbert.com, "Petraeus and Broadwell used the Drafts folder of a joint Gmail account to exchange sexually explicit messages. They were aware enough to want to hide what they were doing by not actually sending e-mails that could be traced, but apparently naïve enough not to realize that this trick is known to terrorists and teenagers the world over."

Ryan Gallagher adds on *Slate,* "If the lovers had only ever logged into their pseudonymous Gmail accounts using anonymity tools like Tor, their real IP addresses would have been masked and their identities extremely difficult to uncover."

overshare, you might make a rule that in the wake of getting enraged or otherwise jazzed up while online, you'll give yourself a little time-out before you let your fingers do any tap-dancing on any keyboards.

A time-out rule is especially important for anyone who uses social media as part of their job. Scott Bartosiewicz, a Detroit-based social media strategist working on the Chrysler account, decided to blow off a little frustration on Twitter when traffic was making him late to work. This turned into the perfect strategy for getting himself canned when he tweeted a message on the Chrysler feed that he thought he was tweeting on his personal account:

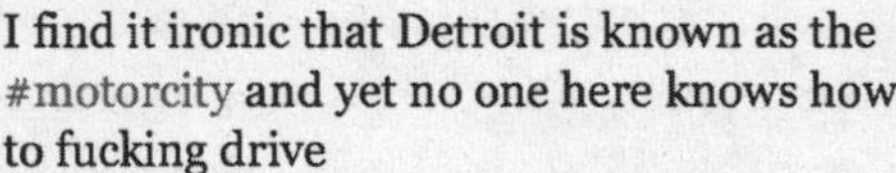

PRIVACY: IT'S REPORTEDLY DEAD, BUT IT SHOULDN'T BE.

Even before our government started logging your calls to your grandma, blogger Greg Swann deemed privacy "an artifact of inefficiency," explaining that what we've thought of throughout our lives as privacy "has simply been a function of inefficient data processing tools." In other words, it's not that we never used to reveal so much because we had better character. We just lacked the technology to depants each other in the Global Village's town square.

Now that we have that technology, many seem to believe that their life and everyone else's are there for the uploading. If something happens, it simply *must* be posted, tweeted, and Facebooked, and if something isn't, it must not matter or maybe doesn't even exist. (If a tree falls in the forest and nobody's around to video it and upload it to Facebook . . .)

But, is it really a matter of compelling public interest that three days ago, while waiting in your car for the light to change, you picked your nose? And just because some guy in the next car was quick to catch your nose-digging with his phone and post it to YouTube, should it really be preserved for eternity like a bug in amber?

Technology's impact on privacy isn't a new issue. "Numerous mechanical devices threaten to make good the prediction that 'what is whispered in the closet shall be proclaimed from the housetops,'" wrote Samuel Warren and Louis Brandeis in the *Harvard Law Review* in the 90s—the 1890s. They were worried about the advent of affordable portable cameras and dismayed at the way newspapers had begun covering people's private lives.

Brandeis and Warren explained that a person has a right—a natural human right—to determine to what extent their thoughts, opinions, and emotions and the details of their "private life, habits, acts, and relations" will be communicated to others. They noted that this right to privacy comes out of our right to be left alone and that it applies whether an individual's personal information is "expressed in writing, or in conduct, in conversation, in attitudes, or in facial expression."

This has not changed because of what's now technically possible: how it takes just a few clicks to Facebook or Instagram an embarrassing photo of a person or blog their medical history, sexual orientation, sex practices, financial failings, lunch conversation, or daily doings. No matter how fun and easy the technology makes immediately publishing everything about everyone and no matter how common it's become to violate everyone's right to privacy, each person's private life remains their own and not a free commodity to be turned into content by the rest of us.

Where privacy ends and content begins

Sometimes it is fair game to yank somebody's privacy: to publish their name, image, or whereabouts or other information about them that they'd rather not have made public. Harvard's Digital Media Law Project advises that the law protects you when you publish information that is *newsworthy*, meaning that there's "a reasonable relationship between the use of the (person's) identity and a matter of legitimate public interest."

Brandeis and Warren pointed out that politicians and other public or quasi-public figures have, to a great extent, "renounced the right to live their lives screened from public observation." They explained that the details about a would-be congressman's habits, activities, and foibles may say something about his fitness for office, whereas publishing something about, say, a speech impediment suffered by some "modest and retiring individual" would be an "unwarranted . . . infringement of his rights."

Still, private individuals sometimes do things that justify our stripping them of their privacy. Say some lady parks her BMW convertible in a handicapped space (sans disabled plate or placard) and jogs over to the dry cleaner. She's gambling that no ticket-giver will come by before she's back. She's also taking advantage of how, anywhere but in a small town, we're largely anonymous to the people around us, removing the natural constraint on rude behavior—concern for reputation—that's in place when people you know can see the hoggy things you're up to. We restore the reputational cost by webslapping her: taking her picture and blogging, tweeting, and Facebooking it in hopes of shaming her (and compelling other inconsiderados who see the posts) into parking like less of a douche in the future.

A webslapping is also in order for rude people who have *voluntarily given up their privacy* by bellowing their cell phone conversation so loudly that everyone seated around them in a restaurant is forced to listen to it, which makes it a public conversation. You don't, however, have the right to blog, tweet, Facebook, or otherwise broadcast a *quiet* conversation you're able to overhear between people seated behind you, assuming they aren't talking about a plot to blow up the State Department.

And say a man is "guilty" only of attending a dinner gathering. In my advice column, I answered the letter of a man, signing himself "Publicized," who is widely known and admired for his business accomplishments but values his privacy. Unbeknownst to him, his presence at a dinner party was tweeted by the host's cousin, a man who "rudely spent most of the evening thumbing" his smartphone. The cousin was maybe trying for status by association (being a guest at the same dinner party as somebody who's somebody) or, like many people, feels compelled to persistently flick information out on social media as a sort of digital proof of life.

"Publicized" only found out about the tweet upon getting home, when he was surprised to receive an e-mail from a distant acquaintance asking, "How was dinner at Elaine's?" Days later, he met a former colleague for lunch at a restaurant. He discovered that the colleague had tweeted about the lunch upon coming home to a handful of e-mails from those who'd seen the tweet. And no, these tweets wouldn't be a big deal—or any deal—to every person, but they were to "Publicized," and rightfully so.

Privacy plunderers will argue that a restaurant is a public place. This is true, but a man's appearance at that restaurant is not "newsworthy" unless he's sticking the place up. And while a man's desire for privacy is valid if he simply isn't comfortable being turned into a newsbit, there may be compelling reasons a person would not want his whereabouts published, like if he turned down three other dinner invitations to go to the dinner he ended up attending.

Of course, because so many people now believe others' privacy is theirs for the violating, if you'd like your private life to remain private, you may need to be proactive about it when you're invited somewhere. Obviously, if you see somebody's about to take your picture, you can either bow out of the shot or tell them that you don't want to appear in social media. Though many people have just resigned themselves to the idea that privacy is over, others are increasingly cognizant that privacy violations can be a real problem for some. The idea of a "what happens at dinner stays at dinner" social media embargo might be worth floating to a host if you aren't near-strangers and if you think they might be open to the notion that sharing everybody's everything goes a little far.

There's a policy like that in place at a monthly writer/pundit dinner I go to—a policy that I think makes those in attendance feel freer to speak their minds, knowing that something they happen to blurt out while sloshed won't be used against them. The policy was announced in the invitation e-mail at one point and then just understood and passed on to future guests by those of us who are regular attendees. As I wrote to "Publicized," in the wake of one of these embargoes, guests will just have to satisfy themselves with being rude in old-fashioned ways: hogging the mashed potatoes, passing gas and looking scornfully at the guest next to them, and rummaging through the host's medicine chest . . . but refraining from uploading a shot of its contents to Instagram or Flickr.

Having regular sex with someone doesn't allow you to roll back their privacy to that of a convicted serial killer.

Getting into a relationship doesn't entitle you to demand your partner's e-mail and Facebook passwords so you can subject his digital life to regular cavity searches. His inner life—and Internet life—still belong to him, as does the decision of which hopes, dreams, and really tasteless forwards to share with you. Anything he doesn't specifically invite you to see should be considered off-limits—even if you can guess his password or seize the opportunity to take a little tour of his browser history while he's in the john.

A common suspicion is, "If you aren't hiding anything, why would you care whether your girlfriend can read your e-mail,

Facebook messages, whatever?" A woman, writing me for advice, asked me that when her boyfriend of two years refused to be bullied into handing over his passwords. I explained that a desire for privacy isn't evidence of sneakiness.[20]

People show different sides of themselves to different people, and her boyfriend would likely feel curtailed in who he is and how he expresses himself if Big Girlfriend is always watching. Giving her access to his e-mail would also be unfair to people who correspond with him, kind of like putting them on speakerphone without their knowledge. If he caved and gave her access to his e-mail, the fair thing for him to do would be the humiliating thing: send out an e-mail to everyone he's ever met and anyone who might ever write him, disclosing the possibility that any message they send him could be read by The Warden. (Subject line: "I'm whipped.")

There is, however, an alternative to turning a relationship into the world's tiniest police state, and that's putting in the time and effort to figure out whether a person is ethical *before* you get into a committed relationship with them. As I wrote to the woman, "if you can't trust your boyfriend, why are you with him? If you can, accept that his information is his property, and leave him be when he closes the bathroom door to his mind."

Your relationship needs a privacy policy.

Each person in a relationship gets to set the standard for what the other partner can blog, tweet, Facebook, Flickr, or otherwise share about them—if anything. That standard should be agreed upon in advance and maintained in the event of a breakup.

Should be, that is. But, keep in mind that breakups caused by cheating tend to make a partner feel less compelled to honor any prior agreements and, at the same time, make them feel more compelled to vent to anyone and everyone who will listen, including

[20] A *sudden* desire for privacy in a person who's always been open may be reason for suspicion.

three fishermen who were able to pick up a Wi-Fi signal on their trawler off the coast of China.

Additionally, consider what you have to lose before you let someone—even someone you love, in a relationship you are sure will never end—turn a video camera on your naked patootie. Remember, times change; videotapes get mysteriously "lost." Your willingness to appear doggy style on video should be directly *dis*proportionate to how much you like your job as an elementary-school principal.

How you unwittingly violate your own privacy—and that of your friends, relatives, and some guy you once e-mailed about the cross-country skis he was selling on Craigslist.

In addition to the government's grabbing more and more of your personal information for "security" purposes (and occasionally losing it on a laptop some government employee has stolen out of their car), corporations are using technology to hoover up everything they can find out about you and everyone you know.

Big businesses info-grope you when you buy things from them, and especially when you get something for nothing. Basically, you get hosed by what you don't pay for, like Facebook, which is far from the free service it appears to be. The same goes for newspaper sites that require Facebook registration, as well as Gmail and other Internet "freebies." You pay for them by giving up some (or a lot) of your privacy, which can, in turn, open the door for a business to every e-mail contact and social media connection you have.

For example, "liking" a product on Facebook or entering some contest that requires a Facebook "like" may shoot out a little ad turd for it on top of the Facebook page of everyone who's friended you—and maybe some of their friends. When you're reading a compelling article on a newspaper site requiring "Facebook Connect" to log in, it's easy to forget that "liking" it or commenting on it may announce your politics or interests to people you'd rather keep in the dark about them.

Beware of the address book hijackers: social networking sites that thank you for becoming a member by raiding your address book and sending out an e-mail (appearing to be from you) telling everyone in it that you want them to join. Goodreads, Pinterest, and Reunion.com have been among the guilty.[21] [22] When you join a site, avoid clicking on any seemingly harmless request like "See which of your friends are members!" This too often acts as a digital "open sesame!" for the site to e-mail everyone in your address book and maybe your entire list of Facebook friends, sometimes despite your not clicking many or any names. In short, if you'd rather avoid pissing off the 36,000 business contacts in your address book, it pays to think of social networking sites both as social networking sites and as giant parasites targeting your personal information like a tapeworm waiting for a move-in special on your large intestine.

HOW TO TREAT OTHER PEOPLE ONLINE AND WHAT TO DO WHEN THEY TREAT YOU BADLY.

The "Behave as You Are in Real Life" rule

It's easy to get bewitched by the power you can have with a few clicks and keystrokes, especially when combined with anonymity. Understanding this, I made a rule for myself that every comment I make on a blog or website I make in my own full name. Now, maybe your job or family situation doesn't allow you to post in your real-life identity, or maybe it just creeps you out. To keep from going ugly on the Internet, resolve to at least post as the same person you are when speaking face-to-face with someone at work,

---

[21] Disgustingly, some sites and phone apps won't even ask before sucking up your address book—a situation some privacy activists have fought to change.

[22] My boyfriend at one point claimed that he was starting a nihilistic social network called Quitter: "Posts are zero characters, and you're asked not to join."

a dinner party, or the grocery store, assuming you aren't in the habit of greeting a grocery-shopping stranger eyeing some out-of-season veggie with "well ur a dum bitch now aren't you?"

The "Behave as You Are in Real Life" rule should also apply when commenting on the rich, famous, and enfranchised. Some movie star might have buttloads more money than you—and international fame, to boot—but it's safe to assume she also has feelings. Marilyn Monroe told *Life* in 1962 about the ugliness she encountered:

> When you're famous, you kind of run into human nature in a raw kind of way. . . . It stirs up envy, fame does. People you run into feel that, well, who is she—who does she think she is, Marilyn Monroe? They feel fame gives them some kind of privilege to walk up to you and say anything to you, you know, of any kind of nature—and it won't hurt your feelings—like it's happening to your clothing. . . . I don't understand why people aren't a little more generous with each other.

Riding the rapids of social and antisocial networking

The great thing about Facebook is how wildly easy it makes it to connect. This is also the not-so-great thing about it. I had an unhappy childhood. I had no friends as a child—not one, until I was thirteen. I was, admittedly, an odd, scrawny, nerdy kid with poor social skills, but it didn't help that I grew up in a neighborhood where my family didn't fit in. A few years ago, I was surprised when I got a Facebook friend request from a guy I grew up with—a guy I strongly suspect was in the group of boys who regularly egged my parents' windows, toilet-papered our trees, and shaving-creamed "Dirty Jew" on our garage. Because I mainly post links to my blog items on Facebook and because I earn a living based on the number of people reading me, I will friend just about anyone who asks (save for any guy whose profile picture is his erect penis), but I declined the guy's friend request. My policy: If you "Dirty Jew" me at eight, you don't get to "friend" me at forty-five.

Whom should you friend or unfriend? There have been countless articles on this subject, handing down what are supposedly the stone tablets on Facebook friending and unfriending, but the truth is, there's no one policy that works for every person. To decide what works best for you, take into account who you are (and, if you're looking for a job, who you want to be); what will get you fired, excommunicated, or disemboweled; the kind of content you post; and what you want your guiding principle to be. My guiding principle is openness and inclusiveness. For somebody who is less promiscuously public or who posts more personal content, privacy might rule.

When it's hard to decide whether to accept or nix a friend request, try to predict which would ultimately cost you more, refusing to friend a particular person or putting up with them online. If you ignore a friend request, it's usually best to avoid any explanation if it was from a stranger or someone you barely know. (You have no obligation to get in a debate with some stranger or distant acquaintance about your turndown, and any back-and-forth about it could ultimately get ugly.) If somebody you do know calls you on refusing their friend request, I think kindness is the best policy. (Honesty is for hardasses.) You could explain your refusal by saying you hope they won't take it personally; you just keep your Facebook circle to close friends and family, or you mainly use Facebook to stay in touch with a few old friends. (This excuse flies best if your privacy settings are tight enough that they can't see that you have a group of "close" friends and family numbering into the thousands.)

If you feel you just can't decline a particular person's friend request, you could always adjust your privacy settings so that person can only see certain posts, but keep in mind human fallibility, which always pops up at the worst of times. Also bear in mind how complex and confusing Facebook's ever-changing privacy settings are, effectively making them "privacy" settings. In a 2010 *New York Times* article, reporter Nick Bilton noted that Facebook's privacy policy was 5,830 words long—almost 1,300 words longer than the U.S. Constitution (without any of its amendments)—and Facebook's in-depth privacy FAQ page was a bulging 45,000 words long, the length of many books.

If you'd like to friend somebody you don't know personally, the polite (and least creepy) way to go about it is to first message them to explain that you're a fan of their work or thinking or that you find their posts on a friend's Facebook feed smart and would like to follow them. Keep in mind that women, especially, are wary of being followed by guys who may turn out to be mashers. If your request isn't accepted immediately, consider the possibility that the person isn't all that active on Facebook and has yet to see it. And if someone you know refuses your friend request, consider, as I mentioned above, that they may use Facebook as a personal bulletin board to share things with a few close friends and family members. If they do write to explain themselves, be gracious in your response. Getting huffy about somebody's desire for a close-knit Facebook circle is like getting in a snit because you knocked on the door of somebody you kind of know and they refused to let you march upstairs and rifle through their underwear drawer.

Unfriending—kicking somebody off your Facebook friends list—tends to go over like a kick in the face, especially when the dumped person is somebody you know in real life or have had a significant level of contact with online. Again, it's wise to weigh the trade-off: What will ultimately cost you more, unfriending a dull or abrasive person or putting up with their dull or offensive comments online?

I will unfriend people who leave frequent ugly strings of comments on my Facebook posts—not because I'm afraid of ugly speech but because I don't have the time to monitor and respond to all of it. If, however, some Facebook friend is just dull or mildly disagreeable, I go back to my guiding principle—openness and inclusiveness—remembering how it felt to be the kid who always got shunned by schoolmates who would have unexisted me if they could.

They're called "friends," not "prey": A few additional points on civilized social networking.

- *Think of your friend's Facebook wall like their garage door.* Tempting as it may be to go over early one Sunday morning and spray-paint your politics across your friends' garage door, I'm guessing you'd at least wait till they wake up to ask whether they'd mind.

  Consider your own Facebook wall your very special place to post your politics, links to your favorite conspiracy theories, and THE CUTEST PICTURE EVER!!!!! of your cat snoring, but consider whether others share your views and your interest in your cat's sleep positions before you haul off and post them on theirs. Some people will adjust their privacy settings so they have to approve what others try to post on their wall, but not everyone knows how or decides to do that. So, the safest, most considerate approach is messaging a friend to suggest a link for them to post—that is, if you are reasonably sure they'll appreciate it and you aren't just looking to hammer them on why people of their political persuasion are ruining the world.

- *Tag with caution.*
  Because you have a tight circle of Facebook friends, each of whom shares your every belief about politics and religion, doesn't mean everyone does. At a party, one of my blog commenters told a naughty joke about the pope to three friends he knew wouldn't be offended. One of them posted it to her Facebook wall, crediting him by name, which made the post show up on his Facebook wall, too—where he said some of his religious friends would have seen it and found the joke "super-offensive." The tagged post was up for an hour before he noticed it and deleted it from his wall.

- *Facebook group invitations: Shockingly, people who share some of your interests may not share all of them.*
  Anyone who knows me in *the slightes*t knows that I am about as interested in playing one of Facebook's games as I am in offering myself for human sacrifice, but those irritations—*uh,* invitations—keep on coming. Luckily, my Facebook friends seem more timid about dragging me into groups I have no interest in. My friend and Facebook friend Virginia Postrel, who describes herself as a "now-secular Presbyterian-turned-Jew," is not so lucky:

  Virginia Postrel
  Periodic reminder: Do NOT put me in your FB group w/o checking first.
  Renegade Catholics? Seriously?[23]

- *The cameraphone is also a weapon.*
  Even if you know that one of your friends has no problem with people posting photos of them to Facebook, there are

[23] I, of course, got Virginia's permission to publish this.

limits—or there should be. In short: Friends don't post photos that make friends look like crap.

Yes, the camera may have captured *you* at the exact moment heaven opened up and the angels wept at the sight of your radiance. Resist publishing the shot if it also captured your friend at the exact moment she's never looked more like a crazy homeless woman taking a brief break from rifling through a Dumpster to smile for the camera.

- *Ask your friends to "like" your venture; don't shine a bright light on them and force them to confess why they can't or won't.*
  When you post a request on your Facebook wall for a "like" for your book, play, or business venture, friends who see your post can choose to click to like it or just sail on past. They can't do that if you message them directly, an imposition that can put them in the uncomfortable position of explaining why they need to decline.

- *Mass-messaging: Don't eat people's time because it's easier for you to send an invite to your entire friends list.*
  Refrain from mass-messaging an invitation to everyone on your friends list unless you will be giving away bars of gold bullion or all of your invitees are actual real-life friends who live close enough to come. I typically won't drive thirteen miles to Hollywood for a party; I'm not taking three planes and a shuttle bus to get to "Karaoke Nite!!!" in Tampa.

- *If you're the boss, think twice before you friend your employees.*
  They are entitled to have private lives and might feel pressured to say yes to your friend request because you're their supervisor and then forget you're on their Facebook feed when they post about having a sexathon on the day they called in near-dead.

- *Moochstarter and other sources of crowdfunding*
A guy messaged me on Facebook, "How the heck are you? Do you still have that pink Nash?" He was referring to the cotton-candy-pink 1960 Rambler/four-wheeled money pit I drove when I moved to Los Angeles—in the 90s. When he messaged me, I hadn't had it for ten-plus years—about as long as it had been since I'd heard from him . . . until he contacted me to ask me to pay into his Kickstarter fund to finance the distribution of some indie film he'd made. My response: "I would like to get a new pair of boots. Please send me $200 via PayPal."

It's the rare person who would do what he did face-to-face—be in a restaurant, spot some person they hadn't seen for ten years, and go over and hit them up for 50 bucks. But, online it takes little effort for people to moochspam everyone whose e-mail address they ever came upon—falling back on what's technically possible as the standard for their behavior and assuming that if the technology exists, it must be cool to use it to mass-milk everyone in their address book.

Sure, some of these crowdfunding requests are for noble causes or—occasionally—ventures that might someday turn a profit for those who invest. And I don't get all miffy when close friends e-mail me about causes or projects they're trying to fund. But for vanity projects—those unlikely to pay off in any meaningful way for anyone but the creator—I think it's in bad taste to ask for what amounts to friend- and acquaintance-supplied welfare. This is too often requested by people who would simply rather spend *other* people's money—and try to get the opportunity to do that by (consciously or unconsciously) preying on people's fears of seeming stingy or having their refusal to donate held against them. If you have a vanity project, perhaps consider funding it the old-fashioned way: by working long hours at some dull job until you can pay for it yourself.

"You've Got Hail!": The nonstop storm of e-mail.

If it were as easy to snail-mail a letter as it is to send an e-mail, the entire United States would be deforested in a week.

It was really cool to get an e-mail back in the 90s, when it was a novelty. These days, some people get fifty or more e-mails an hour. Some of these people are in competitive fields and have bosses who expect them to answer at all hours. But even people in less competitive jobs often open their inbox dreading the flood.

In other words, the guideline for considerate e-mailing is best summed up by the cartoon owl in the old Forest Service ads: "Give a hoot!—Don't pollute." This isn't to say you shouldn't e-mail. It's sometimes the best way to get a particular message across. Just recognize that every e-mail you send eats a tiny bit of the recipient's life, and combined with all the other e-mail they get, the life-eating can add up. Considering that, I offer a few guidelines:

- *Recognize the beauty of brevity—in your e-mail body and your "To:" line.*

  Take the time to say it short. Of course, the shortest e-mail of all is one that is never sent—and never cc'd or bcc'd. So, think twice about whether saying thank you to their thank you to your thank you is really necessary. And before you copy six of your co-workers (who will all likely be copied on every reply), consider whether you really need to cover your ass six ways to Tuesday.

- *Subject: Don't make people guess the subject of your e-mail.*

  Guessing games can be a fun way to pass the time on long car trips, but they put stress on the recipient of your e-mail. In writing your subject line, keep in mind that e-mail is a form of communication, not a game of hangman. Also, if you're quick to complain about not getting a speedy reply, be mindful that you've got competition for a person's attention. For example, if you're e-mailing me for advice, the subject line "advice" does nothing to suggest that your question is interesting and should be opened before all the other advice requests waiting for me. Specificity in the subject line, however—"Should I tell my wife about my diaper fetish?"—piques my interest.

- *Don't send three e-mails when you can send one.* When you're e-mailing someone a bunch of information—times, dates, questions in need of answering—take care to gather it all together in a single message so you won't have to e-mail them three more times with bits you forgot . . . basically reassigning them the task of pulling together the information you should have before hitting SEND. If, after sending, you realize you've forgotten something, go back to the e-mail you sent, include the forgotten bit at the top, resend, and note in the subject line that the person should ignore the earlier e-mail.

- *E-mail people you do business with during business hours.* Many people get their work e-mail on their phone, and many use a single e-mail address for social and business e-mail. Just seeing a work e-mail pop up after work hours can cause work to eat into the life sphere. Patience is not one of my natural virtues, but I am always mindful that the woman who edits my column, the guy who copyedits it, my agent, and my book editor should all have time off when it's time to have time off—no matter how desperately I long to e-mail them about something at 8:37 a.m. on Sunday.

- *Help people who e-mail you respect your time by announcing your e-mail boundaries.*

  These suggestions are mainly for people in jobs with a lot of client or customer contact but can be retooled to be useful to anyone with a psycho friend or family member who expects a response twelve seconds after they've sent an e-mail:

  —Squash the absurd expectation that you will answer e-mail whenever it comes by adding a line just above your e-mail signature: "E-mail will be answered during business hours, from 9 a.m. to 5:30 p.m."

  —Adopt standard times each day to check e-mail, and announce them with: "I check e-mail at 10 a.m. and 4 p.m. and can be reached at 555-555-5555 in case of emergency."[24]

  —Announce a deadline for responding: "I'll do my best to answer all e-mail within X hours" (24 hours, 48, 72, etc.).

- *When you can't respond promptly, just say so.*

  The difference between an asshole and an unfortunately busy person is often a tiny bit of information—for example, responding to an e-mail with "Got this. Swamped. Will respond as soon as humanly possible."

- *Technology makes a nearly instant response possible; it doesn't mandate it.*

  When you have e-mailed someone but haven't gotten a reply, don't immediately go scramble the fighter jets. Consider that the person you've e-mailed may be overwhelmed, on vacation, or in a vegetative state or may have changed their e-mail

[24] A suggestion blogged by "The Four-Hour Work-Week's" Tim Ferriss, fourhourworkweek .com.

address or neglected to check their spam folder. Check that you sent the e-mail to the right address, e-mail them again, or pick up the phone and tell them you're wondering whether they got your message. It's very possible their mail server has become convinced that you're trying to enlarge their penis and not their income with a freelance job.

- *It's called "e-mail," not "soapbox."*
  As on Facebook, avoid trying to "cure" someone's political point of view by barraging them with yours, and don't be sending your meat-eating friends articles about how their lunch is killing them and the planet.

- *Go ahead and use "u," "ur," and "n stuf" in e-mail—if you are twelve and e-mailing your BFF.*
  If you are twenty-two and e-mailing your professor or if you are forty and e-mailing another adult you are not having sex with, take that extra millisecond to tap out the "yo" before the "u." Personally, I don't even use text-speak when texting, because I'm terrified of it leaking into my writing. And besides, as "The Jingoist," one of my blog commenters, noted, "how much time did you really save by typing 'how u bin?' "

  Accordingly, it's considerate when e-mailing to put in that tiny bit of extra effort to write in complete sentences, complete with a capital letter at the beginning of each and attention paid to grammar throughout.[25] People have

[25] David Yontz, host of the podcast "Stop! . . . Grammar Time" and the grammar ninja who copyedits my syndicated column, gave me a short list of commonly made grammatical errors to check for before you hit SEND (and maybe google and read up on so you can internalize what is grammatically correct). In addition to confusing "you're" and "your," people tend to mix up "it's" and "its" and "myself" and "me" and start a sentence with "her" or "him" instead of the correct "he" or "she." And finally, in Dave's words: "Do not sign off with a 'Thanks, (Your Name).' You're not thanking yourself. Make sure you add a paragraph break after the comma."

enough e-mail to read that they don't need e-mail to decipher. Also, keep in mind that grammatically sloppy e-mails can send an unintended message. For example, a common error in e-mailed hate-rants, "your an idiot," tends to convey that *you* are an idiot, or at least not all that literate, turning what was supposed to be a withering attack into a source of amusement for the target.

- *How to stop annoying forwards*

If it's your grandma sending you forwards—especially if she sends really good dirty jokes—take two seconds to send her back a smiley face or "I love you, Grams!" and let that be that. With anyone else—like those who consistently neglect to check Snopes.com before forwarding you something about the supposed danger of dying in a gang initiation involving flashing headlights—make your request that they quit sending forwards about the *volume* of messages you get instead of the asinine content of theirs, which should make them less likely to take it personally. For example:

> I am just deluged with e-mail, so I have to ask you to kindly stop sending me forwards. Of course, personal messages from you are always welcomed. Hope you understand!

- *"Choremail" is less likely to be answered. Ever.*

Choremail is my name for e-mail that assigns some task, like reading and analyzing an article or piece of poetry you've written, to someone who is not your employee. Forget whether you asked them and they said yes. Immaterial. As I write in the "Communicating" chapter, many people will say yes to this sort of task simply because they feel bad saying no. If you must have an opinion on your writing, there are people who will give it to you. They're called freelance editors, and they work for pay.

- *Mass-e-mail failures: It costs no extra to bcc.*
  Bcc is short for "blind carbon copy," referring to a method of document reproduction that predates not only the Internet but the photocopier. These days, it can also be short for what elderly great-aunts don't know to do or careless e-mailers forget to do when sending mass messages, in turn exposing people's private e-mail addresses for harvesting and sometimes announcing their presence in a group they'd rather not go public about being a part of. When somebody does err and send a non-bcc'd e-mail to 147 people, take care not to hit REPLY ALL, which will likely make a number of those people want to stop whatever they're doing, hunt you down, and hurt you.

- *Impose a waiting period on sending any e-mail you've written while foaming at the mouth.*
  I get it: Indignation wants to be free. So, when you get an e-mail you think is seriously out of bounds, you can go ahead and bang out your every enraged thought—*after* removing the sender's e-mail address so there's no possibility of sending it by accident. Once you've got your response together, give yourself a time-out before you send it—an hour or a few hours or even a day or days. Reread it and think about it and maybe run it by a wise colleague or friend and see whether it still sounds more like a righteous reply or a suicide note for your social life or career.

THE NIGHT MY IMAGINARY FRIENDS TOOK ME TO DINNER

In the spring of 2013, I had a fascinating dinner with two people who were in my thoughts a lot but whom I had never met. One of the two, an LA–based tech guy, has been commenting on my blog almost since its inception in 2002, and the other, Alaska-based FedEx pilot Jeff Guinn, has been commenting since 2008. Prior to this dinner, I couldn't have picked the face of either out of a crowd, but I've read thousands of words reflecting how they think and what they care about. The LA–based guy once even came to my rescue in real life in a major way (though we spoke only on the phone and only for about twenty seconds). I would likewise have come to his aid, same as I would for others in my life I care about, because these online friendships are as real and legit as friendships I've made after saying hello to a person face-to-face. The medium through which you conduct the friendship really doesn't change that.

Recognizing this, I have to laugh at all the Chickenpundit Littles wailing about the great harm that the Internet, smartphones, and social media are doing to all of us and fretting that all human interaction will eventually involve our pecking out abbreviated, underpunctuated speech with one giant index finger. Of course, ever since Socrates got his toga in a wad about how the *written word* would surely degrade our ability to think logically and sift out the truth, people have gotten hysterical about the latest advance in communication, predicting that it would mean not just The End of Life as We Know It but The End of Civilized Society.

The Internet *has* meant the end of life as we've known it, because it's erased so many of life's annoying limitations. For example, we three—three people who never would have met—had dinner and a very interesting evening together because Jeff uses his job perk of being able to fly for free to get together with the bloggers and blog commenters around the globe whom he finds interesting and treat them to a meal. (Thanks for the duck and the fumé blanc, Jeff!) What the doomsaying hysterics fail to see is that the Internet is a tool, same as a paring knife. The paring knife can be used to cut up an apple for a baby, to carve "B.L. loves M.C." on a tree, or to stab somebody 300 times. Likewise, the Internet itself doesn't alienate people. It's the most amazing connector of humans we've ever had—that is, providing those of us on it have the guts, imagination, and good manners to use it that way.

— 7 —

DATING

FLATTERY IS SOMETIMES THE GREATEST FORM OF CREEPING A WOMAN OUT

After having a late lunch and doing some writing in my favorite coffeehouse, I went out to the parking lot and found a book—probably off the coffeehouse's "take-one" bookshelf—on my car windshield. It was *Popped Culture: A Social History of Popcorn in America*. I opened it.

I do put some effort into putting myself together in the morning, and I contain my impulse to spend my evenings with my snout in a trough of Häagen-Dazs, so I appreciate when people take notice of that. Just not in a way that says "Some stranger is watching me, knows which car is mine, and wants to bend me over the hood."

A note about the wisdom of grandmas:

If you're a woman in your twenties, some of what I advise in this chapter may make you flash on your grandma swinging a wooden spoon and telling you to lose ten pounds and stop chasing the boys and then lecturing you on cows and the high price of free milk. Guess what: There's a mountain of research that finds that your grandma was right—about pretty much everything.

DATING IS WAR.

Writing a love advice column, I have probably heard a version of every dating rudeness story there is, including ones that led to vomiting, blackouts, global humiliation, and brushes with death. One woman had sex with a man on their third date, fell asleep in his bed, and awoke around 3 a.m. to him trying to strangle her in his sleep. She thrashed and screamed, and he woke up. He apologized profusely, only then revealing that he had "a minor sleep condition"—which is what you get to call it when you sometimes wake up to an empty Oreo bag on the kitchen floor.

Since I only have space for a chapter, I'll stick to some of the most common forms of dating rudeness and perceived rudeness. *Perceived rudeness?* The truth is, in dating, a good bit of the hurt and anger people feel is caused not by rude behavior but by misconceptions about the opposite sex and the way things "should" work as opposed to the ways they actually do. Often, an offended person's bottom-line complaint is something along the lines of "Hey, lady, why can't you act more like a man?!"

It helps to understand that there really is a war between the sexes—one that goes back millions of years. Evolutionary psychologists David Buss and David Schmitt explain that men and women have some "conflicting strategies" in dating, sex, and relationships. These seem to have emerged from our differing physiologies and the ensuing differences in what sex can end up costing us. As I wrote in a column:

> A cave man could do a cave lady behind a bush and just walk away, no child support, no nothing, and still pass on his genes. Consequently, men evolved to have this extremely unsentimental sexuality: getting aroused at the mere sight of a nubile woman. Since women can get pregnant from a single sex act, and since there were few suckier places to be a single mother than 1.8 million years ago on the African savannah, women evolved to care a lot less about a man's looks than his ability and willingness to provide. Although we now have reliable birth control, our genes are extraordinarily slow learners, so these competing sexual strategies remain. As my friend Walter Moore put it, "A guy was complaining to me that women are only attracted to wealthy men. I said, 'That's so unfair, because we don't expect them to be wealthy; all we ask is that they look like models.' "

Attraction: Yes, men want hotties. Women want hotties but will settle for a homely gazillionaire.

Many women think men are pretty rude to care so much about a woman's looks. In a just world, men would have the hots for women simply for the beautiful people they are on the inside. Unfortunately, in the real world, this is just not how male sexuality works. (The penis is not a philanthropic organization and will not get hard because a woman bought a homeless guy a sandwich.)

Because male sexuality is all about the visuals, men's magazines are filled with pictures of naked women with freakishly large breasts and women's magazines are filled with pictures of beauty products and ass-cantilevering $2,000 stilettos. Men evolved to go for signs of reproductively hot prospects—an hourglass figure, youth, clear skin, symmetrical faces and bodies, and long shiny hair: all indicators that a woman is a healthy, fertile candidate to pass on a man's genes. Women co-evolved to try to make themselves look reproductively hot, though that's not how we think of it.[26]

Whether men want thinner or fatter women seems to correspond not to the availability of *Maxim*, *Hustler*, and the Victoria's Secret catalog but to the availability of food in a society. Population ecologist Judith L. Anderson and others have done research on this, finding that where grub is scarce, like in parts of Africa, men go for the meatier ladies. In our culture, where there's a 7-Eleven, a Starbucks, and a supermarket the size of Rhode Island every few miles, men tend to prefer slimmer women (arm candy, as opposed to the whole candy store). Obviously, character counts in a relationship, but women need to accept how much looks matter to the opposite sex and keep up their curb appeal or, if they decide to slack off or resign from general groundskeeping, accept that it'll be harder to land or keep a man.

Because men are turned on by disembodied photos of boobs, butts, and coochies, they're quick to pull down their pants, click

[26] I wrote in a column, "Men are told it's a thought crime to ever view women as sex objects. Of course, that's exactly how women think of themselves when they're dressing to attract a man. Oh, did you think women wear plunging necklines and a little gold charm dangling in their cleavage to frighten away mosquitoes?"

their cameraphone, and text some woman they just met a close-up of their zipperwurst. Really bad idea. Men who've done this should pick up a Harlequin romance,[27] which is basically porn for women (from the ravishing by some hot gazillionaire to the final commitment-gasm). See any photo spreads of male crotch shots tucked in there anywhere, boys? This is not an error of omission. Women aren't fantasizing about seeing your willy; they're fantasizing that somebody in the royal family will pluck them out of suburbia and marry them in Westminster Abbey.[28]

Although women will go for man babes if they can get them (and studies show that most do at least want men who are taller than they are—by about six inches), they prioritize seeking men with status and power. In one of the more hilarious studies reflecting this, anthropologist John Marshall Townsend and psychologist Gary Levy showed women photographs of attractive and homely men wearing business attire or a fast-food worker outfit. The women overwhelmingly went for the ugly man wearing a Rolex over the handsome guy in the Burger King uniform, whether they were pairing up for the long haul or the short roll. In other words, if you're a man seeking a woman, your first step should be seeking extremely gainful employment, which tends to be far more productive than lying on the couch in your parents' basement pounding a six-pack and whining about how "shallow" women are.

Pursuit: Life will not always give you a cookie—especially when you're on the make.

- *Getting dates*

  There are a number of tactics for meeting people you can date. One is waiting for them to come to you. If you are a

[27] I love how crime novelist Elmore Leonard described romance novels: "full of rape and adverbs."

[28] *Note:* Although a photograph of an erect penis initially makes a poor calling card, some women *are* into getting bonerpix *after* they've slept with a guy.

heterosexual man, this tactic can be very effective—that is, if you are Robert Pattinson, Clive Owen, or George Clooney. Otherwise, you'll need to approach women and ask them out—and without seething with resentment that women rarely (or never) pursue you. Being pissed off and bitter will not get you laid. It will only get you more pissed off and bitter.

Women will not always be nice to you when you ask them out. This sucks, but it will hurt less if you ask a lot of women out instead of, say, spending a year sneaking furtive glances at one from across a coffee shop before squeaking out a request for a date. To get comfortable asking women out, give yourself an assignment: Hit on and ask out two hot women a day for two weeks in a row (and by asking them out, I don't mean giving them your business card and telling them to give you a call sometime). The idea is getting to the point where getting rejected is boring more than anything else. At that point, "Actually, I'm a lesbian" from the straightest-looking woman you've ever seen will merely be a sign to move on and hit on the next girl.

If you're a woman, the direct approach—asking a man on a date—is a risky tactic. Men will insist that they love when women ask them out—and they do. They love the ego-rub, but they tend to devalue the woman who gives it to them, just as they'll often lose interest in a woman who has sex with them right away. Once again, the evolutionary explanation applies. Women evolved to be the choosier sex because of the costs of pregnancy and feeding and raising any resulting child, and men co-evolved to expect female choosiness, and they value women they have to work to get.

This isn't to say it's always a bust when a woman straightforwardly pursues a man. But, if you'll hate a guy when he becomes a booty call instead of your boyfriend or gets into a relationship with you but only half-heartedly wants you, you should do what tends to set up the best dynamics for long-term success: flirt with a man to let him know you're interested. By flirting, you're also being considerate to the guy—signaling to him that you want him to ask you out, and that if he does, you won't mock him or scream, "Rapist! Rapist in Aisle 2!"

The fact that a guy seems shy is no excuse for a woman to do the asking. If he's too wimpy to endure thirteen seconds of rejection, he's too wimpy to date you. Dating behavior is a microcosm of what you can expect in a relationship. If you don't want to find yourself screeching at a ball-less boyfriend you have no respect for, make a basic show of balls a requirement for going out with you.

Some guys can be a bit flirtation-blind—especially the nerdboys I've always gone for. Some get so used to women kicking them out of the way when they are in their early twenties—typically the dark ages for one of these guys—that they can't imagine that a woman who doesn't resemble the thing under the bridge being interested in them. You can feel sympathy for them, but your methodology with them should remain the same. Instead of making moves on them, make flirtatious moves on them. Touch them, tease them, look them in the eye a little too long, play with your hair, touch them some more, and maybe some more after that. Good news: It seems that you can flirt yourself practically radioactive with obviousness about your interest in a guy and still not be seen as the aggressor—providing you stop short of "Hey, how about taking me to a movie on Friday night?"

- *When a wink becomes a wank*

On dating sites, a woman can probably get away with a "wink": sending a doofy winking cartoon face to a man she's interested in. A wink from a woman comes off as a form of flirting. A wink from a man to a woman sends a slew of messages, all of them wrong. Since winks are free to nonmembers of fee-based sites, a guy who winks suggests he's too cheap to join. Other possibilities: He's too lazy, wimpy, socially primitive, or lacking in intelligence to express himself in the written word. Or, he's contacting women in volume because for him, just about anything with a vagina will do. In other words, when a woman doesn't reply to a wink, this should be considered not a sign that she's rude but a sign that she isn't missing many teeth.

- *An unambiguous rejection is a good thing.*

Men should ask women out in a way that gets them as firmly and unambiguously rejected as possible, if that's what's ultimately in the cards.

Technology has allowed men to resort to wussy hit-and-run ways of asking women out: leaving messages on their voicemail, e-mailing them, and texting them. If you're a man using these methods and you don't hear back, you don't know whether you've been dissed or whether your message got deleted, your text went to the wrong number, or your e-mail went to her spam folder. You should instead get on the phone with a woman and ask her out.[29] This lets you know where you stand—or don't—which means you'll know to move on to the next woman instead of mooning and wondering endlessly and ultimately seething with resentment.

Women, too, are guilty of wimping out. They use the ambiguous shutdown, telling a man asking them out that they can't date him "right now" when they really mean that they

[29] This is one of those times to break the "Do Not Ever Call" rule I wrote about in "The Telephone" chapter.

won't ever, or they say they "have a boyfriend" or they're "really busy," which suggests he just needs to cool his heels until they break up or their workload gets lighter. A woman typically soft-pedals her rejection like this to avoid hurting a man's feelings and having an uncomfortable moment, but this approach can eventually make for many bad moments and much bad feeling when an obsessive or socially clueless guy keeps pursuing her.

Unless you know a guy well enough to be pretty sure he'll take an ambiguous shutdown as a no, the best and most considerate turndown is one that leaves a man with no hope for an opening—ever. You do that, gently but firmly, by saying something like "Thanks so much. I'm really flattered, but I'm sorry to say that I'm just not interested." Most guys will eventually get it if you reject them in an ambiguous way, but there are those who won't, who will turn into annoyances or worse. As security expert Gavin de Becker points out in *The Gift of Fear*, "men who cannot let go choose women who cannot say no."

- *Dealing with unwanted attention*

When a stranger you aren't interested in hits on you in public, be kind—assuming you aren't in a dark alley at the time, in which case you should just be fast.

A Southern California blogger, "UnWinona," often commutes from North Hollywood to Long Beach on the train. She avoids speaking with other passengers, wears a ring to imply that she's married, and buries herself in a book. Yet, on "at least half" of her train rides, a man will (*horrors!*) interrupt her reading and ask her about her book. She explains:

> This serves the double purpose of getting my attention and trapping me in a conversation. If I stop reading the book I enjoy to

> talk to you, random stranger, you hit on me or just stay way too close to me. If I tell you to leave me alone, you get mad at me. Because I somehow, as a woman, owe you conversation.

One summer evening, a boy, about eighteen, seated nearby with two guy friends, made the fatal error, asking, "What are you reading?"

She went straight from zero to nasty: "I told them loudly and firmly that I wanted to be left alone to read my book."

The trio didn't take that well, sneering "I bet she's reading *Twilight* or some shit!" and otherwise taunting her. Not because they thought that she "owed" them conversation but because she treated the guy who spoke to her as if he were too insignificant to deserve the perhaps ten-second effort of a considerate response.

After they got off the train, a guy with a bike got on. And yes, he had the gall to ask it: "What are you reading?"

She again went straight to cold bitch mode: "Please leave me alone. I am reading."

Again, she couldn't extend herself just a little by saying "It's just *Blah Blah Blah*" and making some excuse: "I'd love to talk with you, but I'm reading this for work and I'm a little behind" or "Sorry, but I'm married and my husband gets a little jealous when I talk to other guys." These maybe sound like bullshit excuses, but that's not what matters. Just that there's *some* sort of explanation that gives the guy an out for his ego. *(This perhaps seems a contradiction of my advice on the unambiguous shutdown, but a stranger who's hitting on you in passing in public can be shut down less definitively than a guy who has your phone number and can keep calling to ask you out.)*

Bike Guy wasn't about to be shit on and go quietly. Glaring at her, he bayed in an "angry baby talk voice,": "PLEASELEAVEMEALONEI'MREADING."

He marched back and forth in front of his bike, yelling that UnWinona was "a slut, a ho, a bitch." The few other passengers offered no help, and she feared that he might turn physically violent.

Bike Guy didn't touch her, but he went full-on scarytime, punching the walls of the train car, screaming right in her face, "SUCK MY DICK, BITCH. . . . IF I HAD A GUN I'D . . . FUCKING KILL YOU, BITCH."

Finally, the train pulled in to a crowded station, and she bolted out, shaking and barely able to breathe, and nearly vomited. Even after she got home, she cried long and uncontrollably and remained on the verge of throwing up.

Afterward, unbelievably, she blamed her situation on "nothing more than being female and not wanting to share," adding, "I just wanted to read my book. It's not my fault I'm pretty."

Outrageous.

These guys didn't lean over her and sneer, "Hey, sugar tits . . ." or say they wanted to grab her ass and ride it all the way to Compton. Sure, they were hitting on her, and their attention was unwanted and a bother. And no, she had no obligation to carry on a conversation with any of them, but she also seemed to feel she had no reason to make even the most minor effort to politely duck out of one.

Unfortunately, not "blaming the victim" has come to make it taboo to explore how and why certain people and not others are victimized and whether they were randomly preyed upon or whether they might have done anything differently to keep themselves out of harm's way. This encourages some women to adopt the attitude that they can do whatever they want and nobody's "allowed" to do anything back. Lovely thinking but very inapplicable to the real world, where it's important to take a little responsibility for how you talk to people, especially when you're a lone woman riding late at night on an almost-empty train. In UnWinona's case, things would likely have turned out very differently if only she'd treated these guys with a little dignity—as if they have value as humans and their feelings matter.

A safer and more compassionate response involves calling up a little empathy for a guy who's trying to chat you up. Think about some time when you had to approach a stranger—how you had to work up the courage, how you fretted about what they'd say in response, how you maybe even felt a little queasy walking over and sputtering out your piece. And then, with those feelings in mind, maybe you can respond as I did to a huge nose-wiping guy in dirty overalls in 7-Eleven who spewed little flecks of spit on me as he asked me out. My reply: "Oh, darn! I really wish I could, but I'm married."

The Date

- *Who pays?*

Dating turns some men into amateur accountants. They complain that it isn't fair that they're often (or usually, depending on their age) the ones paying on dates, especially at the start. Well, it also isn't "fair" that being a woman involves so much upkeep. Remaining blonde is like having a second car payment. While men buy underwear three to a pack from a bin, a single bra and underwear set can set a woman back over $100. And then there are all the lotions, potions, and pots of makeup. A pot of eye shadow smaller than most hors d'oeuvres can set a woman back $30—or more. Some eye creams are so pricey they should come with an upgrade to business class. Being a man, on the other hand, is much like being a golden retriever. To get ready for a date, a guy pretty much just has to run through the sprinklers and shake off.

But, let's all put away the calculators. There's actually good reason for a man to pick up the tab on at least the first few dates, and it goes back to Ye Olde Evolutionary Psychology and how women evolved to feel compelled to seek men who are "providers." This hasn't changed, not even for powerful women making a lot of money. Research by evolutionary psychologist David Buss and others has shown that even when women are high-flying big earners, they seem to want men who are higher-flying bigger earners. This is even true of women who consider themselves feminists. Another evolutionary psychologist, Bruce J. Ellis, wrote in *The Adapted Mind* of fifteen feminist leaders' descriptions of their ideal man—descriptions that included the repeated use of terms connoting high status, like "very rich," "brilliant," and "genius."

In other words, men need to accept that dating costs money and that just because a woman can afford to pay on the first date or first few dates, that doesn't mean she should. When a man pays, graciously and seamlessly, for the first and second date, he's meeting a woman's psychological need to seek a man who is generous and willing to invest.[30] That said, this is the twenty-first century, and studies show that on average, young urban women in their twenties are now making more than men. So, after two people have gone out a few times, the woman needs to unbolt her wallet and start taking turns picking up the tab. And not just the cheap parts of it but the whole tab, on every other date. Of course, the

[30] When a guy who isn't exactly a Mr. Moneybags is treating a woman to dinner, he'll be afraid of looking cheap, which will make him easy prey for every waiter upsell in the book. A woman needs to be the one to lead with the frugalities, such as, "Tap water is fine for me," when the waiter proposes the $112 bottled water, collected from dew that fell off angels' wings.

exception would be when the man owns a mansion and a yacht and the woman's a barista who can either buy their drinks or pay her rent.

But there's an important caveat: Even if a man is very wealthy, his investment on the first few dates should be *more symbolic than substantial*. In fact, so there isn't a terribly imbalanced initial investment, it's important that the first few dates be moderately priced—the sort where the point is getting to know each other over a coffee or a couple of drinks, not introducing the woman to the limit on the man's American Express Platinum Card.

- *First dates should be cheap, short, and local.*
On the first date and maybe even the second, you should meet for coffee or happy-hour drinks for an hour or two—*at most*. This helps keep things from going too fast (a big source of misery and resentment) and keeps the guy from needing to shell out much money. Also, if a date turns nightmarish, it will at least be a Hobbesian nightmare: nasty and brutish but also short.

Casual sex: A horny woman can do anything a horny man can do, but there's a good chance she'll feel like stepped-on crap afterward.

The feminist message that a woman can do anything a man can do is great for girls who are aspiring NASCAR drivers or U.S. presidents, but let's not confuse "equal" with "the same" and what a woman *can* do with what actually works. Casual sex is particularly problematic for many women, again probably stemming from women's evolved drive to seek providers and its neurochemical underpinnings. Some women find that they feel especially emotionally connected to a sex partner upon orgasm, probably because of the release of the bonding hormone oxytocin. Although the most conclusive research is on sexed-up prairie rodents and casual sex often fails to produce orgasms in human women, oxytocin has also been shown to be released by touch and cuddling. This means that whether a woman has an orgasm or not, oxytocin may have an effect, putting her on an emotional leash to the man she slept with. (In a man, testosterone bitchslaps the oxytocin, probably making it easier for him to roll over and be on to the next.)

Anthropologist John Marshall Townsend has done interesting research in this area, finding that even when women were just horny and simply wanted to use and lose some himbo, many felt vulnerable after sex, and "thoughts crossed their minds like 'Does he care about me, is sex all he was after, will he dump me in the morning?' These thoughts were difficult to suppress."

Beyond how unsettled hooking up makes many women feel, it's a risky gambit unless a woman knows that all she wants is a little nail and bail. There are hookups that lead to happily ever after, but because men tend to devalue women they don't have to chase, there's a good chance a hookup will be the fast track to "He's just not that into you . . . (but he'll use you for sex while he's looking for a woman he is into)."

Ready, set . . . curl up in a fetal position!

Acknowledging the ugly realities of what men and women want might seem to suck some of the romance out of dating. But actually, being mindful that there's this war between the sexes and understanding that it's not personal, just evolutionary, is probably the best way to keep from hating the other side—in addition to possibly being a little kinder in going after your own evolutionary imperatives. Ultimately, being mad that men act like men or that women act like women is like being mad that your dog sniffs other dogs' butts instead of reading aloud to them from literary fiction.

SOME DATING RUDENESS IS UNISEX

(This is also for all you gay people, who got shafted in the last section.)

Don't date people you aren't attracted to.

A reader wrote to me saying she is tall and is really only attracted to tall men—six foot two and up—and was having a hard time finding a boyfriend because of it. Her friends suggested she be "more open-minded" about dating shorter men—which is terrible advice.

I acknowledged that "it's what's inside that counts"; it just doesn't count enough if you don't want to get naked with what's on the outside. And think of the guy. What guy wants a girlfriend who's with him because her friends say it's the "open-minded" thing to do?

Equally ill-advised is the notion that you should date somebody you aren't physically attracted to simply because they're "a good person." People will suggest that you can work up the hots for somebody like you can get better at playing "Greensleeves" if only you keep pounding it out on the piano. In reality, trying to get attracted to someone is one of the unintentionally crueler things you can do. At first, you can mistake the heat of novelty—of being with someone new and all the exhilaration inherent in that—for the heat of attraction. But no matter how exemplary a human being somebody is, if you find them physically unappealing, they'll just get more and more repellant to you over time, until you'd arrange to get pecked to death by crows just to avoid having sex with the person.

The realistic (and thus kind) approach is figuring out your minimum standards for attractiveness and sticking to them—as the tall girl did, recognizing that she'd have the lukewarmies for guys under six foot two. You should also figure out any other important must-haves or must-have-nots, like if children or certain fanatical eating habits happen to be a no-go. And remember:

If you aren't attracted to flat-chested women or blond men, this isn't a character flaw, just a fact. Know it, accept it, and don't be tempted when the sweetest pea-breasted woman ever or a much-sought-after underwear model named Sven looms on your dating horizon.

Online dating: It should be called "online meeting."

On a positive note, I have yet to hear of anyone on a dating site who's misrepresented their species. People do, however, misrepresent just about everything else. Most commonly, they show up on dates looking nothing like their pictures, although one angry reader complained to me that his date wasn't in the advertised gender. (No, being a woman isn't "just a state of mind.")

It's obviously rude to engage in false advertising, but this can be a relatively fleeting rudeness—if the person it's perpetrated on doesn't have online dating practices that help it become an extended and much bigger one. They do this by using the Internet not just for what it's great for—meeting people to date—but for trying to get to know them at length before ever going out on a date with them. As I've written in my column, the same woman who'd go home with a stranger she spent a couple of hours talking to in a bar will spend weeks exchanging e-mail and texts with some online dating prospect to assess how good his grammar is before she'll feel safe having a coffee with him. In the meantime, she's getting attached—not to the actual guy but to her idea of the guy and maybe to how smart and funny she is when she's talking to him. Investing all this time and emotion can make it somewhat devastating when she finally meets the guy and finds that he looks wrong, talks wrong, and smells like the Dumpster behind the meat market.

A wiser approach is assuming that everyone you meet on the Internet is lying their ass off until proven otherwise. You'll find out the real deal with a minimum of emotional and other costs by getting your interaction with them into the real world as soon as possible. If, after an e-mail or two and maybe a brief phone call, a person still seems appealing, meet them for a brief date. (Refer back to the bit earlier in the chapter on first dates being "cheap, short, and local.") If, for some reason, you can't meet right away, at least video-chat on Skype—once, maybe twice, only. Each chat should be a half-hour or so, *at most*. Remember, the point is getting an idea of who they are, not falling down a digital rabbit hole into a week-long live-chat webisode.

Blister Wonderful: The rules on STD disclosure.

If you're going to give your date something to remember you by, make it some funny little trinket, not painful urination and weeping genital sores.

A woman wrote me for advice about a guy she'd started seeing. She was worried that he wasn't that interested in her because when they fooled around, he kept stopping short of actual intercourse. She wondered whether he'd figured out that she has genital herpes—a fact she hadn't felt "ready" to disclose to him.

Horrible. Seriously, outrageously rude. And the stuff lawsuits are made of. A number of people with herpes—mainly people with herpes who also have a lot of money—have been successfully sued for big bucks ($6.75 million, in one case) for hiding it from a partner or lying and claiming to be clean.

I pointed out to the woman that surely she'd tell the guy pronto if she had a cold, and colds go away; herpes is forever. That *is* a selling point for diamonds, but unlike an engagement ring, a big honking genital pustule isn't something anybody wants to be showing off to their cubicle-mate: "Look at it gleam under the fluorescents!"

Still, herpes isn't the horror that it's made out to be thanks to media hysteria that got whipped up in the early 1980s. For most people, it's basically "cold sores down there."[31] The problem is, if a person's herpes is active and their naked parts are rubbing against somebody else's naked parts, that person could become infected. And people with herpes may *think* they know when their herpes is active—but they actually may not.[32]

If you have herpes, genital warts, or any other communicable disease, you don't need to reveal it before the bartender throws down the coasters on the first date. There's no point in spilling to somebody you may not end up seeing again. But, you do have to tell a person *before* they fool around with you. It might help to arm yourself with a fact sheet you pull off a reputable medical website and then talk in nuances rather than leading with symptoms.

For example, if you have genital warts, that's not what you tell them. Genital warts are just one of the *potential results* of HPV—human papillomavirus. Explain that you have HPV, and then list the possible consequences (including warts), and let them know the stats, like that they should assume that anyone who isn't a forty-year-old virgin is a carrier. (The U.S. Centers for Disease Control and Prevention says that 50 percent of people who are sexually active will have it at some point.)

Those with other STDs should take a similar approach. For example, as I told the girl with herpes, you launch the conversation with a partner by saying something like "Ever gotten a cold sore? I get them sometimes . . . but not on my lip!" Next, as

---

[31] The first outbreak is often the worst, and beyond some tingling and itching (and those yucky sores), the symptoms are similar to the flu—fever, headache, and muscle aches.

[32] As I wrote in my column in 2011, approximately one in six U.S. adults between ages fourteen and forty-eight are afflicted with herpes, and 80 percent of them don't show visible symptoms, according to herpes researcher Dr. Anna Wald. In research by Wald and her colleagues, even when herpes carriers showed no symptoms, they were contagious 10 percent of the time—on average. Wald explained to me that there's a range: "Some people may be contagious 1 percent of the time, and others 30 percent, but we don't have a good way to predict who is who."

DatingWithHerpes.org advises, don't say "I have herpes," which makes you sound like you're having an outbreak right then. Instead, say "I carry the virus for herpes" and explain how often you have outbreaks, which should make it sound more like a manageable annoyance than a ticket to a lifetime of Crusty Pustules Anonymous meetings.

Endings that lead to beginnings: Dating again after the death of a partner.

I answered a question for my advice column from a guy whose girlfriend had died in a car crash four months prior to his writing me. Friends were concerned about him because he wasn't grieving big, long, and showy. They told him that he needed to stop suppressing his feelings, that he needed to work through the "stages" of grief in order to recover, and that if he didn't, grief could "come back to bite" him. The poor guy started to worry that he wasn't grieving right. He said that he had really loved his girlfriend and was really broken up at first, crying hysterically, and still misses her terribly. But, he wrote, "Despite what's happened, I still like my life and my job. I even find myself laughing at stupid stuff."

This doesn't point to a problem; it points to resilience, which grief researcher George Bonanno says is actually the norm in people whose loved one dies. (We seem to have evolved to be able to process a loss and go on with our lives.) Bonanno explains in *The Other Side of Sadness* that there's no evidence to support many widely held beliefs about how we grieve—or "should" grieve—such as the truly awful idea that a person probably didn't really love the deceased if they aren't downing Zoloft like Cheerios and that notion that there are five "stages of grief," all of which a bereaved person supposedly must go through before they can move on.

Elisabeth Kübler-Ross's "stages of grief" were actually based on her observations of people who were themselves dying, not those who'd lost a loved one, which Bonanno points out isn't the same thing as facing your own mortality. Bonanno, Camille Wortman, and other grief researchers actually find a great deal of variability in how people recover from loss. Likewise unsupported by research is Sigmund Freud's notion that the bereaved must do "grief work" in order to heal—slog through every memory and hope about their lost loved one as if sorting through clothes at an industrial laundry. In fact, research suggests that doing this *strengthens* the bereaved person's connection to the deceased, keeping them from healing. Yet another myth is the idea of "delayed grief"—grief postponed (as if you could decide to put it off for a while) that comes back to "bite" people. Studies find delayed grief extremely rare—almost to the point of nonexistence. As I wrote in my response to the guy, "if you have a problem, it's that your friends think you have a problem."

The same goes for anyone who has well-meaning friends who are trying to micromanage their grieving. Tell these people in a kind way that you truly appreciate their concern, and explain some of the myths about grief to them. Because we're biased to keep believing what we already believe and toss out information to the contrary, they may not be willing to listen. The important part is emphasizing that it means a lot to you that they care and not buying into the notion of "Whoa, mister, you're way too functional!"

To keep from burning new people you're dating, be honest about your situation so they know what they're getting into, and recognize that it's possible to think that you're ready to date before you actually are. (The same goes for people who've gone through a devastating divorce or breakup.) Because it's easy to get carried away by wanting to be ready, along with the excitement of having a new person in your life, consider taking things slowly—not seeing someone night after night but instead spacing out your dates and conversations with them over a period of weeks, perhaps with one date a week and one or two conversations (say, no more than an hour total of phone time). This may help give you time and space to sit back and process your feelings and see whether you're truly ready for new love in your life.

As for advice for those dating someone widowed, I think a woman who was widowed and also married a widower—and who blogs at anniegirl1138.com—said this wisely and beautifully:

> My advice to anyone considering a relationship with a widow/widower is do NOT try to make us forget who we are, who we loved, and how we got here. If you truly love us, you would embrace our lost love as much as we do. Because that person, that loss, that event made us the person you supposedly love. Think about it.

How to Ditch Someone

- *Someone who's messaged you on a dating site*
  If somebody you have no interest in writes to you and has clearly put some effort into their message, you should do them the courtesy of writing back, just to say, "Thanks, but I don't think we're a match." It's the gracious thing to do. Sure, you can just ignore their message. But, have you ever talked about how you longed for "closure"? Everybody feels better when they have it.

- *When you're on a date and you'd gnaw your right arm off at the wrist to escape*
  Even achingly dull or otherwise-objectionable people have feelings. If somebody is so wildly unbearable that you just can't suffer through a meal with them, stay as long as you possibly can and then feign illness—believably—apologize for being sick, and leave. (So believability doesn't necessitate much acting ability, I suggest saying that you feel a migraine

coming on and need to go home before it gets full-blown.) This should be more plausible than the phone call "from the office" supposedly summoning you back for some emergency and is thus more kind.

- *After your date when you want nothing more to do with the person* Sometimes, right on the date, it's stone-cold obvious to both people that there's no tomorrow for the two of you. In that case, after the date, you can say nothing (other than "thank you") and just walk off separately into your respective sunsets.

If, however, you're on a date you want to be your last with a particular person and they say "Let's do it again" and seem sincere, don't give them the heave face-to-face. It's humiliating. Just nod and smile and clarify your lack of a future together by e-mail the next morning. In your e-mail, thank them for the nice evening, and then tell them that you've been thinking about it and you don't think you're a good match but that you wish them the best.

Accordingly, men aren't rude to say "I'll call you" after a date—even when they know it's the last thing they want to do—providing they straighten things out afterward, when not face-to-face. (The morning-after corrective, "Actually, I've been thinking . . ." again applies.) Don't let the truth telling wait any longer than a day, as every day that passes allows your date to get her hopes up a little higher.

If a person you're no longer interested in asks you out again, don't just try to duck all communication from them. That is mean and violates their dignity. Having gone out with them previously, you owe them a polite goodbye—letting them know it *is* goodbye and not just hoping they'll get the message when you fail to return any of their 300-some texts, phone calls, and e-mails.

- *After you and someone you're dating have removed essential articles of clothing in each other's presence*
  Many people like to avoid an uncomfortable conversation by texting a person to tell them it's over—a degrading way to be dismissed after you've shared more than a latte. As I wrote in a column, "once you've spent more than a few naked hours with somebody, you can text them to tell them you're late, but not that you're never coming back." At least "do them the solid" of breaking the news in a telephone call. And yes, you do have to talk to them directly; you don't get to tell it to their voicemail.

  If you've been dating a person for any length of time (three to six months, for example, or any amount of time where it's started to feel *relationshippy*), it's respectful to break the news face-to-face. Do not, however, do it in a public place. No woman wants to be weeping before an audience in a packed restaurant. Double or triple that for any man.

- *In breaking up, the waiting is the makes-it-harder part.*
  Whether you've been seeing somebody for two weeks, two years, or ten years, the absolute kindest time to tell them is *as soon as you know it's over.* The longer you wait the more attached they're likely to get and the more painful it will be. The sooner you tell them the sooner they can get on with their life and maybe meet somebody who does want them.

- *What to say when you dump someone*
  No matter what stage of a relationship you're in when you're ending it, the point of a breakup conversation is simply to communicate that you will no longer be together. To that end, the best breakup excuses are broad, vague ones like "I am just not feeling the spark" or "I realize that this isn't working for

me anymore." No matter how hard the person presses you for "the truth" and tries to convince you that they will be much better off for having it, don't give it to them. Once you no longer want to be in a relationship with them, it is not your job to tell them they are a conversation hog or bad in bed. It will make the split even more hurtful and may give them information they can use to try to wedge their way back in. Remember, this is a breakup—a procedure to extricate you from a relationship—not a sex therapy session or a public service announcement.

DON'T OVERLOOK OR DISMISS BAD CHARACTER

- *Trust isn't birdseed. Don't throw it around.*

A lot of people looking for love ask, "Oh, what's the big deal in closing your eyes and taking a leap with a person?" More often than not, they eventually get the answer, as one guy did after he broke off his engagement to a woman he'd been seeing and then left on a business trip. She went over to his house, stuck the hose through his mail slot, and turned it on.

Shocking and awful—but not unpredictable. In fact, she was *always* a person capable of this. He just chose not to look. So did the woman whose ex-boyfriend let himself into her apartment and fed some high-grade oleoresin capsicum (pepper extract) into her tube of lube. She and another guy ended up in the emergency room. Not because her ex suddenly became a guy who does this sort of thing. He always was. She just didn't want to know.

There *are* some clever douche-iopaths out there who can hide their malevolent nature.[33] But, much of the rudeness that

[33] My boyfriend, the armchair psychologist, says, "Make a guy sit through *Old Yeller*, and if he doesn't cry at the end, he's a sociopath."

people suffer in dating (along with any ensuing flood damage and intense burning and itching in their special place) could be avoided—if only they'd figure out what a person's made of before they let themselves get seriously involved. This actually isn't all that difficult. Therapist Nathaniel Branden once told me that people will let you know what they're all about—if you're willing to look and listen.

Of course, digging up the ugly truth is the last thing we want to do. We meet somebody, and the roar of our hormones drowns out any small voice in us cautioning us to be rational and sensible. And if our hormones don't entirely do our reason in, romanticism will bat cleanup. For instance, we're quick to claim we've found "love at first sight," which makes us sound romantically lucky, instead of referring to ourselves as "two people who know very little about each other rushing into a relationship," which makes us sound like idiots.

- *Yes, you really do need a list.*

To assess what somebody's made of, you need standards for what you require in a partner. We all *believe* we have standards, but often, what we really have is just the hazy idea that we'd like somebody "nice."

Coming up with standards takes figuring out who you are and what you value. You then need to articulate what your standards are, especially on ethics, and look for a partner who meets them. And when I say "look for," I mean watch a person over time to see who, exactly, they really are, and admit it if they fall short of your standards instead of pretending all is well so you don't have to go back on Match.com.

You'll probably be tempted to settle. I know I was when I wandered alone in the desert for forty years—sorry, wrong story—but that's pretty much how it felt. In my thirties, I spent eight long years in Los Angeles largely alone, going on a series of sometimes-horrible, occasionally degrading, and mostly disappointing first dates.

I would sometimes meet guys who were kinda-sorta in the ballpark, but I was holding out for a guy who had what I called my "man minimums," which I figured out, very LA-ishly, in a sort of movie log line: "Tall, evolved man of character who thinks for a living and cares about making a difference in the world." Eventually, I met my boyfriend of ten-plus years—truly the best person I know (and everything on my list)—but I might not have been free to go out with him had I gotten together out of loneliness with some kinda-sorta-in-the-ballpark guy.

Six months into dating him, wanting to make sure that I wasn't with *him* out of loneliness, I did something I now advise everyone to do at the point they're starting to get serious with someone: I figured out all his faults and any little annoying things about him. This probably sounds horribly unromantic, but we all have stuff about us that will bug the hell out of somebody. When you're looking to have a person in your life for more than an occasional movie date, taking stock of the less-than-ideal things about them allows you to reasonably predict whether you can deal instead of eventually finding that you can't. (Nobody breaks up with somebody because they're really witty and great in bed.)

Figuring out who a person really is involves seeing them when they let down their guard, when they forget to keep up their party manners. The classic advice on assessing character is right on: looking to see how they act when they think nobody's looking and observing how they treat the waitress, the busboy, and the taxi driver.

- *Forget tea leaves. Let spilled wine tell the tale about a person's character.*

One Saturday, a bunch of my friends and I got together for happy-hour drinks. Lawyer Tom, who was seated next to me, got animated in conveying some point and knocked my entire glass of wine into my lap. What didn't go into my lap went straight into my open purse under the table. My *new* open purse. Well, laps and new purses eventually dry, and I didn't want Tom to feel bad, so I just laughed, tried to soak up the wine with napkins, and ordered another glass.

Later, when I was walking to my car with filmmakers Courtney Balaker and her husband, Ted, Courtney told me I'd passed "The Spilled Drink Test." The term came out of the time that Courtney and Ted were at a film networking event and a guy spilled his *entire glass of red wine* down the front of her white sundress—and then continued talking to the man he was with as if nothing had happened.

Courtney, who's a sweet person but nobody's pushover, said, "Excuse me, but you just spilled red wine all over my dress." The man stared at her, said "Oh, sorry," and went back to his conversation.

Courtney explained, "I'm not the emotional type, but I have to admit, I wanted to get right back on the bus, cry, and go home. He was mean, my dress looked ridiculous, and I had the entire night ahead of me." But, she instead went to the bar, got fizzy water, took out as much of the stain as she could, and then decided she was "going to have a lovely time" despite everything.

Later in the evening, her husband turned to her and said, "It takes someone with grace to handle it the way you did." And what was an ugly experience ended up making her feel good about herself—and understood.

"Anyhoo," Courtney wrote me in an e-mail, "my theory

(and I think Ted would agree) is that if you are a woman who can have a drink spilled on you in the midst of a social event and handle it with humor and grace, that this is the sign of a solid, grounded woman that men will admire."

Now, of course, I'm not advising that people go around dumping drinks on their dates. But, it's important to find a way to observe who they are in a situation—camping, hiking, doing a project together—where there's more stress put on them than when the waiter in a fine restaurant doubles back to ask whether they'd like their filet mignon *au beurre* or *au poivre*.

THE DATING-AVERSE

The Girl with the Imaginary Boyfriend

Sometimes a really bad experience puts a person off dating for a while. I've had numerous dating-avoidant people write me over the years, but none so avoidant as the nineteen-year-old woman who asked me for advice about her nine-year relationship with her imaginary boyfriend.

Of course, my first thought was that she was pranking me, but the more I exchanged e-mails with her the more convinced I was that she was for real. And no, it didn't appear that she was hallucinating him, nor did she report that the neighbor's dog speaks to her and tells her to do very bad things. In fact, she explained about her Prince Nonexistent-But-Charming, "I understand that he isn't real and that I'm supposed to have had real relationships with real men by now. (I have the complete capability to get a real guy and have let lots of opportunities go by because of him!)"

I acknowledged that an imaginary boyfriend does have his merits. He will always be loving and supportive, and he will never fart in bed or cheat on you with your best friend. He can also be a useful tool for getting a pesky flesh-and-blood suitor off the phone—forever: "Sorry. Gotta go. Just heard my boyfriend's unicorn pull up outside my apartment."

But, I told her, an imaginary boyfriend also never challenges you in the good ways a real boyfriend and a real relationship do. A real relationship requires compromise and empathy. It's also an interpersonal flashlight of sorts, pushing you to grow as a person by highlighting what's less than ideal about you—stuff you can't learn by spending your nights going to second base with your pillow. Also, it's got to be pretty awful to wake up at forty and realize that you've been pretending to have a love life for thirty years.

The trade-off, for anyone who takes their chances with a flesh-and-blood partner, is that you could—and most likely will—suffer some heartbreak. And when I say heartbreak, I mean feeling kind of like you were run over by a truck and then backed over a few more times. On a positive note, it's an imaginary truck, and though the feeling really sucks, with time, tears, and dozens of pints of ice cream, it eventually subsides. The person you were sure you couldn't live without becomes the person you can live without—as well as the person who helped you figure out what stuff you need to choose better on the next time around. At this point, you lick your wounds, go back out, and try to be better at identifying the assholes—and to *be* less of an asshole yourself—in hopes that you'll someday have real love in your life from somebody who is flawed and human just like you but is mostly pretty great.

— 8 —

GOING PLACES

Cars, sidewalks, public transportation, and airplanes

If a scratch is that big a deal, you aren't rich enough to drive it.

Piggy parker the day after Christmas at the packed Irvine Spectrum mall, Orange County, California.

THE NAKED APE GETS A PRIUS

It's the twenty-first century, and we're going places—while exercising our baser instincts. Our cars have backup cameras and back-seat movie theaters with surround sound, but nobody's come up with spiffy new technology to advance civility. In fact, when offended while driving, we're quick to turn to the old familiar weapons: the screamed obscenity, the flipped bird, and occasionally (standing in for the club brandished by our loincloth-wearing ancestors) the golf club through the windshield.

Sometimes we go off like that because some other driver has nearly cost us our life. Other times, it's because they've cost us a whole two or three seconds by tearing through a stop sign out of turn. Although the cost from that is minuscule, someone who imposes it on us is stealing from us (as well as turning us into a chump for obeying the rules), and psychologically, even tiny fairness violations are a big deal.

Anthropologist Robert Trivers explains in his famous 1971 paper on reciprocal altruism that our sense of outrage at cheaters and rule-breakers probably developed when our ancestors started living cooperatively in small, stable hunter-gatherer bands. In an environment where group members survive by trading food and favors, there's a need to guard against the shifty-ass cheaters whose idea of reciprocity is give-and-take—you give; they take. To keep the two-legged rats at bay, our psychology evolved to include a cheater detection and punishment department, logging who owes what to whom and dispatching that information to the enforcement division, our emotions. When somebody's done us a good deed, guilt wells up in us, reminding us that we'd better hop to it and repay their kindness. In response to a take-take-taker, anger rises in us, messaging us that somebody seems overdue for a beatdown.

Trivers calls the rage we evolved to feel in response to an injustice "moralistic aggression" and notes that it's often way out of proportion to the offense committed. One of its functions, Trivers explains, is to "educate" a nonreciprocator "by frightening him with immediate harm or with the future harm of no more aid." In extreme cases, it puts a stop to any future possibility of unfair treatment from the offender by injuring, killing, or exiling him. A fierce reprisal also "educates" others that the person administering it makes a poor patsy.

Of course, back in the ancestral environment, the need for moralistic aggression was tempered by the fact that we were interacting with the same people every day. Living among people we know in a small, consistent, interdependent band deterred exploitative behavior, even by born users, who needed to maintain a reputation as good and fair to avoid getting shunned or booted from the group. Today, however, on the highway, on an escalator in a public building, or on the urban sidewalk, we're just one more stranger among strangers—which means we have no say in the reputation of the roadhogs, the line-jumpers, and all the other adult bullies on the go.

People in cars, especially, have license to treat us badly. The "automotive bubble" distances them from not only other drivers but also the visual cues that they're taking advantage of another *person*—cues that they'd have if they, say, took cuts in the office building coffee line. Further greasing the wheels of rudeness, that automotive bubble can speed them away from the target of their abuse at seventy miles an hour. And besides, as I noted in chapter 2, only a few among us are what economists call "costly punishers"—people (like me) who get so enraged by injustices they see that they can't help but go after the perpetrators, and never mind the potential costs.

Unless you and your vehicle manage to radiate a certain white-supremacist motorcycle gang member *je ne sais quoi*, the pathologically self-serving find that it often *pays* to ignore what's fair and polite and park so they block your car in while they run an errand or endanger your life by making a right turn from the left-turn lane. If you're like most people, you will just suck up the abuse and drive on. These motoring rudesters make a gamble—sometimes calculated, sometimes subconscious—that you will not be that rare fed-up driver who ends up tailing them home, bludgeoning them with her "World's Greatest Mom!" mug, and crucifying them on their trellis, explaining somewhat apologetically: "I know, they say Jesus died for our sins. I like a more direct approach."

Driving Miss Crazy: How and why to rein in your vengeful impulses.

If "blue language" actually came out that color, the ugly things I've snarled from inside my closed car at rude drivers and willfully sluggish pedestrians would long ago have transformed the interior from Honda gray to a singed hellfire blue. But I've managed to stop throwing these in-car tantrums. Understanding moralistic aggression helps me understand why I get so enraged and why my rage at some rude passing stranger no longer does the job it would have on some similarly ill-mannered member of the hunter-gatherer band way back when. Understanding biochemistry reminds me of the negative health effects of flying into a rage—sending my blood pressure skyrocketing, poisoning myself with surging stress biochemicals like cortisol, and sometimes giving myself the jitters and a sour stomach for hours afterward.

This isn't to say I now—*poof!*—magically transform into Becky Buddha when some driver, upon spotting my car trying to enter into traffic, hoggishly darts forward, stopping squarely over big white words on the pavement, KEEP INTERSECTION CLEAR FOR CROSS TRAFFIC. Not vaulting into a rage takes preplanning—reminding myself in unheated moments about the pointlessness of getting all bent up. For example, unless you have a rocket launcher on top of your car—and precise aim, to boot—the driver who's just taken a big crap on your existence will likely just keep tooling along with little or no idea of the bug-eyed, mouth-foaming lather you've worked yourself into. And how completely unsatisfying is that?

But let's say some rudeness-inflicting driver is more accessible, maybe getting out of their vehicle in a parking lot or driving alongside you in an adjacent lane. It becomes enormously tempting to fly out of your car and send your tire jack on tour in a place with less sun than Iceland or at least roll down your window and speculate loudly on their mother's sex practices. In such moments, ask yourself whether you want to give some person with all the gentility of a cockroach a say in shaping who you are—which is created through the sum total of how you behave. If not, the answer is not just swallowing whatever they did to you but channeling the adrenaline wave pushing you to do something awful to them in response and instead doing something extremely nice for some nearby stranger. You'll still get some physical and psychological release from taking action—the warm fuzzy that comes from surprising a stranger with an act of kindness or generosity plus the satisfaction that you didn't let some lowlife turn you into their rage-bot.

Finally, it can help to recognize that whether you excuse a driver's behavior as a result of simply being confused or preoccupied (rather than flagrantly rude) often depends on whether you happen to be that driver. This is called "attribution bias" and describes how we tend to think far more charitably about ourselves and our own behavior than other people and theirs. It's something to remember the next time the light turns green and the driver in front of you is just sitting there growing roots—just like he did at the previous light. Consider the possibility that he is lost and looking down at his directions—tempted as you are to believe that he knows who you are, sat outside your house waiting for you to leave, and then followed you down the road just to screw with you.

IMPOLITE AT ANY SPEED

The following sections cover the specific dos, don'ts, and how-to-get-them-to-stop-doing-thats in a variety of transportation arenas: sidewalks, moving sidewalks, elevators, escalators, public transportation, streets, parking lots, street parking, police traffic stops, and airplanes. Subjects grudgingly excluded are sleepwalking, driverless cars, jetpacking, and teleportation. But, about that last category, just a reminder that it's always nicer to say "Beam me up, *please*, Scotty," providing you aren't about to be eaten by something with one big purple eye.

HAVE YOU BEEN RUN OVER BY A FORD LATELY?

Stopping the spread of cur culture in driving, parking, and traffic cop stops.

One car, one parking space. Even if your car is a Ferrari.

My 'hood-adjacent Venice, California, neighborhood became "hot" a few years ago, which is great for people who like to be in walking distance of both a $10 cup of coffee and a $10 hit of heroin, but it's become really hard to find parking.

One day, my boyfriend drove over with cheeseburgers he'd picked up for us to eat before we went out. For twenty-some minutes, he drove round and round looking for a space, but there was not one to be had anywhere remotely nearby. Knowing I wasn't ready to leave, he phoned me from his car, telling me to come outside for a moment. He put his flashers on, handed me my burger, and drove a half-mile to the big office supply store on the boulevard to eat his in the parking lot.

The memory of our drive-by lunch makes it especially maddening when somebody with fancy-ass wheels parks on my block like the Porschehole taking up two spaces in Irvine (in the photo at the start of this chapter). Parking like this is not just hoggy but idiotic. Although the person's Bentley or whatever *could* get a boo-boo on its bumper while taking up only one space, taking two is like taping a note—"KEY ME!"—on the hood of the car. And no, I'm not suggesting that's okay to do.

My friend Doug knows how to park a really nice car. He had driven over to my house so we could walk to a bar in my neighborhood and grab a drink. When I came out of my gate with him, it was like my little Venice shack had gotten caught in a tornado and landed in Bel-Air. Sunning itself directly in front of my house, between my neighbors' little beatermobiles, I saw this gleaming black ocean liner of a Mercedes—Doug's new car.

Uh-oh. It would surely get scraped by somebody parking or pulling out, and he would hate me a little every time he saw that scratch. "Um, this street is probably not a good place for you to park," I said.

Doug laughed. "It's just a car."

Right on.

Absolutely right on.

And if *that's* not how you think of *your* ritzywheels, whenever you're contemplating driving to an area where the parking is scarce, you really should think again—and then build your car a velvet-lined, temperature-controlled garage and leave it there to be dusted on the hour by its nanny.

The self-crowned queen of the parking lot and the beauty of positive shaming

If you are a frail 9,000-year-old lady or you just had your knee replaced with four steel pins and sixteen thumbtacks and you lack a handicapped placard for your car, you get a pass for waiting for a primo parking space near the door of the drugstore. Otherwise, you don't get to back up traffic behind you while you wait—and wait and wait—for some other car to pull out, you lazy cow.

When people do this and, once in the store, don't look the type to cause me disfiguring injuries, I'll call them out on their rudeness if I can catch their ear. I do this both to make them pay for being rude with a hassling conversation and because I'm a big fan of shaming as an inhibitor of future rude behavior. Otherwise, I like to leave a shaming note on their windshield, and I keep a pad of Post-it notes and a pen in my glove compartment for this purpose. Here's one of the notes I left on a car in my neighborhood—parked dead-center in a two-space spot between a driveway and a red zone:

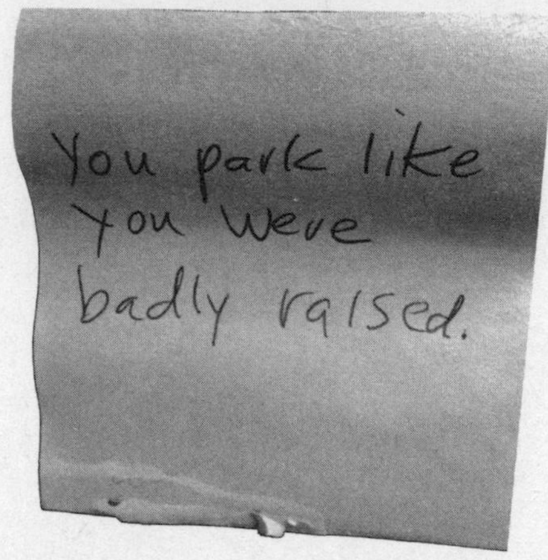

The shaming note is at its most powerful in a residential neighborhood, where the rudely-parked car is likely to belong to a rude resident. If that person has any conscience or concern for their reputation, they have to wonder whether their neighbors strolling or walking the dog saw the note on their windshield about what an inconsiderado they are.

For those worried that they'll be struck with writer's block when it comes time to shame the parking piggy, there are packs of temporarily sticky bumper stickers like "I park like an idiot" for sale on the Internet.[34] The beauty of these or the shaming note tucked below the lip of a car trunk is that the offender may unwittingly drive around with it for quite some time, announcing to the world exactly the sort of ill-raised jerkus they are.

Neighborhood parking culture and when shaming notes go too far

Shaming notes should go after people for their rotten behavior alone. Those that go further—attacking a person's looks or size—usually end up being ruder than any rudeness or perceived

[34] Google this: "I park like an idiot stickers." The stickers to get use Post-it-type stickum so they won't damage cars.

rudeness they're responding to, as evidenced by a cruel note left on the car of an Oregon woman's sister. The sister had driven over to stay with the woman for the weekend and had parked in front of the house across the street simply because she'd come from that direction. (That's the sister's car in front of the neighbors' house below.)

The woman explained in an e-mail to me that her sister's car was "the only car parked on the street for three whole blocks, and there was easily room for another five cars in these people's driveway. Plus there's the little detail that she was parked legally on a public street." Yet the neighbors saw fit to tuck a hateful rant under the sister's windshield wiper blade, addressed to "the idiot owner of the green Pontiac."

"I realize that you're probably too busy stuffing your face to care," wrote one of them, going on to inform the sister than they have a busy household and lots of cars coming and going, including those of clients. The neighbor told the sister to move her "P.O.S. car" further down the street or across the street where she would be "all weekend long," or they'd "block her every time." The neighbor couldn't pass up a final opportunity to go mean: "I figured that a fatty like you would want to park as close as possible to your destination anyway!"

The woman told me that her sister was "completely mortified," which clearly was the neighbors' aim, as anybody with an IQ topping the speed limit in a school zone doesn't expect to say to somebody "You stupid, ugly piece of shit!" and then have them respond, "Oh, sorry! I'll do my best to change!"

In fact, if I were the sister, I'd be tempted to park squarely in the middle of these cruel creeps' front lawn, if not in their living room. And if I were the woman living across from the cruel neighbors, I would have sent a note back, stapled to a copy of the original (so the neighbors would have to revisit their ugliness), but swap an expression of sympathy for the neighbors' low blows. Something along these lines:

> You could have written a polite note requesting that my sister park on my side of the street, though on a public street you have no right to dictate where anyone parks. Still, a respectful request would likely have been honored. I'm going to assume there's something terribly wrong in your life or marriage for you to feel the need to lash out at another person as you did. This allows me to feel sorry for you instead of angry with you. I hope things get better for you.

By taking action—sending a note rather than just casting hurt looks in the direction of the neighbors' living room—the woman is refusing to act like a victim. Keeping the note free of low blows says that the neighbors don't get to pull her strings, directing how she acts or the kind of person she is. And showing sympathy rather than anger, though still a reaction and maybe not an entirely believable one, removes much of the satisfaction the neighbors would surely get from a response in kind and sucks a good deal of air out of any feud the neighbors may have been hoping to incite.

Now, there is such a thing as parking culture in a neighborhood—unwritten but often widely accepted rules about how people should park. Weirdly, the rules are usually the most rigid in neighborhoods where the parking is most ample and typically involve the dictate that residents and their visitors must always park in the resident's driveway—or at least in front of their house.

Even if you think it's ludicrous that there are rules about parking on a public street, it might make sense to respect them. Consider the trade-off: whether it might be worth it in exchange for keeping civil relations with persnickety neighbors. The nastier your neighbors are the more it might pay to go along with their odd minor demand. (More about this in "The Neighborhood" chapter.)

Should you move to a new neighborhood, it's wise to find out about the parking culture, if any, by asking a neighbor or two whether there is one. And if you're annoyed that one of your neighbors seems to be ignoring your neighborhood's parking, just gently mention in the course of general conversation that there *is* a parking culture, explain what it is, and add that they "probably didn't know." Leave it to them to take the reasoning to the next step—that you'd like them to follow it—which makes them less likely to defiantly do the opposite, as does having some previously-established friendly relationship with them. Of course, there is one surefire way to control who parks right in front of your house, and that is to buy either an island or a gated mansion set back a mile from the street.

Sign language: The wave, the horn, the flipped bird.

Obviously, laying on the horn and flipping the bird are not examples of the best in adult manners. Also, it's good to remember that giving in to these impulses can make another driver suddenly drop all their life goals in favor of turning you into roadkill.

The wave, on the other hand, is an important tool for keeping the peace on the road, both by acknowledging when other drivers do something nice for you and also after you do something idiotic and endanger them or unwittingly do something that seems piggy. If you just wag your hand apologetically to them—conciliatory body language that's readable even a car's length away—it tells them that your cutting them off wasn't intentional. Ideally, that's also the truth; you didn't just have second thoughts after looking in the rearview mirror and noticing that they look like they've done time.

•*Traffic cop stops: Drawing the line between politeness and self-incrimination.*

There's this thing called the "California stop," referring to how just about everybody in California (or at least Los Angeles) either can't be bothered to stop at stop signs or simply feels too stupid being the only one doing it. (I know—Jersey, Georgia, and a host of other places claim this, too.) So, when you, like everybody else, *alllmosst* come to a complete stop, and then see flashing lights behind you, it's easy to vault right into Bad Attitudeville and imagine that you're being singled out for persecution, probably because the officer hates middle-aged women in Hondas.

Obviously, it pays to keep your interaction with the cop snippiness-free, but one school of thought says you should say nothing at all. In civil liberties circles, there's a much-viewed YouTube video by Regent University School of Law professor James Duane, titled "Why You Should Never Talk to the Police." Yes, Duane's position is "Never." He explains that by answering a police officer's questions—even if you are innocent, even if you got pulled over for something minor like an unsafe lane change—you can incriminate yourself, giving the police evidence to use against you in court that can maybe even be used to send you to the slammer.

Duane's thinking seems legally sound, and I would follow it in many situations—for example, if cops wanted to question me in respect to some crime that had been committed, even if I had nothing to do with it. But in regard to traffic stops, I had my suspicions that his advice would play poorly outside a law school auditorium, in the auditorium of real life, so I reached out to a few cops and a civil liberties lawyer whose judgment I respect. One of these cops is a Washington state patrol officer with twenty-one years on the job who asked me not to use his name. He says he'd probably find it really odd, even suspicious, if a driver he'd stopped refused to say a word. "It's almost impossible for a human being in that situation to not get a little bit overly gabby. Their heart rate's up, they're nervous, those red and blue lights are heating up the back of their head, and we have a tendency to stammer in situations like that."

Retired California cop Tracy Ambrico agreed. Ambrico, a thirty-year law enforcement veteran who spent eleven years as a patrol officer, says that by saying nothing, you "set off certain warning bells in an officer: What's wrong with this person? Why aren't they interacting?" It gets the officer "way up on their guard."

First Amendment lawyer Marc J. Randazza likewise finds the advice to just clam up seriously unrealistic. Randazza is both a civil liberties bulldog and a guy who appreciates fast cars—and not just from behind a velvet rope as a lingerie model dusts them at car shows. He drives his "to their tolerances, not the law's tolerances," when he's on the Southwest's desolate desert highways.

"I get pulled over going arrestably fast on a regular basis," Randazza told me. "In fact, I can't remember the last time I was pulled over for speeding and wasn't going fast enough that the cop *should have* taken me to jail." So, when a cop comes up to him and says "Do you know why I pulled you over?" he knows better than to say, "Nope, no idea." Recognizing that people hate being lied to and treated like they're stupid, Randazza will adopt a sheepish tone and concede to the officer, "Yeahhhh . . . I was speeding a little bit there, huh?"

Randazza explains, "That is legally inadvisable because you are making an admission and right there you got rid of your ability to plead not guilty." He acknowledges that "the textbook legal response is 'I have no idea why you pulled me over, and if you want to charge me with something, it is going to be your burden to prove it.' That's all well and good on a law school exam and nice if you want to write a legal guide. But, let's be practical. And let's be smart." Unless you look like a typical felon, the cop "probably didn't pull you over to see if he could make something up." The cop probably already knows you were speeding and probably has evidence of it, too—on radar or by estimating your speed—a technique Randazza says holds up surprisingly well in court.

The Washington cop confirmed what Randazza said about not straining credulity. "I don't expect everybody to [say], 'You're right. I was doing forty-eight in a twenty. Why don't you get me out of the car and I'll do some push-ups?' " But to have him maybe go easier on you, "owning what you did is a good start—accepting responsibility."

Of course, attitude management is essential in minimizing a traffic stop's bite. Randazza advises that it's especially important to be congenial if you have something to hide: a roach in the ashtray, a dead hooker in the trunk. "You've already behaved very impolitely if you have a dead hooker in your trunk. You're probably off Amy's 'nice people who say fuck' chart. But, you want to minimize the chances of a search . . . or the impoundment . . . of your vehicle," so: "Smile! Be nice!"

The Washington cop says that he, like many cops, gives many more warnings than he gives tickets. "The tone of the stop is often set by the driver as we walk up to the car," he explains. "For example, if we get you on radar doing seventy in a thirty, you're going to get a ticket. If we walk up to the car and you're maybe ten, twelve over the speed limit and it's a pleasant beginning—'Hi' or 'I know, I'm so sorry, I didn't see the red light'—there's time for decision-making in the officer's head."

Ambrico echoes his remarks and notes that an officer may intend to give a warning—until a driver starts arguing with them. Since we aren't able to listen well when we're angry, "they think you're not going to understand the warning, so they ticket."

Crying can sometimes soften an officer's heart—if you're a teenage girl and it's your first time being stopped by the police. "If it's a twenty-five-year-old meth addict whose driving status is suspended and who has a glass pipe on the dashboard, it's not gonna slow me down much," the Washington patrolman says. In fact, not surprisingly, faking it is likely to backfire. Ambrico explains that cops "become adept at figuring out whether someone is crying because they had a really bad day. If an officer feels the person is trying to manipulate them, they are more likely to get a ticket."

A wiser approach is actually *asking* for a warning, in a way that reflects respect for the officer and for whatever traffic law you just broke. The Ticket Assassin website advises you say something like: "I'm always a safe driver, officer, and now that I see that sign [or understand this law], I'll certainly never violate it. Would you please give me a warning as a reminder?"

When an officer's looking to check your cavities—and not the ones the dentist fills

Say a traffic stop is going badly—badly in that the officer asks to search your car. Even if you have nothing illegal in your vehicle, allowing a search may be a bad idea, considering the increase in recent years in civil asset forfeitures—the term for when the government seizes property or money on the grounds that it *might* have been used to commit a crime. Disgustingly, in these cases, it's guilty until proven innocent—with the burden of proof on the person whose asset was seized to show that it could not have been used to commit a crime. Those without the means to mount a costly legal defense sometimes find themselves waving goodbye to their cash, home, place of business, boat, or car.

Ambrico, acknowledging that you have every right to refuse a search, points out that there are times when allowing one might make sense. For instance, she says, if your vehicle is subject to being towed, like if you're driving on a suspended license, that officer can take your car on the spot. But "in most cases, if you are cooperative and let him do what he's going to do," he'll give you the option of having somebody other than a tow truck operator get your car out of there.

Keep in mind that the officer is *asking* to search for a reason: He has no probable cause—no reasonable suspicion you've committed a crime—or he'd already be searching *without asking*. It is your constitutional right to refuse his request. If you do so, Randazza again advises you to avoid doing it combatively: "If they say 'Well, you got something to hide?' just say, 'No, I believe in the Constitution, and with all respect, I really don't want to give up my Fourth Amendment rights voluntarily. If you're going to search the car, I realize I can't stop you, but I want it to be on the record that it's a nonconsensual search.' "

In *Arrest-Proof Yourself*, ex-cop Dale C. Carson advises declining a search by giving a plausible reason that you need to leave. He suggests saying "Officers, I apologize for the traffic violation," noting that you have cooperated with them, and adding "However, I am late and urgently have to be going" and then explaining why—for example, you are diabetic, asthmatic, or otherwise ailing and must go home to take your meds; your spouse or child is sick, and you need to go care for him or her. He notes that cops may call to verify your reason, so don't give an excuse that can get you caught in a lie.

A prelude to a search is often a series of prying questions. Though it seems a good idea to be politely forthcoming when asked things like "Do you know the speed limit on this road?" the cop may also try to get a little more personal, asking you where you live, how you feel about our drug laws, etc. He probably is doing this not because he finds you fascinating but because he's trying to find something incriminating. You don't have to answer these questions. You will need to wait for him to give you the citation before you drive away, but in response to his attempts to probe you further or get you to agree to a search, you can say these magic words: "Are you detaining me, or am I free to go?" (Unless you explicitly announce that you want to leave, the law considers your continuing encounter with a cop voluntary.)

But, again, let's get real. An unscrupulous cop can use your exercising your rights against you, as did an Idaho officer who pulled over one of my blog commenters for speeding (going seventy in a sixty-five zone—wow). The officer asked this guy—a twenty-two-year-old poli-sci major at the University of South Dakota—to stick around and answer a few questions. This guy, who told me he'd viewed his share of civil liberties videos, asked, "Officer, am I being detained?" The officer said no. The guy told the officer he was going to leave and walked back toward his car. The officer then told him he *was* being detained and called in other officers to tear apart his vehicle in a search on the grounds that his refusal to answer questions was "suspicious."

Where people go wrong is in thinking they're powerless to fight back against an abusive cop. Ambrico says that if an officer does violate your rights or is rude or otherwise out of line, it's important to recognize that you have recourse—*just probably not there*, while the stop is taking place. She does say that you can ask for a supervisor to come out during the stop or go afterward to the counter at the police station and ask to file a complaint. Ambrico suggests keeping in mind that officers are being videotaped and audio-recorded during traffic stops. "Nobody does anything anonymously anymore." (Check your state or locality to be sure.) She says the cop's supervisors and the DA "are going to look at tape [and] listen to the audio recording" to see whether your rights were violated or the cop behaved inappropriately. "The DA will not [bring a court case against you] if the search is bogus."

I think it's also a wise idea to protect yourself by making your own recording. Steve Silverman, founder of the nonprofit Flex

Your Rights and co-creator of the film *10 Rules for Dealing with Police*, wrote for Reason.com in April 2012 that it is legal to record the police in every state but Massachusetts and Illinois. That said, it's probably best to turn on your cell phone recorder or video camera and place it discreetly out of sight well before the officer gets to your car. Even the most fair and even-tempered officer is unlikely to be charmed and amused by the notion that he could soon go viral on YouTube.

Traffic stop etiquette basics: How to set the right tone, even before the officer gets to your car.

When you get "lit up" by a police cruiser, put on your blinker or flashers and look for a safe place to stop nearby. With emphasis on "nearby." The Washington patrolman says, "I don't want to follow for a mile and a half while someone looks for the perfect spot to pull over, because that makes me think that they're swallowing four pounds of methamphetamine."

Once you stop, if it's night, turn on your car's interior light and sit there with both hands on the wheel so the officer will be reassured you aren't going for a weapon. Stay in the car unless told to get out. Roll down the driver's-side window and the passenger's-side window, too, if two officers are approaching you. Wait for the officer to ask you to get out your paperwork, and whatever you do, do not be talking on your cell phone when they get up to your car. They might not be able to put you on death row for that, but they'll probably want to.

Finally, if you do get a ticket, sign it when the cop asks you to. As ex-officer Carson writes in *Arrest-Proof Yourself*, the ticket is "merely a receipt" acknowledging that you've received the traffic citation, not an admission of guilt. You can still go to court to contest it. But, in some states, refusing to sign it is a criminal offense—one that can get you arrested and sent to jail.

THE DESCENT OF MAN—INTO RUDENESS ON SIDEWALKS, MOVING SIDEWALKS, ELEVATORS, AND ESCALATORS

If there's a guiding principle of polite conveyance on foot, it's this: "The barrier method" is a type of contraception, not a form of pedestrianism.

Walkblocking

The considerate thing to do on the sidewalk seems obvious: Whenever you are walking side by side with one or more people and someone's approaching or you hear hurrying footsteps behind you, go single file to let the person or people pass. But when I mentioned this during a talk, a girl, about twenty, couldn't help but interrupt: "But, wait! If my boyfriend and I are holding hands, do we really have to let go?"

Tragically, yes. Spend some time apart. Like, three seconds.

It's actually a sneaky form of bullying when a bunch of people strolling together form a human wall across the sidewalk, showing no sign that they'll separate to let pedestrians through. Don't enable their rudeness by pasting yourself to a storefront until they pass. Instead, use a trick I learned in the 90s in Rome, where traffic laws are seen more as traffic suggestions and the locals all drive like they're on a lifelong coke bender.

I was a little tentative in crossing the street there because cars didn't seem to stop for pedestrians—sometimes not even at a red light. "Don't worry if traffic's coming," my Rome-dwelling friend advised. "Just walk across, but be sure you don't make eye contact with the drivers. If they can't be sure you see them coming, they'll stop."

I was terrified to put this into practice, but to my amazement, he was right,[35] and I've found that the same psychology applies on

---

[35] I wouldn't do this now in Rome, with all the drivers on cell phones.

the sidewalk: Avoid making eye contact, by looking either at the pavement or into a store window, and a wall of rudewalkers bearing down on you will part like the Red Sea for the Jews.

If you aren't moving, move over.

- *Texting while walking isn't* always *rude.*
  If you live in a rural area and you're in the mood to text while on a stroll, have at it. In any place more citified than Tenney, Minnesota (population: 5, last I checked), step aside. Remember, it's called a "side*walk*," not a "side*stop* suddenly and make everyone walking behind you leap around you."

- *The Empire Hate Building: Sightseeing without making people who live there want to kill you.*
  If you're part of a group of tourists, sure, stop and look up, but first back up—against the buildings or to the curb—so you don't take over the entire sidewalk like a bunch of grazing cows.

- *Moving sidewalks and escalators: A poor place to do one's impression of paralyzed livestock.*
  This is especially true in the airport, yet people the size of industrial refrigerators constantly plant themselves and their bags squarely in the middle of the walkway, making anyone hurrying along behind them feel like a colonoscopy camera meeting an intestinal impasse with ugly luggage. There are plenty of areas in which Europe has cornered the market on stupid, but somehow many Europeans seem to get it about moving walkways and their older cousin, the escalator: Walk left, stand right.

  As for your exit strategy, upon coming off a moving sidewalk (or emerging from an elevator, subway stairs, or building) remember that your job is not done.[36] Don't just stop in your tracks and pick your teeth or check your phone, much as you might like to help the people behind you improve their reflexes by giving them a human obstacle to leap around.

For some, the sidewalk is a side-roll.

It's easy to forget that curb ramps at intersections and ramped pathways to businesses have an essential purpose for some of us. The handrails on both sides of the wheelchair ramp outside one Culver City, California, Starbucks look like the perfect place to lock your bike or tie your dog—unless you know Thom Fritz, who can only get into that Starbucks by rolling up that ramp in his motorized wheelchair. Thom has this rare muscle-attacking disease called Friedreich's ataxia, moves parts of his body with great difficulty, and has a hard time speaking and seeing objects in his path until they're right in front of him. So, when somebody blocks the ramp, even a little with their locked bike wheel, Thom gets trapped there and has to wait until somebody sitting in Starbucks notices him and helps him through.

Amazingly, Thom hasn't let his disease stop him from getting out of the house. In fact, he went across Australia in his wheelchair and published a book about it in 2006, *Rollabout Australia*. But, back in Southern California, along with bikes in the handicap ramp, carelessly placed shopping carts are one of Thom's fiercest daily impediments. This blog item he wrote makes me mindful to always go that extra few steps and push the shopping cart back to the store:

> Often, I go zipping along minding my own business, lost in my thoughts, and I come across a shopping cart left lackadaisically in the middle of a walkway or

[36] The same goes for grocery shoppers who plant their shopping cart squarely in the middle of the aisle and orphan it there. My boyfriend says, "That's why grocery carts should have horns."

> sidewalk. I am bound to run into it, or be forced to make a last-minute maneuver to keep from running into it. These unexpected maneuvers lead to collisions of a catastrophic moment, leaving me with a broken and bloody foot or sending me careening off the sidewalk or walkway into the flower bed or even off the curb.

Thom wrote that he sees the shopping cart as having two purposes—convenience in transporting our groceries and reminding us of the relationship we have with others. In Thom's words, the latter "must be looked at a little more."

The world is neither your oyster nor your giant spittoon.

Certain sidewalks in midtown Manhattan can become a hockaloogie obstacle course. One look up at a bird or a building and you're sure to find some stranger's DNA wet-mounted in the treads of your shoe.

These spitters do this where everyone else walks because they're disgusting and because nobody ever follows them, removes a shoe, and returns their slobber to them by wiping the sole on their coat. (I'm not recommending, just fantasizing.)

Yoo-hoo, spitters . . . your saliva belongs one of three places: in your mouth, in the toilet bowl, or speeding down the drain. Also, you might want to get that checked out—whatever's in your mouth that's so odious that you feel the need to be all "bombs away!" with your saliva everywhere you go.

Do you mind if I fart?

Sorry, smokers, but the entire great outdoors isn't one big "screw you if you don't like my smoking" section. Guidelines for polite smoking in public are akin to those for passing gas. If you wouldn't stand just upwind from a sidewalk café or a public bench lighting your farts, don't stand there and light a cigarette.

My favorite café is unfortunately situated in respect to Southern California wind patterns, turning it into a walk-in ashtray whenever some passerby with a lit cigarette sits down in one of the four little metal folding chairs in front of the place. When their smoke (and occasionally ash) starts blowing in the door, one of the other regulars always looks (pleadingly) to me to go out and say something. I, of course, don't tell the smoker what to do, being mindful that bossiness tends to make a person long to do just the opposite. Instead, I simply give them the air pollution report—along with the benefit of the doubt: "You probably didn't know this, but your smoke is blowing right into the café." There was only one guy in an entire year who *didn't* say something like "Whoops, sorry. I didn't know" and then move away from the doorway, and that guy looked like my voice wasn't the only one he was hearing at the time.

THEY CALL IT THE "F" TRAIN, NOT THE "EFF YOU!" TRAIN

Considerate conveyance on public transportation

It doesn't take much to be polite while riding the bus or subway—just remembering that public transportation is shared transportation and that there's a good chance that you're already torturing another passenger near you simply by existing.

It's public transportation, not a public restroom.

While riding public transportation, do not pick your teeth, floss, apply nail polish, clip your fingernails—or, worse—your toenails. During my years living in New York, I not only witnessed several men clipping their toenails on the subway, only one of whom looked homeless and insane, but once saw a man remove one of his shoes and begin biting his. And as long as we're puttering around in my mental archives, no, you don't get to save time during the workday by masturbating under a magazine while en route to the office—and besides, remember all the people these days with smartphones.

Unfortunately, it seems there were too few photo- and

video-equipped phones back in 2009 to cramp the personal care efforts of the DC subway rider whom blogger Unsuck DC Metro deemed the "Metro Arm Barber." Yes, just as it sounds, a guy seated on DC's orange line was snipping off all of his arm hair with a pair of scissors and then brushing his trimmed fur onto the seat and floor as horrified riders stared on in shock.

Dealing with public transit pervos: Is that your erect penis in the small of my back . . . ?

It's sometimes hard to tell whether the train's just crowded or your commute is being turned into a sex crime. Be mindful that you can ruin a person's life on a mere suspicion. It's better to maybe let a grope-grabber get away with it than to accuse somebody who's only guilty of squeezing into a packed train car at rush hour and then needing to reach down into his pocket for his phone.

If you are creeped out by somebody pushing up against you but really can't be sure whether you're being victimized (or if it seems dangerous to say something), move away from the perp immediately by announcing that you're about to be sick. Not only should this get others on a crowded train to quickly clear a path for you but the potential to be vomited on also seems likely to rapidly shift a perp's priorities and state of mind.

Once you move away, clue in any sympathetic riders who come to your aid. You'll feel less alone, and they may support you and help you assess the situation. Clandestinely videotape the perp, or at least take a photo of him if you can do that without endangering yourself, especially if he seems to be rubbing up on the woman who took your place. (This almost always happens to women, not men.) If you can, after you get off, approach that woman to see whether she feels she was victimized and whether she'll join you in filing a report with the transit cops. The blog *Gothamist* and other sites report mass transit butt- and boob-grabbers being found and charged thanks to photos and video passed on to them by victims and witnesses.

Even when women are certain that they've been sexually touched—like when somebody grabs and twists their boob—their gropers often slip away to grope again because their prey are too shocked or embarrassed to do what one woman in the New York City subway did: bellow, "He groped me!" In July 2012, the *New York Post* reported that a thirty-year-old Bronx man allegedly grabbed an unnamed thirty-five-year-old woman around the waist and copped a feel of her butt as she got off a Queens-bound G train. The *Los Angeles Times* added that she chased the man onto the L train, pointing him out to other passengers, who pulled him off the train and held him until transit cops arrived and arrested him on charges of forcible touching. (That part of the incident was captured on video and posted on YouTube with the title "Subway Grabber.")

New Yorkers have an undeserved reputation as people who won't get involved. I've read research on the "bystander effect"—how being in a crowd causes people to do nothing for a stranger in trouble, sometimes because of "diffusion of responsibility." People in the crowd tend to assume someone else will intervene or, if they haven't, there's good reason they haven't. And, sure, there are stories of subway gropees' cries being ignored by other passengers, but the portrayal of New Yorkers as a cold, look-the-other-way bunch is exactly the opposite of my experience during my years living in Manhattan. My sense then was that New Yorkers realize that life in the city is tough for everyone, and they'll come to your rescue, especially if you call out and especially if you're a lady in jeopardy. That said, you'll increase your chances of overcoming the bystander effect and getting help if you do more than announce to the train car, "He groped me!" Be specific about the help you want and from whom.[37] For example, say, "This guy in the red groped me! You two big

[37] I got this idea from British psychologist Dr. Richard Wiseman. See his terrific book *The As If Principle*.

strong dudes over there by the door, please help me: Grab him and hold him for the police!" By calling out to them as individuals, you'll make them more likely to intervene and help you get the scumbag's creeping hands around a set of bars, where they belong.

Ear invasions: When somebody's iPod becomes an Everybody-in-the-Train-Car-Pod.

You get on the Lexington Avenue line at 14th Street. It's crowded, so you can't really move around. This is a problem because no sooner does the train groan to a start than the lady next to you starts spilling a tiny but continuing trickle of her Sprite down your leg and keeps spilling it . . . 23rd Street . . . 28th Street . . . the trickle continues.

Sprite does not stain, and your pants will dry, but few people would find you unreasonable if you not only were extremely peeved at the Sprite spiller but told her to cut it the hell out. But if you so much as admit to being irritated at riders who continuously spill a trickle of their music into your ears—that angry-mosquitoes sound of leaky headphones—you're likely to get sneered at by many who share the sentiments of a commenter on a *New York Times* blog-rant on iPod volume by reporter Ray Rivera:

> I hear rent is dirt cheap in Idaho, move your complaining behind over there and go complain to a potato.
>
> —*Jason*

The truth is, no matter where you are, other people's attention doesn't belong to you. This is especially important to remember in a contained shared space like a bus or subway car, where people often can't get away from the persistent annoyance of leaky headphones (or obnoxiously loud conversations) except by getting off before their stop and walking forty blocks. Talking at a polite volume takes recognizing that all those strangers are riding the bus with you because they need to get somewhere, not because they want an update on you and your day. Listening to music politely might mean spending more than $3 on headphones and getting a friend to tell you whether they're leaking sound. Using your cell phone politely means only using it for texting on public transportation or in any contained space rather than following "norms" set by the self-important who force a busful or trainful of strangers to listen to their phone conversations. And be sure to turn off the sound on your phone so the world will not—*bing!*—be apprised every time you get a voicemail or—*clickety-clickety!*—spell a word. Putting one's device on silent is also a huge must for riders playing games on their devices sans headphones, the noise polluters the rest of us most long to tase and watch writhing in agony on the spit-, gum-, and urine-spattered train car floor.

As for whether you should say something to public transit noise polluters, it depends. If you're endlessly asking noisy jerks to put a damper on it, you'll spend your whole commute being a scold and probably annoy other passengers in the process—perhaps more so than the noise polluter already was. Also, although some people just don't realize that they're being noisy and will respond apologetically and even gratefully when you let them know, many absolutely know they're rude but would lick the subway car from end to end before admitting to it. So, if you're sensitive to noise pollution, it's probably best to take proactive defensive steps, like wearing what I call "asshole-canceling headphones" (or, as they're more commonly known, *noise-canceling*). The top-of-the-line models with the big, ugly over-the-ear cans (like the Bose QuietComfort 15s my boyfriend got me) are expensive, but they're worth every cent, as they do a remarkable job of quieting or even muting noise entirely.[38]

[38] For added protection, because the Bose headphones are better at blocking out low noises than they are at blocking out voices, I sometimes pair mine with industrial-use earplugs and an iPhone app that plays white, pink, or brown noise.

But say you've left your defensive measures at home and you're stuck on a long commute with somebody leaking *Angry Birds* or inane pop the whole way. As I've noted elsewhere in the book, telling a stranger what to do can be very effective . . . if your desired effect is having them keep doing what they were doing, only louder or otherwise more bothersomely—after they get done yelling at you about what a stupid, ugly, meddling bitch you are.

For more effective effectiveness, take the no-blaming/"just the facts, ma'am" approach I suggest for getting smokers, loud cellphoners, and drivers parked outside your house with booming car stereos to stop bothering you. Smile, get the attention of the person with the leaky headphones, and tell them, "You probably didn't know this, but your earbuds leak quite a bit of sound." You aren't giving them orders; you're simply pointing out a helpful fact. You aren't suggesting that they're rude, just temporarily unaware. If they care at all about being considerate or at least being perceived as considerate, you've just put them in the best possible mind-set to voluntarily turn their device off or at least turn the music down.

Hey, Seathogs: Did your purse pay a fare, too? Did your penisaurus?

If your penis is so huge that you are forced to spread your knees and take over half the space of the people on both sides of you, you aren't well-endowed; you have a frightening medical condition in need of immediate attention.[39] SeatHogs.com calls this space invasion "mansitting" (though women occasionally do it, too) and scorns the "selfish or clueless individual who deprives another individual of any reasonable or unimpeded opportunity to sit down."

Accordingly, no, your purse or backpack doesn't get its own seat on the train or bus—not even if it isn't terribly crowded. Someone may want that seat, and turning it into a throne for your bag forces that rider to have an interaction with you in order to sit

[39] The porn star called "Tony Titanic" doesn't have to spread his legs that wide.

there. This isn't to say it's impossible to keep strangers at bay and have an entire bank of seats to yourself. Just hire Jeeves to drive you around in a Bentley.

If somebody seated has given their bag or their hat a seat of its own, avoid showing anger. Using a calm tone, just point to the item and say, "Excuse me?" They will know exactly what you mean and should move it—perhaps grudgingly—which marks them as even more of a jerk than they already were by giving their hat its own seat.

I've even had success getting those subway leg-spreaders to stop invading my space. I pull my bookmark from my book and prod their knee in the direction I want it to go, sometimes chirping "Excuse me!" while prodding. You could also just ask them to move their knees. (They probably count on most people being too uncomfortable or too scared to say anything to a stranger.) Again, attitude is important. If you don't come on all bitchy and aggressive, they're less likely to get angry back, and it would probably seem embarrassing to try to kill you.

THE AIRPLANE

Flying with old-fashioned manners—like from the 1950s, not from when the Neanderthals were running around.

It's seriously cool that a whole bunch of people can get into a big metal tube in Los Angeles, hurtle through the sky, and be in New York five or six hours later. We're all so used to airplane travel that we mostly forget to be amazed by it. Of course, these days, we're sometimes just too angry to be amazed by it. Just getting through the airport to the gate is an ugly ordeal, thanks to the "security theater,"[40] security expert Bruce Schneier's term for our wildly wasteful and idiotic pretend security that treats every American with a plane ticket as a plausible suspect.

---

[40] Actually meaningful security would involve trained intelligence officers using probable cause to root out terrorists long before they ever get to the airport or another target.

In 2010, I was flying home from Toronto (where you go through American security), and the TSA supervisor at the X-ray machine told me I was "lucky" that he wasn't going to take away my dull little drugstore tweezers. Take away my tweezers? Because I might use them to break in to the cockpit and overpluck the pilot's eyebrows?[41]

In 2011, a female TSA worker's lawyer (unsuccessfully)[42] demanded $500,000 from me after I dared complain on my blog that her client had jabbed the side of her latex-gloved hand—four times—up somewhere you don't get to go unless you at least buy me a drink and tell me I'm pretty. My stay-at-home-mom neighbor, pulled aside for a TSA "pat-down" at LAX, got felt up almost to the point of nipple play. It was so intimate she felt compelled to explain to her TSA groper, "They're a little lumpy because I'm still breast-feeding."

Beyond all the "security" indignities, people are fatter than ever, seats are smaller than ever, and airlines are stopping just short of charging for use of the restroom in flight. Airplane travel increasingly feels like a cross between factory farming (from the chicken's perspective) and being thrown into an airborne Turkish

---

[41] In July 2013, novelist Cory Doctorow blogged about the TSA's Instagram account, where they show off all the "dangerous items" that they, as Doctorow puts it, "~~steal~~ confiscate from air travelers." Their intended message—they're keeping us safe from danger in flight—is clear. But Doctorow, at BoingBoing.net, notes the essential missing detail:

> What they don't show is all the grand-jury indictments for conspiracy to commit air terrorism that they secured after catching people with these items—even the people who were packing guns. That's because no one—not the TSA, not the DAs, not the DHS—believe(s) that anyone who tries to board a plane with a dangerous item is actually planning on doing anything bad with them. After all, as New York State chief judge Sol Wachtler said (quoting Tom Wolfe), "a grand jury would 'indict a ham sandwich,' if that's what you wanted." So if there was any question about someone thinking of hurting a plane, you'd expect to see indictments.

[42] I'm thankful that First Amendment lawyer Marc J. Randazza and his team of associates came to my rescue, defending me pro bono, or my groper might be driving to her job at LAX in a Ferrari, which I'd be spending the rest of my life paying off.

prison.[43] But, don't despair. It's still possible to take a flight that isn't hellish—and maybe even one that's pleasant—even if you can't afford an $8,000 first-class ticket or a working time machine to take you back to the days before Pan Am went out of business. As you'll come to see, a pleasant flight has three elements: one part luck, one part polite behavior by us, and one part knowing how to play it upon encountering some airborne unrepentant boor.

Baggage manners: Buying an airplane ticket does not entitle a person to challenge the laws of physics.

Because most airlines are now charging to check bags, some have gotten very strict about the size of your carry-on. Or, so I hear. Whenever I fly, the gate and flight attendants all seem to turn their backs on any rollaboard smaller than a sarcophagus. Sure, it sucks to pay $25 or $30 to check a suitcase, but whether or not the flight attendants stop you, there's carry-on baggage and then there's douchebaggage: coming aboard with two huge wheeliebags and a bulging backpack and making room for them by asking three other passengers to pull their reasonably sized bags out of the overhead and stick them under the seat.

It's good to be kind and generous and *voluntarily* move stuff under your seat for some late-boarding passenger who needs space for their single, reasonable-sized bag. But, if you've stowed a moderate amount of stuff and then some bag-caravanning hogaboard asks to colonize your little section of overhead space (eradicating leg room you're especially in need of if you're tall), don't be afraid to politely refuse. Just avoid responding to "Can you put your bag under your seat . . . ?" with a definitive no, which will give them room to attack you as "selfish" and maybe get other passengers to take their side. Instead, deflect them with an indirect approach (in the guise of being helpful)—something like: "Actually, I paid to

[43] Think Midnight ExpressJet.

check *my* large rollaboard, and I think the flight attendant can help you check yours." Remember, tone and manner count. If you don't get angry, you're more likely to prevail, deftly emphasizing the difference between *sharing* space and giving it up entirely.

After stowing your stuff in the overhead, your butt cheeks should meet your seat and remain there until the plane is at cruising altitude. If you have a tendency to pop up multiple times during boarding to rummage through your bag for your headphones or a stick of gum, plan ahead: While waiting at the gate, gather all the items you'll use in flight in a small bag so you can toss it under your seat fast and maybe help that cute honeymooning couple make their connecting flight to Hawaii.

Tempting as it may be to stow your carry-on over the first seat of the plane when you're sitting in the last one, that's not fair to the guy in the bulkhead seat who'll end up having to check the bag holding his laptop. Yes, tragically, you must glide your wheeled suitcase a whole fifty feet to your seat at the back of the plane and, upon landing, endure a similar Bataan Death March–like struggle to get it off.

Family planning: How to be seated with your spouse and children on a plane.

I have "motion sickness issues," which is to say I get carsick on any street with more than five turns in it—for example, the winding mountain roads of Washington, DC—and I often feel airsick when seated anywhere on a plane but up near the front. This means that I am an advance-planning fiend when flying and that I often pay $25 to $75 extra to sit in the "premium" coach rows near the bulkhead. Should I screw up and forget to buy my ticket soon enough and get stuck near the back of the plane, I'll sometimes end up feeling pretty crappy, but what I don't do is try to press some other passenger to trade seats with me. Just asking them would be an imposition, as my frequently flying First Amendment lawyer, Marc J. Randazza, pointed out in a blog item about how peeved he is when he's asked to give up his window or aisle seat and take somebody's middle seat:

> A woman (it's always a woman) gets on the plane and sits in the middle seat next to me. She wants me to trade seats with her or her husband/child—who is in a different row, but ALSO in a middle seat. I always decline. I am never polite about it, and I damn well should not have to be. Often, I've paid extra for that seat. If not, I at least had my head out of my ass when making the reservation, and I took steps not to get crammed in the middle seat. So, since you were too cheap to pay the $25 for the window or aisle seat, or because you failed to plan, I'm an asshole for saying "hell no" when you want me to spend three hours in a middle seat? This is asshole behavior. I know I sound like a dick when I say "no way." You don't get to put me in that situation. Worse than that, you don't get to ask until you find some poor sap who thinks he needs to be a gentleman. You fucked up. YOU sit in the middle seat. If you want to switch with an aisle or a window passenger, you had better have at least $50 to sweeten the deal. I would not accept $50 for it, but someone might. That should be the minimum charge to trade with a middle seat fool.

It *is* somewhat different if you aren't asking somebody to switch to a substantially crappier seat. If you're just, say, asking them to move from, say, 7D to 6D, you could ask in a way that gives them an out, like, "I realize that it might be inconvenient for you to move, but if it's not a big deal, my husband and I would love to sit together." Then again, if it isn't a long flight and your husband isn't being sent off to war when you get to your destination, maybe you can survive sitting a row or two apart. Although for some people, it might be no big deal to swap with you—and some may actually volunteer without your ever asking—others may have a bunch of belongings to move and some issues with climbing over other already-seated passengers. Keep in mind that by asking somebody to move, you're basically saying, "I don't know you, but I'd like to inconvenience you because it would make things better for me." Also, many people really just want to be left alone; that is, unless the question is, "Would you mind giving up your coach seat and taking my wife's seat in first class?"

They're flight attendants, not Teamsters, bouncers, biohazard cleanup workers, or your mother.

I got upgraded to the very last business-class seat on a Delta flight, and the only meal left by the time the flight attendant got back to my row was one I don't eat—pasta. And I was hungry, too.

"Don't worry about it," I told the flight attendant. "You can just give it to me, and I'll eat the salad. And if you have an extra piece of cheese back in the galley, maybe I could have that."

"Oh, my God," he gasped. "Thank you for being so nice about it."

I wasn't exactly thrilled about the situation, but I wasn't quite sure what else I'd be.

"A lot of passengers get furious at me," he explained. "They really take it out on me."

Well, there's some ugly. As big a bummer as it is to just sit there while other passengers scarf down their meals, does anybody really think the flight attendant got with the catering people and hatched a plot to screw 4D out of dinner?

Yet, this flight attendant and all the others I spoke with told me that passengers are increasingly going off on them for anything that goes wrong on a plane, including mechanical problems, a broken seat, and how airlines now provide little bags of pretzels instead of peanuts (lest passengers with peanut allergies go into anaphylactic shock in flight).

The more beaten down the flight attendants feel, the uglier flying gets for all of us. But making them feel less like one of the Christians thrown to the lions doesn't take much. It starts with saying hello to them when you board instead of wordlessly blowing past them to your seat. The same goes for when you leave the plane. Don't forget to thank them and the pilots, if you see them, and say goodbye. They're people, with feelings, not skybots.

Elizabeth Coulter, an Atlanta-based AirTran flight attendant for seven years, talked to me about how awful it feels to greet people boarding with a friendly "Good morning . . . good afternoon . . . welcome aboard" and to then have twenty-five people just ignore her and walk on. She's not even looking for much. You don't have to say hello, she said. "Just give me a man nod."

What many passengers don't know is that flight attendants don't start getting paid until the door of the aircraft closes. That's right: They aren't even getting paid to be snubbed. So being pleasant to them and showing them consideration from the moment you get on can actually mean a lot to them. There are pissy people in any job, of course, but probably many flight attendants are looking for reasons to like you and be nice to you. Do your best to help them out.

They're asking you to turn off your phone, not sacrifice your firstborn. When flight attendants give you instructions, like telling you to turn off your phone or other devices, understand that it isn't because they're really mean and they're looking to deny you your special moment with your electronic binky. They are required to do this by the airline, and many flight attendants believe they can personally be fined by the FAA—perhaps even $10,000—if they don't ask you to comply. This is a myth, according to FAA spokesman Ian Gregor. Unfortunately, it seems to be a widely believed one that has many flight attendants living in fear of some secret-shopper FAA inspector being on board. Luckily for these flight attendants, even according to the myth, they just have to *ask* passengers to follow the rules. For example, if the seat belt sign is on during turbulence and you get up anyway, Coulter said, "all I'm required to tell you is, 'Ma'am, the seat belt sign is on.' I can't tackle you, much as I'd sometimes like to."

Even without FAA fines, passenger misbehavior can end up costing flight attendants by causing them to spend even more time working without pay. "Any kind of incident that happens on the plane, you have to document within twenty-four hours, and all three of us [flight attendants] have to write the report," Coulter said. Flight attendants aren't compensated by the airline for the time it takes to do that.

"Get another job if you don't like it!" some will sneer.

Sure, the flight attendant could quit a job she may love . . . go for career counseling, apply for student loans, go back to school for two to four years, and try to get hired somewhere or open a new business. But wouldn't it be a whole lot easier—and nicer—if passengers would just turn off their phones when asked?

Flight attendants are supposed to provide food and beverage service, *not* servitude.

Once in flight, if you need something and a busy-looking flight attendant is passing your row, say "When you have a moment . . ." getting your message across without also sending the message that you're yet another economy-class princess who expects her foot rub and expects it NOW.

Unless it's your first time on a plane, you know that big metal box the flight attendants push is not a roving puppet show. When it comes to your row, have your earphones off and some idea of what you'd like to drink so the flight attendant doesn't have to stand there while you meditate on it. Also, be a dear and say how you'd like your beverage—i.e., "club soda with ice" or "coffee with two creams, no sugar, please"—so they only have to ask whether a passenger wants ice or cream or sugar 299 times instead of 300. This is a small thing but doesn't go unnoticed, and it's especially appreciated when the flight attendant has just had some jerk shake his glass of ice cubes at him or her, as if this is an acceptable way to demand a refill from the airslave.

Coulter said one of flight attendants' pet peeves is parents using drink ordering as a teaching moment for their toddler, "asking their two-year-old what they want to drink out of a choice of seventeen—'Do you want juice? Do you want Dr Pepper? . . .' "—and expecting the flight attendant to just stand there as the kid puzzles it out. "I don't have forty-five minutes," Coulter said. And although passengers tend to see flight attendants as sky waiters and waitresses, Coulter explained that her primary job is not slinging drinks but "to make sure, from takeoff to landing, everybody's safe . . . [to] get everyone calm, [and] get people safely off the plane in an emergency situation."

It's also good to take note of a flight attendant's attire and how little it has in common with that of the guys in the coveralls and heavy gloves who dump your trash cans into a garbage truck. Just before landing, when a flight attendant asks whether she can take "any" trash off your hands, she means a granola bar wrapper or a newspaper, not any medical waste or poopy diapers you've accumulated in flight. Don't hand her anything you wouldn't want to be handed, and don't leave that big ball of snotted-up Kleenex in the seat back for the next passenger, telling yourself that the airline hires people to pick up the trash. Pick up the trash, yes—not go on a scavenger hunt for it.

Mediation at 30,000 feet is not in a flight attendant's job description. Too many people start looking for the flight attendant at the first sign of a dispute with another passenger. A flight attendant on Flyertalk.com complained: "Passengers are always coming up to me and tattling on each other. 'Can you tell him to put his seat up?' 'She won't share the armrest.' What am I, a preschool teacher?"

If, on the ground, you resolve conflict by implementing valuable preschool lessons like "use your words," make that your first course of action in the air. As soon as somebody starts doing something rude, ask them to stop—politely and without anger in your voice. Waiting leads to hating and to suggestions (usually about forcing some item up the offending person's rectum) that are ultimately counterproductive. On some occasion that you're unable to solve the problem and it's truly making your flight a nightmare, you're better off asking a flight attendant to move you than to try to referee. (A willfully inconsiderate lout doesn't transform into Citizen of the Year because he's asked by a lady in a blue uniform with a pair of wings pinned to it.)

When you notice others being abused by some rudester, don't be afraid to be part of the solution. Since we're all frisked to the point where we have anything more lethal than dull tweezers[44] removed from us, probably the worst-case scenario if you speak up is that somebody will clock you. More likely, they'll either growl at you or heed what you're suggesting they do. And should you observe another passenger trying to squeeze a little human decency out of a boor, you might pipe up in support. Because we evolved to care about preserving our reputation, group dismay at our behavior weighs heavily on us—even when it's just a group of two. Even the tiniest squeak of "He's right, you know!" can serve to temporarily civilize the airborne savage.

Lack of space: The final frontier.

If the airlines continue shrinking passenger space at the rate they have the past few years, coach-class seating will soon be patterned

[44] Except when the TSA is too busy removing diapers and the dignity of grandmothers with leukemia to notice the occasional machete or AK-47 slipping through.

on the mass grave. What airlines haven't taken away is the ability to recline, which means you can sometimes be pressed as far back as possible into your seat and still be able to lick the bald spot of the man seated in front of you.

If your airplane seat reclines, you do have the *right* to recline, but that doesn't mean it's the polite thing to do. Some claim reclining is a must to alleviate their back problems, but the way I see it, I don't get all that much out of reclining and the person behind me gets a lot out of my not reclining, so I almost never put my seat back. My big-guy boyfriend feels similarly: "Unless I look back and see Kermit the Frog, I don't recline. If it's a slighter adult, I might recline a few notches, but not all the way."

If you must put your seat back, give warning to the person behind you and recline slowly and gently, lest you crack them in the nose or turn their laptop into a doorstop with USB. But, say the person in front of you reclines, giving you room to do little more than breathe in flight. To have some chance of getting them to give you a little space, swallow your hatred and ask very nicely, "Hey, I know you have every right to recline (killing what's likely to be their first objection), but is it possible for you to maybe meet me halfway?"

The other seating element that causes much on-plane hatred and strife is the armrest. Many people contend that the armrests belong to the person in the middle seat. The truth is, each passenger has paid for the space that spans from one end of their seat cushion to the other, plus the corresponding under-seat space. Everybody's entitled to an edge of a shared armrest—the one on the inner edge of their seat. Nobody's arm—especially nobody's gross, hairy, bare arm—gets to take up residence in anybody else's paid space. One's legs, likewise, should remain unsplayed (subway rules apply), and one's feet should not be allowed to graze in another passenger's under-seat space. The "No Grazing in Others' Seat Space" rule also applies if you've got 200 or so extra pounds you keep meaning to lose. If you take up two seats, buy two—or at least offer the passenger next to you a couple hundred dollars for colonizing half of theirs.

Other passengers' eardrums should not be considered shared space. Assume that you are not fascinating and that we all hate the music you love. If you've got one of those big voices that carry, make like the iPhone and put your voice on airplane mode—both while in flight and while making pre- and post-flight cell phone calls. As on the bus, when taking the skybus, you need to see that your headphones don't leak. And although using an electronic device with the sound up is not a federal crime, it should be—or at least reason enough to have you thrown off the plane at any altitude.

For some people, a total stranger's striking up a conversation on a plane is an atrocity akin to that stranger's plopping his head on their shoulder and taking a little nap. It is nice to say or nod hello to the people beside you when you first sit down—because it seems cold to say nothing whatsoever. But, if your seatmate responds with a brief hello and nothing more or otherwise shows signs of wanting to remain mum, save the exciting news about everything that's ever happened to you for friends, relatives, and strangers who are coma patients. Even when a seatmate seems open to chatting, you should look for signs suggesting his openness has closed, such as fidgeting or a little trickle of blood coming from his ear. When in doubt, ask—something like: "Am I keeping you from your reading?"

If you are an introvert or just don't want to talk to strangers on planes, pack a full set of boundaries in your carry-on: earplugs, a book, an eye mask, and asshole-canceling headphones. Despite your precautions, should your seatmate start gnawing on your ear, if the brevity of your responses—"True!" . . . "Uh-huh," . . . "Mmmhmm"—doesn't shoo him off, ramp up to tactful excuses:

"I'd love to hear more, but I really need some think-time right now." If these attempts, too, are a wash, point at the blowhard's seat pocket, gasp "Airsickness bag?" and stick your face in it.

It's an airplane, not a drum circle.

The passenger seated in front of you will thank you for small kindnesses like recognizing the difference between "touch screen" and "poke-really-really-hard-throughout-your-ten-hour-overseas-flight screen." You should also avoid using the seat of the person in front of you as a giant handle when getting out of your seat, as this can cause their seat to snap forward and slam them in the head when you let go. This is unpleasant even if they're reading a book or watching the movie, but there's nothing quite like being startled awake by whiplash-lite.

If the kid (or ill-raised forty-five-year-old brat) behind you keeps kicking your seat or banging the tray table, speak up immediately—before you build up so much rage that you turn to the parents and hiss, "A pity you weren't forcibly sterilized!" No, you shouldn't have to ask parents to actually, you know, *parent*, but if you'd like to increase the possibility of it happening (or of any passenger's doing your bidding), ask as nicely as possible and incorporate a reason—for example, "I just had back surgery." The eighteenth-century economist Adam Smith explained that evoking sympathy is a strong human motivator, and studies have shown that giving a reason behind a request makes people more likely to fulfill it. (See chapter 9, "Eating, Drinking, Socializing," page 223.)

Nose hairs are burning.

As Emma Lazarus pointed out in that poem on the Statue of Liberty, the huddled masses are yearning to breathe free. This is especially true of those packed into coach like shrink-wrapped cocktail wieners. Ease their suffering by bathing before flying, and not in cologne. Besides the fact that it's unpleasant for anyone with a working set of nostrils, some people have these crazy fragrance allergies. Forgoing the Axe the day you fly (and not applying that stinky, perfumed lotion on the plane) will allow the allergic to enjoy special little in-flight perks like continuing to breathe.

While you're on the plane, don't be waving your smellier parts around. There are places your stinky-ass bare feet belong, like in a cool stream in the country. Places they do not belong include the bulkhead wall, the seat back, and, horrors, the armrest of the person seated in front of you. (*P.S.* Lightly covering your stinky-ass bare foot in an acrylic sock doesn't make it any more party-ready for the elbow of another passenger.)

Take care not to bring smelly things on the plane. It's understandable that you don't want to fork over 6 or 7 bucks to the flight attendant for crackers and a wedge of "cheese food," but the people seated around you likewise don't want to spend four hours smelling airport food court Thai. Maybe work a compromise and score yourself a ham sandwich instead?

Applying or removing nail polish is one of the rudest things you can do in an enclosed space like an airplane cabin—basically gassing everyone in a dozen or more rows in front of and behind you with toxic fumes. A woman (or mannerless drag queen) doing this should immediately be told to stop by as many passengers as possible if a flight attendant isn't immediately available to scold her. Of course, if life were fair, she would subsequently be dragged from her seat and be given a swirly in the airplane toilet. Suggested musical accompaniment: "Blue Bayou."

If you're a farter, kindly plan ahead. Here's a little secret known to low-carbers like me: Carbohydrates—sugar, flour, starchy vegetables like potatoes, and anything sweet, including fruit—cause gas. Eat none before flying and you will likely be gas-free on the plane. Maybe consider the day of your flight the first day of your low-carb diet? Your cardiologist will thank you—as will anybody who'd otherwise be trapped on a packed plane with your nonstop ass-bombs.

Potty politics

Be mindful of the places your butt does not belong while waiting for the toilet:

1. The flight attendant's face as she's seated on the jump seat trying to eat her lunch.
2. Other passengers' faces.

If the laws of physics dictate that some part of your lower extremities *must* go in somebody's face, crotch is preferable to ass.

Spawn on a plane

There's something to be said for snakes on a plane: They're quiet. Your kids are more likely to be if, when flying, you occupy them with more than your wagging finger and *"Shhh!"*

When my supermom neighbor flies with her kids, she operates under the assumption that there will be no one but her to meet their needs (packing their carry-ons as if there will be nothing to eat and the video screens will be broken or the movie will be just this side of porn). She brings DVDs, iPods loaded with games, books, puzzles, paper and pencils, new little toys, and a new comic book or sticker book for each child. She packs sucking candies for the ear pressure and fresh clothes in case of spills. She preps the kids with naps so they won't be tired and cranky and finds that "a bag of cookies goes a long way toward buying quiet."

If you're taking your kids on a plane, be mindful of this weird partial deafness some parents develop, allowing them to ignore shrieks by their children that could shatter the plate glass in an entire block of storefronts. Should one of your children start wailing or babbling the same phrase over and over, other passengers will be less enraged if you appear more concerned with stopping them than with continuing to read your magazine. You might even mouth "Sorry!" to those around you while trying to quiet your kid or take her into one of the bathrooms and try to calm her down. Any show of consideration actually goes a long way in eliciting generosity of spirit from other passengers. Of course, offering to buy a drink for everyone in your immediate vicinity will go even further.

If it "takes a village," maybe that's where you should leave your screaming-prone children.

I can guess what you're thinking: "Hey, Cranky, weren't you young once?" Sure I was, but until my parents were sure I could sit for four hours on a plane without blowing out other people's eardrums with my screams, they limited my air travel to any place I could get to by vigorously flapping my arms.

I know . . . since I am not a parent, I cannot *possibly* understand how hard it is to keep a child from acting out. And I do hear claims that some children are prone to tantrums no matter how exquisitely they are parented. If this describes your child, there's a solution, and it isn't plopping him down in a crowded metal tube with hundreds of other people who cannot escape his screams, except by throwing themselves to their death at 30,000 feet.

Granted, there sometimes are extenuating circumstances—reasons a parent and their little hellraiser simply *must* take a plane. Well, actually, there are two:

1. Dire family emergency. (Granny's actually dying, not just dying to see the kid.)
2. The wee screamer is urgently in need of a liver transplant that, for some reason, can only take place on the opposite side of the country.

In all other cases, if there's any chance your child is still in the feral stage, pop Granny on a flight or gas up the old minivan for your next vacation. It really does come down to this: Your right to bring your screaming child on a plane ends where the rest of our ears begin.

— 9 —

EATING, DRINKING, SOCIALIZING

Julia Child, the warm, welcoming late chef and culinary camp counselor to millions, called dining with one's friends and beloved family "one of life's most primal and innocent delights."

Ever the realist, Child also noted that "every kitchen" should have a blowtorch.[45] The imposing *whoosh* of the host's turning it on and the sight of a strong and uninterrupted flame can bring one's guests to their senses when other primal urges come out—those that cause one brother to chase the other around the dining table with a carving knife.

To be fair, Child was most likely thinking of singeing off any remaining feathers from a plucked chicken or making those little hardened-sugar ice-skating rinks atop crème brûlée. But eating, drinking, and socializing often highlight (and even bring out) the worst in people, from outlandish cheapness to cross-table insult-hurling to the occasional murder-suicide. As excellent as a blowtorch

---

[45] Child's remark has been widely misquoted as "Every woman should have a blowtorch."

Child's actual remark came from an episode of her TV show, when her guest, pastry chef Mary Bergin, pulled out a blowtorch to put a crème brûlée crust on a chocolate Bundt cake. Child, looking on, exclaimed about the blowtorch, "That's wonderful! Every kitchen should have one."

Bergin answered: "I think so. I think every woman should have a blowtorch because men listen to you when you have a blowtorch in your hand."

"I can imagine," said Child.

can be for halting a felony in progress, to prevent some of the smaller crimes and repulsivities at the dinner table—and bars, restaurants, and parties—there's the rest of this chapter.

On the off chance you were raised in the wilderness by a family of coyotes, I'll touch briefly on the essentials of at-the-table etiquette.

1. Wait for everyone to be served before you start eating. Try to come off more like someone who's eaten a meal or two in his lifetime than like a feral hog loose in Home-Town Buffet.
2. Chew with your mouth closed. The view from across the table should not be the same as the view from your esophagus.
3. Put your silverware down between bites. Clutching your knife and fork in your fists throughout the meal makes you look like one of those oafish guys in some B movie about the Middle Ages.
4. Talking while chewing is not like juggling while riding a unicycle. Nobody will be excited that you can do both at the same time.
5. Coyotes lick their paws while eating for good reason—because animals that die on the side of the road rarely do so next to place settings complete with a napkin.
6. If you want some item located across the table, ask, "Could you please pass . . . ?"; don't knock over two drinks and bloody the nose of the person next to you while stretching for it.
7. You can try somebody's food—if they offer you a taste. Extend your bread plate to receive it instead of reaching over and sending your fork (or, worse, your fingers) souvenir hunting on their plate.

8. Like hostages held by terrorists, some gristly bit you've put in your mouth may require an extraction. Put your napkin to your mouth, smuggle the offending inedible into it, and either keep it hidden there or, when nobody's looking, tuck it under something on your plate.
9. If you don't know what to do with some exotic utensil, wait for somebody else to do something with it and hope they aren't just too drunk to care.
10. Avoid licking your plate clean unless there's a power outage or you're dining with the blind.

People put a lot of emphasis on table manners, which can be acquired or polished with fifteen minutes of googling, but most of the conflicts that lead to hard feelings in social situations have nothing to do with how you pilot a fork. As in other areas of our lives, rudeness in eating, drinking, and socializing almost always comes down to a failure in empathy—neglecting to consider how our behavior will affect others. The lack of empathy is apparent when a supposed friend doesn't bother to respond to your party invitation, but it's also what allows some guy to do that big honking nose-blow right at his table in the middle of Applebee's. The thought he never considers: *Gee, wonder whether the sound of my high-velocity snot ejection might gross out other diners.*

And take the wealthy woman who's secretly cheap. (We'll call her Jane Dough.) She dines out at fancy restaurants like it's her birthright but always comes up with creative justifications for docking the waitress on her tip when the service wasn't actually lacking. It seems that Jane, despite all her money, has some fears about running out of the stuff and likes to cut corners in her spending where she can get away with it. Well, she wouldn't be the first person to have a pang at parting with a dollar, but not everyone sees merely having a pang as reason to follow it wherever it leads. What enables Jane's chronic undertipping is a lack of empathy, which allows her to avoid any inconvenient thoughts of the waitress as a person and the panic she'll feel when she can't pay her electric bill.

TIPPING: PART OF THE TRUE COST OF GOING OUT

Tipping is the area we have more quandaries about than any other sphere of going out, perhaps because our tipping behaviors are about as far away from rational economics as we can get. Take, for example, the way most people tend to tip the same percentage—15 percent (or, increasingly, 20 percent)—whether they're eating cheap or fancy. This means that the waitress at Denny's will get, say, 43 cents for bringing you your plate of food, while the waitress at SnootyAss Bistro will get, oh, $14. Did the SnootyAss waitress really smile $13.57 more broadly when she delivered your order?

Why we *think* we tip and why we actually tip

Most people will tell you they decide how much tip to leave based on the quality of the waiter or waitress's service. The truth is, some actually do, but a whole lot just believe they do. We like to believe we do things for good reasons, but a good deal of social psychology research finds that we're often poor judges of what motivates our behavior. The relationship between the quality of service and the size of the tip diners leave is actually extremely weak, according to the research of Cornell University social psychologist Michael Lynn, a former Pizza Hut waiter and the author or co-author of over fifty papers on tipping.

Lynn acknowledged to me that customers who get better service do tend to tip better, "but not much better." In fact, his research finds that on average, only 2 to 4 percent[46] of the variation

[46] Two percent within a restaurant and 4 percent between restaurants.

in tip size is explained by the customer's assessment of the quality of the service (like server attentiveness, promptness, and knowledgeability). For example, people will often tip a higher percentage on a lower bill. In fact, when I asked Lynn what he typically tips, he told me that he normally leaves 20 percent on a restaurant check at an upscale establishment, but when he goes to his local diner and gets a $10 check, he'll leave $15 total—a 50 percent gratuity. No, the waitress doesn't deliver a happy ending with his hash browns. "I know the servers. I really like them. I show up there a lot," he told me.

As for some of the subconscious influences on tip size, if you're male, you're likely to tip bigger if your waitress is blond, wearing red lipstick, wearing a red dress, and/or wearing a flower in her hair, according to research by French behavioral scientist Nicolas Gueguen. Other research finds that many customers leave bigger tips when a server does little things that seem to invite or reflect a familiar relationship between themselves and the customers. For example, in a study by experimental psychology student Kimberly Garrity, a waitress serving Sunday brunch got 23 percent more in tips when she introduced herself by name. Squatting down by the table—coming down to the customer's level and making the conversation seem more intimate—increased the size of the tip by 20 percent for a waiter and 25 percent for a waitress, per research by Michael Lynn and Kirby Mynier. Giving out mints or chocolates with the check—even just Hershey's Miniatures—has also been shown to significantly increase the tip, perhaps because giving a gift tends to trigger feelings of obligation to reciprocate.

But Lynn says his research suggests that the single biggest factor beyond check size in the amount tipped is a desire to "buy social approval" (including that of the server) by complying with tipping norms: to tip at least 15 percent of the bill, before tax, and perhaps 20 percent, which Lynn finds is increasingly being considered the minimum standard. Other factors that increase the tip size include discomfort about social inequity—having somebody running around and doing our bidding while we're sitting back like pashas.

How come you have to tip your waiter if you don't have to tip your dental hygienist?

Many people take issue with how the tipping norm forces them to take part in employee compensation—an obligation we're free of when shopping for, say, office supplies or groceries or when we go to the dentist. The U.S. Department of Labor allows restaurants to pay tipped employees a "sub-minimum wage"—$2.13 an hour as of spring 2013—although employers are required to make up the difference between the sub-minimum and the federal minimum wage ($7.25 in 2013) if the employee isn't pulling it in in tips. (Some states require the restaurant to pay a higher minimum base. In Arizona, it's a whole $3; in California, it's $8.) Before anyone sniffs "Hah! The waiter's going to make at least the minimum wage!" note that a waiter's tip is usually not entirely his own. Waiters very often must share their tips—15 or 20 percent of them—with busboys, bartenders, and counter personnel. And in some restaurants, how much the waiter must share is determined not by their total tips but as a percentage of the total of each check. In other words, if some patron really cheaps out on the tip, the waiter may end up paying out more money than he's made from serving that particular stingy-ass party.

You should expect to leave a 15 to 20 percent tip for the same reason people eat pork chops but not poodle chops: Because that's just what's done.

Clearly, our system of paying those who serve us is imperfect, but it's the system we have. This means we need to factor in the tip as part of the true cost of eating out (in any establishment where you don't line up for a bag of burgers). The same goes for having drinks in a bar. As for what is a *fair* rate for refilling a water glass, reciting the specials, or bringing a side of mayo, who can say? And as for why the tipping standard is 15 to 20 percent, before tax, there's really no reason for those particular percentages. A 15 to 20 percent tip is simply the social norm—the understood, customary price for service when one goes out to eat. Because many or most people comply with the norm, there's a reasonable expectation by the waiter that a customer will leave at least the standard percentage, providing that the service is not lacking in some glaring way. In other words, leaving 15 to 20 percent should be the default—or as Steve Dublanica, a former waiter, restaurant manager, and the author of *The New York Times* best-selling book *Waiter Rant*, put it to me, we need to think of the tip as a "15 to 20 percent commission on the sale of food."

For those people who snarl that they're not about to base their payment for service on monkey-see/monkey-do economics, well, that's their choice. But because the 15 to 20 percent norm is the generally accepted price for service, you are cheating the waiter if you don't let him know beforehand that you're a 5 or 10 percenter (or if you plan to leave only a Bible, a smileyface on the check, or a snarky note about what a "loser job" being a waiter is) so he can give you all the service you're willing to pay for.

What if the service is bad?

Tipping less than 15 percent tells the waiter he sucked in some way. And sure, maybe there were issues. If the waiter stands outside smoking pot or is laughing and texting at the bar when he should be serving you, don't wait to reprimand him by docking him at tip time. Make an immediate complaint to the manager. (Too many people let bad service go on and on, making their experience at the restaurant a miserable one.)

Understandably, some diners just don't want to deal with the drama or interruption of complaining in the moment. If you're one of those people and a waiter turns your meal into an ordeal—

making a planned forty-five-minute lunch take two hours because he never comes around and you can't even ask for what you need—he obviously doesn't deserve the same tip you'd leave for bright-eyed, bushy-tailed service. So, maybe you leave 8 to 10 percent. (You spent your lunch looking all over for him; now he can look all over for the rest of his tip.)

Sometimes people will feel compelled to leave a good tip for a lousy waiter because they can't afford to be seen as cheap by those they're dining with. If you're taking somebody to lunch on business, you may just decide it's safest to suck it up and pay the customary tip amount, even if a waiter seems quite undeserving, and consider it a reputation maintenance fee. But Dublanica has what I think is a graceful alternative: giving your tip to the busboy instead of the waiter. This means you haven't cheaped out on the standard but you also haven't gone all Stockholm syndrome and rewarded somebody for treating you terribly, either. Should the waiter chase you out the door to complain, as sometimes happens when a customer leaves no tip, you can tell him you gave it to the person you saw doing all the work.

But, let's be honest about what should be considered terrible service and what are more likely to be ways people justify behaving like cheap bastards at tip time. Did the waiter say certain magic bad words[47] that hit you in your pet-peeve zone like "Are you still working on that?" Did he recite the specials in a cheesy way?

---

[47] People born before 1960 have a weird tendency to feel almost homicidal when others, typically those in more recent generations, respond to "Thank you" with "No problem!" instead of "You're welcome." A friend's husband, who's in his late fifties, explained, "The person who says this is indicating that you are not inconveniencing him. This is aggressive rather than polite."

Um, actually, it's just lingo, thought by some linguists to be influenced by the Australian "No worries" or similar responses to thank you in languages other than English (such as the French "*de rien*"—"it's nothing"). Unless somebody says "No problem" in a surly tone, they're probably indicating a cheerful willingness to be of service. They may also feel "You're welcome" sounds a little stuffy. So, maybe just try to accept it as a quirk of an age group you are not a part of, tempted as you may be to see it as reason to dock your waiter's tip or clock him over the head with a bar tray until he sees the light.

(Chances are, the restaurant makes him do that.) Are you sticking him with demerits he doesn't deserve, say, for food that wasn't to your liking? (He doesn't prepare the meal; he just delivers it.) And are you sure he's willfully ignoring you, or does it look like he's rushing around to cover three other tables, maybe because some other waiter quit without notice or called in sick?

Before you dock a waiter's tip, it might help to consider "attribution bias," our tendency to judge the motives and behavior of others more harshly than we judge our own. (This is also referenced in chapter 8, "Going Places," page 153.) Imagine if you, in doing your job, were judged as severely as some judge a waiter—with your every failing or apparent failing noted in the form of dollars taken out of your paycheck. Projector breaks during your presentation? *Gong!* You take home $200 less this week! Wasn't your fault? Tough tacos. Your sales pitch wasn't your best work—maybe because you didn't sleep well the night before. *Gong!*—$500 less in your check, buster!

Now, maybe your pay *should* be based more directly on your exact moment-to-moment merits—but if that isn't how it works for you, maybe you can extend the same munificence to your waiter. If, however, in the face of occasional human fallibility, it's simply too galling to you to pay the customary tip amount, there's an obvious solution: Stay home and snap your fingers at your cat to bring you your martini *chop-chop*.

From bartenders and baristas to hot dog stand workers: When, where, and what to tip.

Yes, there are now Styrofoam tip cups at hot dog stands, and it shouldn't be long before there's a beg jar at the hardware store. Dublanica calls the expansion in the occupations that solicit gratuities "tip creep." He says that whether to tip for something we've never tipped for before is the source of much social anxiety, as well as some anger at the expectation that we pay more money on top of an item's cost—rather like a tax. Dublanica writes in his book on tipping, *Keep the Change*, "Our country might have been founded on the principle of 'no taxation without representation,' but if Thomas Jefferson rose from the dead, bought a double mocha latte at Starbucks, and saw the tip jar, we might have another revolution."

When you aren't sure how much to tip, your approach should be the same as I advised in deciding how you'll behave on the Internet and elsewhere: Think about the sort of person you want to be, and act accordingly. I am very frugal and spent less on my favorite jacket ($2, on sale at the Santa Monica Salvation Army) than a lot of people will pay for a single vegetable, but there's a difference between frugal and cheap. It's worth it to me to tip 50 cents at the coffeehouse, even when I get a $1.50 self-serve coffee, and to do as Michael Lynn does and leave a generous tip when I get a plate of eggs at a diner. Forking over a little extra money doesn't cost me all that much per year, but it makes the person waiting on me feel good, which makes me feel good, and it fosters the sort of world I want to live in—the kind where you *can* work as a waitress in a diner and still pay your electric bill.

Dublanica says he is pretty free with a dollar come tip time—unless you're making him a hot dog. Dublanica confessed that he tips nothing at a hot dog stand. "It's what I'm used to," he explained. But, he agreed with me that how much you tip "boils down to who you are as a person." You have to ask yourself, "what's in your heart?" But in case your heart isn't all that talkative when you come to the tipping crossroads, Dublanica helped me out with a few guidelines:

- *Alcohol served at the table in a restaurant*
  People grouse that the alcohol is a rip-off—that they're paying $22 for a bottle of wine they could get at Trader Joe's

for $7 and then tipping on the $22, to boot. Some don't tip on alcohol served at the table at all or tip a reduced rate. (Unfortunately for servers waiting on such people, they may have to tip-share based on the price of the entire check.) Dublanica reminds that you're paying not just for that bottle of wine but for the atmosphere and the experience in a restaurant and says you should tip 15 to 20 percent on *everything you order*, including the alcohol. "A bottle of wine costs what a bottle of wine costs in a restaurant," he says. "That's the game in going. If you don't like it, don't buy it."

- *When drinking at the bar*

In *Keep the Change*, Dublanica writes that he always went by the old standard of tipping a dollar per drink until he talked to Seamus, an "older Irishman" tending bar in midtown Manhattan. When he asked Seamus about what the standard should be, Seamus said 20 percent—same as you'd tip if you drank the two martinis at the table with your food. "Why am I any different from a server?" Seamus asked. "On a $10 drink, I should get anywhere from $1.50 to $2."

What about the argument that the bartender (if not providing you with counseling or complicated drinks) isn't doing much? Dublanica again counters, "If you want to save money, drink at home." (Also keep in mind that bartenders, like waiters, typically must share their tips with busboys, food runners, the host or hostess, and other nontipped employees.)

I also think there are times when you should leave more than 20 percent, such as when you're drinking a drink that costs very little—like a soda water—or if you sit at the bar a long time and drink very little. My favorite bar in LA is Hal's Bar & Grill in Venice. When I go there, in the amount of time others would pound back a few pricey mixed drinks, I'll sip a single glass of wine ($8) and leave $4, which is my way of making up for how I drink like a fish—a goldfish.

- *Table-squatters*
  If a waiter doesn't "turn the table"—if you just sit there for hours and hours sharing a single Caesar salad and five glasses of water with your lunch companion—the waiter is probably losing money. There's a Spanish proverb, "Take what you need, but pay for it." The tip line is the perfect place to do that—generously.

- *Restroom attendants*
  Dublanica says the standard for men is "a dollar to pee. That's it for the night." But, he says, if you're a woman and you use those goodies the attendant has on hand—hairspray, bobby pins, etc.—you should leave more. Sure, he said, you can get that paper towel they hand you by yourself. "No kidding—we all know basic hygiene since we were four. But why do you not want to give that person a tip? They're there to keep the bathroom clean. . . . Is it going to kill you to leave a dollar?"

  It's asking myself that question that has me *sometimes* tipping the bathroom attendants—while resenting being pressured to have a financial transaction with somebody in the bathroom. I carry a purse the size of a gymnasium, well-stocked with beauty supplies, so I use none of those provided. Also, I was born with a stainless-steel spoon in my mouth, so I'm uncomfortable being served when I'm capable of serving myself.

  That discomfort nearly led to a minor disaster for me one night at a monthly dinner I used to attend at the upscale Hollywood Japanese restaurant Yamashiro, where they had a bathroom attendant. I so dreaded that moment of pay/don't pay after being handed a paper towel that I didn't want to be handed that I once decided to postpone going to the toilet till

I got home. I then got stuck in a traffic jam and nearly wet my pants.

- *The coat check*

  Tip a dollar a coat, Dublanica says.

- *The restaurant's parking valet*

  Tip them when you *drop off your car*, Dublanica says, pointing out that you're handing over "probably the most expensive thing you own, after your house." He says, "$2 is standard; for $5, they're going to remember where they parked your car." And in case you're someone whose monthly car payment bill has the word "Ferrari" on it, Dublanica adds, "$20 means you want your car there"—right in front of the restaurant. "You won't have to wait for it. And then just slip 'em a buck when you leave."

- *Pizza or other food delivery*

  "Tip 15 percent or the cost of a gallon of gas, whichever is greater," Dublanica says.

- *The takeout counter at a sit-down restaurant*

  Dublanica suggests leaving 10 percent but adds, "That's a 'What kind of person are you gonna be?' question. You're under no obligation to leave a gratuity."

- *Buffet restaurants*

  Tip 15 percent, Dublanica says, explaining in *Keep the Change*, "Well, someone has to clear your dishes and refill your sodas."

- *On a comped or discounted meal or drink*

  Tip on what it would have cost at the regular price. (I suggest maybe sharing your good fortune at getting a freebie by leaving a little more than you would otherwise.)

- *Baristas*

  "A lot of work goes into making these caffeinated chemistry experiments," Dublanica notes. He thinks people should treat the barista more like the bartender when it comes time to pay. "You drive up to Starbucks and you order 72,000 calories of coffee and it costs you $37 and then you go 'Bye' and you don't leave them anything. You're a jerk." He says that people who work at coffee bars don't expect to be tipped, but what he heard from people who work at Starbucks is that the change on a cup of coffee—say, 27 cents—is appreciated. That's how Dublanica tips on a cup of coffee. "Whatever is left over [in change], I give to them. If it comes out to $1.97 . . . I'll look for [more] change."

- *Adult entertainment*

  I asked Dublanica what strippers should get. "Anywhere from a dollar to a Mercedes-Benz . . . where do we start? If you're sitting at the rail and she shakes it a little, give her a dollar. A tip on a lap dance should be 20 percent."

LORD OF THE FRIES: HOW TO KEEP DINING FROM GOING DYSTOPIAN

It's unlikely that during dinner, somebody's going to off somebody with a boulder, like one of the boys did to poor Piggy in William Golding's *Lord of the Flies*, but the following guidelines should help you manage the uncivilized behavior you encounter (or may be tempted to engage in) while dining at a restaurant or as a guest at a dinner party.

Too gross for comfort: Which behaviors are okay at the table, and which belong in the bathroom?

One etiquette auntie will claim that a woman may apply lipstick at the table if she's quick about it; another will sniff (à la the *Downton*

Abbey dowager countess),"The dinner table is not to be used as a vanity, my dear."

Although there seems to be solid agreement from the aunties on "no flossing while dining," the standards for hygiene and grooming behaviors largely seem a matter of she said versus she said—as in, arbitrary and mainly dependent on whether you bought a book by this etiquette auntie or that one.

I suggest we instead go by an age-old standard: the evolved human emotion of disgust. Evolutionary psychologists Joshua M. Tybur and Debra Lieberman point out, in their paper "Microbes, Mating, and Morality," that disgust seems to have evolved to help us avoid disease-causing microorganisms, a threat to human survival and reproduction. Disgust acts as a psychological "Keep Out!" sign when we encounter things and substances that can infect us, like poo, bodily fluids, spoiled foods, insects and rodents, and dead and decomposing bodies.[48]

Decomposing bodies probably aren't a big issue for you when you dine out. But, consider how pathogens are spread from person to person. If whatever behavior you're contemplating could cause some bit of something—a piece of chewed food or some bodily icky—to go airborne, it's bathroom behavior. So, since applying your lipstick will not cause any to land on another person or their food, you can do it at the table. Nose-blowing, teeth-picking, ear-digging, nail-clipping (yes, disturbingly, it is necessary to include this), eyebrow-plucking, applying powder or false eyelashes, or removing your fake eyeball, sadly, requires a bathroom visit.

---

[48] Researchers Paul Rozin, Jonathan Haidt, and Clark McCauley are better-known for their work on disgust, but Tybur and Lieberman, in this paper, point out the holes in their thinking, including the odd and unfounded notion that our sense of disgust is based, in part, on not wanting to be reminded of our animal nature.

When food meets its maker: Guidelines on sending food back.

I used to have a policy of not sending food back in a restaurant unless there was something six-legged using it as a jogging track. Sending food back felt princessy, and I was afraid of seeming like the sort of woman who orders a Diet Coke with *exactly* three ice cubes.

Well, I like my beef "very rare" (as in, "faintly mooing") and ordered a cheeseburger that way at a nice restaurant I frequent. Uncharacteristic of this place, it instead came to me very well-done—as in, partially cremated.

I signaled to our waiter, a sweet guy who's been working there for years. Pointing to the hardened puck on my plate, I said, "I don't want to be one of those picky-wicky customers who sends food back, but this is seriously well-done . . ."

"You're absolutely right to send it back if it's not the way you asked for it," he said. "You're paying for your meal. You should get what you ordered."

And he's right.

If you're unhappy that your food is substantially different from what you ordered and if you can't easily correct the problem yourself (say, by extricating a few croutons from your salad), it's fair, not fussy, to return it to the kitchen. Other examples of food you're right to repatriate include chicken that's rare or undercooked inside (or any food that's unhealthy to eat), food that includes some allergen that you specifically asked them to leave out, and food that's supposed to be hot that arrives cold.

If you know good food and you know what you've been served doesn't qualify, it's okay to do as a foodie friend of mine has on occasion—say to the waiter, "You know, this is just not good. Can you do anything for me here?" My friend told me, "It has always worked out with them saying, 'I'm sorry you don't like this. What can I get you?' The tip goes to 30 percent immediately."

If, however, the mistake is yours—like if you took a gamble on some exotic food or didn't really pay sufficient attention when ordering—you should, as they say, eat your mistake (or order another item, with the expectation that you'll pay for it).

As for rumors that sending food back will cause the kitchen staff to spit or pee in it, that is possible, but per all the waiters I talked to and their blog comments I read, it happens rarely to never. Again, keep in mind that the kitchen staff is less likely to long for revenge on a customer the waiter portrays as nice, polite, and trying to be reasonable.

They're called "reservations," not "possibilities."

Sometimes when a person with a dinner reservation can't make it and doesn't let the restaurant know, they have a very good reason, like that they're in a coma or dead. Others simply can't be bothered to pull out their phone and take twenty seconds to do the right thing.

This means that nice restaurants in urban areas can have between five and twenty-five no-shows at reserved tables a night. For a small restaurant or one operating on a tight margin, even two no-shows can mean they're operating in the red. Yes, sometimes a reservation must be canceled, but it's considerate to do it as much in advance as possible because many restaurants will hold a reserved table for between fifteen and thirty minutes, honoring their end of the commitment and losing money in the process.

If you are planning on showing but are running late, call the restaurant and apologize and let them know (realistically) when you think you *can* get there. If doing the right thing isn't motivation enough, keep in mind that many restaurants have computer systems that track everything from reservations to a customer's allergies and favorite waiters. If you are a poor tipper, have no-showed for your reservations, or have made an annoyance of yourself, they've got your number, and there's a good chance they won't put it beside a reservation there again.

That wouldn't exactly be a huge deal for anyone who doesn't live in a fifty-person, one-restaurant town. But offenders should consider the possibility that they'll cross paths with a restaurateur fed up enough to engage in a little customer-shaming. Noah Ellis, owner and general manager of the Los Angeles restaurant Red Medicine, Twitter-shamed one night's no-shows by name, leading off with, "All the nice guests who wonder why restaurants overbook and they sometimes have to wait for their res[ervation] should thank people like those below."[49]

A classier and more amusing form of punishment comes from New York City chef and restaurateur Dewey Dufresne, who nails the no-shows while sounding like he's giving them the benefit of the doubt. His restaurateur son, Wylie Dufresne, told Eater National's Amy McKeever that his dad "has been known to call people late at night who haven't shown up hours after their reservation—and well after they closed—and say, 'Hey, we're still holding a table for you. Should we let it go?' "

Sweet dreams, rude people!

"Waiters" should describe restaurant staffers, not customers with reservations.

If you have a reservation, "fifteen minutes is about the tops you should be asked to wait," advises Nick Coe, a Los Angeles–based chef who has also owned restaurants. This assumes that your entire party has arrived, which he says is legitimate for a restaurant to ask, lest diners sit down and play table hockey for an hour while waiting for somebody to arrive and only then place their orders.

But if you're all there and you're kept waiting an hour at the bar, Coe says something has gone very wrong and you need to speak to

[49] It's possible somebody hasn't shown up or called because they had something terrible happen to them, as was reportedly the case with one of those whose name Ellis tweeted.

the manager. He "ought to comp you on something—anything from a bottle of wine to your whole dinner." If something "fairly substantial" weren't offered, Coe says he would walk out. "I wouldn't want to give a restaurant like that my money. They've been totally unprofessional."

Coe acknowledged that a smaller restaurant without many tables can have a harder time making space for those with reservations when there are "campers," people hanging out long after they've paid. Still, he says, "it's really not an excuse to say, 'People are sitting there and won't get up.'" A professional manager has tricks to make that happen, for example, saying, "We'd love to have you stay, but there's somebody booked for this table right now, so why don't you have a drink at the bar on us?"

There will be times when you'll realize that it's simply a better bet to keep waiting than to leave, like on a Saturday night when you're unlikely to get a table at any restaurant where the maître d' isn't a redheaded molded plastic clown. Your impulse afterward will probably be to go tar and feather them on Yelp. But Coe suggests giving them a chance to fix their mistake: writing them a letter, letting them know what happened (since it's possible that, say, the regular manager was out the night you were dining and your experience wasn't business as usual). If you aren't a letter writer, you could call and ask to speak to the manager. Coe says, "A good restaurant will offer you some inducement to come back and give them another chance."

Fine-dining atmosphere-eaters: Underparented children, glowing screens, ringing phones, flash photos, shower shoes, and adult bigmouths.

People dining in fine restaurants could just as well get gourmet carryout and eat it at the wild monkey den at the zoo or at the New York Stock Exchange at the opening bell. But few people go to fine restaurants just for the food. The atmosphere is an essential part of the experience, with the dimmed lights, elegant floral arrangements, and waiters speaking in hushed tones instead of hollering across the place, diner-style, "Yo, put a rush on that partridge confit!" This means it's absolutely unfair for any restaurant patron to force a transformation of this environment on the other patrons with any of the following creatures or items:

- *Underparented children*
  Legend has it that there are young children in this country who can be counted on to behave as if they were merely short adults. If this describes your toddler, there seems to be no good argument for barring him or her from fine dining. If, however, your wee treasure is at all likely to fidget, flail, howl, run up and down the restaurant aisles, chirp her favorite word twenty-five times in a row, and unscrew the salt shakers and spread tiny dunes across the table, she and those dining around you will be much happier if you leave her at home for a fun night of "Let's Try to Institutionalize Another Babysitter!"

- *Underparented adults*
  Mommy's admonition—"use your inside voice"—also applies when you are fifty-one. Unless you are giving out winning stock tips, nobody wants to hear you at the next table.

- *Hairy man-toe revealing footgear*
  Flip-flops are also known as "shower shoes," not "fine French restaurant shoes." Gentlemen, nobody wants to see your hairy toe knuckles while dining.[50]

[50] As for flip-flops on the ladies, one of my blog commenters, "Katie," noted that they "can look really cute!" Cute is good if you're twelve, but keep in mind that there's no such thing as "fuck-me flip-flops." Also, they'll be serving your dinner at a table and not in a sauna. Dress accordingly.

- *Glowing screens*

  In a dimly lit restaurant, brightly lit phone screens, iPads, and laptop screens are eye grabbers, stealing people's attention away from their companions and dinner. Should you be tempted to send, oh, "maybe just twenty-six or thirty e-mails," consider that there's probably a reason restaurants advertise "fine dining" instead of "fine data entry."

- *Flash photos of food or friends*

  If you can't take your photo without a flash and without getting into the lap of the people dining next to you (for a better angle on your sister or your salmon), you should satisfy yourself with memorializing your evening in your mind alone. If restaurants thought blinding flashes of light would enhance the dining experience, they'd hire someone to make them. (Got epilepsy? Come to Joe's Bistro, and we'll see if we can't trigger a seizure.)

- *Answering phones or texting during dinner*

  If you are Cary Grant and it's 1940 and you're saying a few words on the house phone that the tuxedoed maître d' brought over to your restaurant table, you look pretty smooth because, well, wow—getting a telephone call while dining. These days, however, if you're on your cell phone in a restaurant, you just look like all the other people yammering into theirs while shoving fries into their piehole at Mickey D's.

  Letting your cell phone ring in a restaurant (or another shared space that is not a loud foundry) is completely rude. It also seems ill-advised to annoy other patrons around you who not only have been drinking but may just have been given sharpened steak knives. Assuming you aren't the government official with your finger on the "Nuke North Korea" button, your cell phone should be turned off and stowed away while dining. Merely putting it on vibrate will likely tempt you to make it—and not your dining companion—the center of attention every time it buzzes. This is a lovely way to tell the person with you that they are too dull and unimportant to command your attention.

If there's a possibility that some true emergency will arise during the meal, leave your phone on vibrate, give your companion advance warning, apologize, and promise to keep any call as short as possible. Should the emergency call come, answer in a stage whisper, ask the caller to hold on, and then excuse yourself from the table to take it outside or back by the bathrooms, where the phone booths used to be and still should be. (*Yoo-hoo,* restaurateurs—isn't it time some of you started a trend?)

It's best to avoid engaging with restaurant cellboors and other atmosphere-eaters. A restaurant is not a venue for do-it-yourself justice.

Believe me, when some underparented brat (of five or fifty-five) is given the run of a place, there's nothing I long to do more than turn to the cur's sorry excuses for parents and hiss something really helpful like, "A pity you didn't use birth control!" But, even a less offensive and utterly justified remark, such as "Do you mind asking your little boy to stop driving his toy truck across our appetizer?" can cause a crossfire of ugliness, since rudesters who act out or allow their children to tend not to fall all over themselves to be accountable for their shortcomings.

Whenever another restaurant patron's rude behavior is outrageous and persistent, your best bet is seeking out a diplomatic emissary—the manager—whose ultimate job is acting as the guardian of customers' pleasant dining experience. More important, he'll come off to the louts as more of an authority figure than you. (Even the rudest patrons are more hesitant to snarl "Fuck you!" to a restaurant manager than they are to some annoyed biddy at the next table.) The manager may not have the superpowers to stop the awfulness right there in the moment, but he can blacklist the cause of it from future visits, and he may comp you on some of your meal to make up for how your table has turned into a receiving station for hell.

The Check Republic: Paying the bill when dining with others.

It's a group dinner. One person orders a green salad and a glass of water. The guy drinking glass after glass of fine scotch orders a steak—the sort that comes from that kind of cow they hire somebody to read poetry to and give daily massages. Eventually, the check comes, and the steak eater glances at the total and says, "Let's just split it." The greens eater, not wanting to seem stingy, gulps and forks over for the most expensive dinner salad in the history of dining.

When dining with a group, unless your friends favor asking everybody to pay what they owe, you should assume that the check will be divided by the number of people in attendance. If you can't afford that or will feel cheated, send regrets. It's simply easiest to divide the check into equal parts, and the pleasure of dining with friends can turn very displeasurable when followed up by a United Nations–style negotiation about who ate what and who owes what, down to the penny.

That said, a dinner check should not turn into a form of wealth redistribution. The person whose meal and drinks cost substantially more than somebody else's should take the lead and make things fair. If that's you, you might turn to the vegan next to you who had only the $12 tofu platter and a Coke and say, "You just put in $20, and I'll put in the other $70 of your share since I had that glass of port from the bottle wept on for three decades by a French monk."

Some people think the solution is asking for a separate check for each person at the table. This request is easiest on your waiter if you make it before you order and if the restaurant has a computerized ordering system. Even if they don't, it's probably not a big deal if there are just two of you at the table. But when dining en masse, be advised, as Los Angeles chef and restaurant business veteran Nick Coe points out, that many places put a limit on how many ways a check can be split. "Usually, four is about the max." And maybe reconsider whether laziness about math or your failure to weed out your "friend," the hard-core freeloader, really justifies turning your waiter into your accountant. "The guy has to take back a stack of credit cards and cash and run it all," Coe explains. "It's a bit of an imposition."

Yelp is supposed to be a reviewing site, not a step stool to power.

Before you post that one-star rating and the scathing review, take a moment to consider your motivation. Did the restaurant or other business really fail you in some egregious way? Or, is it that you're a frustrated comedian and Yelp is the best venue you can book yourself into? Or, could it be that you have always wanted to open a restaurant and know you could have done it better than this schmo?

Chef and restaurateur Coe, who has worked everywhere from froufrou eateries to a beachfront biker bar, thinks the best (and fairest) reviews by patrons are on dining-specific blogs and sites, like Eater, Grub Street, Chowhound, Open Table, and Urban Spoon, which tend to attract serious foodies. Yelp does, too, but the foodies' reviews are mixed in with those from people seriously angry at their corner hardware store who decided to pop off a quick dig against the bistro next door as long as they happened to be logged in.

Coe notes that "a lot of people fancy themselves [professional] restaurant reviewers when they hit Yelp" but slam places "without a whole lot of expertise about restaurants or knowledge about food or dining or anything else." He explains that professional restaurant reviewers typically go back to a place a few times and understand that there's a startup curve. But amateurs will go to a brand-new place that's just getting on its feet and trying to work the kinks out. Thinking that they'll build their credibility as a reviewer, they'll "just rip it apart for what are actually minor transgressions."

Coe also feels that in the past ten or twenty years, restaurant customers "have lost what their side of the bargain is, which is to behave like decent human beings and not like petty tyrants because they pay the bill." Many go into a restaurant with "a set of bizarre expectations," like the notion that the kitchen of a place with some special, complex cuisine should drop everything and rework a dish to cater to their dietary whims. When the waiter explains that this is impossible, the patron may stick it to the place in the form of a negative review—and never mind how busy the kitchen was or whether the request was impossible in the realm of culinary physics.

Others posting reviews don't limit themselves to assessing the restaurant. They'll knock stars off their review of a place they liked because they went out to their car afterward, blocks away, and there was a homeless guy next to it—"totally extraneous stuff," says Coe, that unfairly cuts into a restaurant's ability to attract new customers.

To write a fair review, Coe advises that you make it reflect your actual level of knowledge. If you aren't a restaurant expert or a foodie, he suggests you say something like "Well, I've never had this before, but I didn't really care for it" or "I loved it" or "It tasted salty to me."

"That's fine," he says. "It tasted salty *to you*. But to say 'Naw, these guys don't know how to cook; this thing had way too much salt in it; they're idiots,' well, then you'd better know how much salt *should* have been in it."

Consider also that a restaurant review site may not be the best place to resolve your disappointment with a meal. Coe, like tipping expert and former waiter and restaurant manager Steve Dublanica, points out that many people don't realize that "in any halfway-decent restaurant, if you have a problem with *any* aspect of your meal, you need to talk to somebody"—ideally, the manager, whose job it is to see that customers end up happy. As Coe suggests doing when your reservation isn't honored in a timely manner, you can call or e-mail the next day if you're uncomfortable saying something about a problem in the moment. Of course, this tack takes accepting that the people who run and work in restaurants make mistakes—same as we all do on the job. We should maybe give them the chance to make good on theirs before we destroy them on the Internet.

PARTY MANNERS: WHAT TO DO TO HAVE THEM AND WHAT TO DO WHEN OTHERS LEAVE THEIRS HOME

It's an invitation, not an invitation to be rude.

For many party hosts, the disappointing discoveries about one's friends, colleagues, neighbors, and even family members start well before the party—weeks before—when they send out, oh, twenty or thirty invitations and get only two or three replies.

Documentary producer/director Courtney Balaker, who sends e-vites, says, "In the old days, if someone didn't respond to your snail-mail invitation, you could at least give them the benefit of the doubt that they never received it or that it got swept under the couch, eaten by a possum, etc." But apparently unbeknownst to some of today's nonresponders, some electronic-invitation sites allow the sender to know which guests have read the invite. "When you see that it was opened a week and a half ago and [there's still been] no response, it feels like a blow-off," says Balaker, "which maybe it is."

We're all busy, and there's a lot competing for your attention in your e-mail inbox, so it may help to look at every invitation you get as a quick test of friendship—or at least decency. All it takes to keep your host from feeling that you don't give a bent crap about them is maybe twenty seconds of your time to either respond right away or put a note on your calendar to respond in a few days. At the very least, say *something*, like explaining that you have a conflict, telling them when you'll let them know and then coming through on that, too.

If you're on the inviting end, you actually might want to rethink using an e-invitation. They do make it easier to create the invitation and log RSVPs, but sadly, requiring the smallest task of someone—just clicking on a link and waiting for a page to load to reply—may cause them to put off responding, increasing the likelihood they'll forget entirely. People may also feel more compelled to reply when the invitation appears to come directly from a person rather than an invitation system. Because of this, e-commerce and social-media expert Jackie Danicki, like me, favors putting the entire invitation into an e-mail, meaning guests only need to click REPLY and type in a quick message.

Some will perhaps find the rest of Danicki's approach too hard-line—but perhaps just until they plan a sit-down dinner party and send out invitations and only three out of fifteen people have the courtesy to RSVP. Danicki explains: "I give a cutoff date for RSVPs in the original invitation. If they try to RSVP after that, no dice. Those who accommodate bad guests have only themselves to blame. I set it up so I don't have an excuse to be annoyed at anyone. I'm not looking for violations of basic etiquette; I'm preventing them. I don't browbeat people in advance, either, and I decline invites from hosts who include preemptive etiquette lectures in the original invite."[51]

[51] If you opt for Danicki's approach, I would suggest putting the RSVP cutoff date in the e-mail subject line to strike, um, consideration in the hearts of one's friends and beloved family.

When you're invited to a party at someone's home, always bring a bottle and/or a gift—and see that it remains there when you depart. Do not leave the party with alcohol you brought or, even worse, alcohol you didn't—or—worse still—the silver or the host's wife or girlfriend.

Barefoot in the Party: No, you don't get to make your guests take their shoes off at the door. Yes, they take their shoes off before entering a residence in Asia. Good to know for when you are throwing a party there. In much of America, asking your guests to remove anything more than their coats is appropriate only if the party you've thrown is the kind where everyone goes off to a bedroom with somebody else's spouse. Otherwise, you should refrain from asking your guests to take off their shoes or any other parts of their ensemble.

And no, you don't get to make your guests slip paper crime-scene booties over their shoes. They surely would have dressed like CSI techs if they thought that enhanced their look. Also, these booties tend to not grip well, and causing your guests to leave the party as quadriplegics isn't exactly the mark of gracious hosting.

"But . . . but . . . what about my white carpets?!" you ask. Well, either don't have parties or hire a carpet cleaner afterward. You should also get your hardwood properly sealed so you won't feel tempted to try to separate the ladies and their stilettos. Your goal when throwing a party should be making your guests as happy and comfortable as possible. At most, if you are worried about what people might track in, you can place a big doormat in your entranceway with a small sign beside it, "Please wipe feet well before entering."

Can you bring your dog? Well, is the party taking place in a kennel? Unless the invitation says "all species welcome" or you are sure this is the host's attitude, you cannot bring your dog, your cat, your ferret, a swarm of tsetse flies, or any creature requiring a pooper-scooper by John Deere. The same goes for bringing your offspring. Think twice about even asking to bring them, because many hosts will feel pressured to say yes when it's the last thing they want. The fact that you were unable to find or afford a babysitter or a bull wrangler (which, for some kids these days, could be one and the same) does not entitle you to singlehandedly shift the ambience at a party from adult-centric to kid- and animal-centric.

When you are the one throwing a party, be advised that the earth shifted its orbit a few decades ago and now revolves around many people's children and animals. Be prepared to be pestered by some parent or pet fancier to allow their darling to come to what you intend to be a sophisticated, adults-only, *humans-only* affair, and be prepared for a tantrum (from the parents or pet owner) when you say no. But do feel free to say no and to calmly stand your ground. Adult parties should be thought of like R-rated movies—an environment inappropriate for young children and livestock. Also, parents who can't fathom why their children shouldn't come to cocktails at 8 p.m. tend not to understand the need to actually, you know, *parent them* once they're there.

The problem with throwing a birthday party in a restaurant

Unless all your friends are hedge-fund kazillionaires who shred dollar bills to line the hamster cage or you are picking up the entire dinner and drinks tab, think twice about having a birthday party for yourself or a friend at a restaurant. Consider having birthday cake and cocktails at your place or another friend's, or at least celebrate with birthday drinks in a bar—one where those short on finances can order a single glass of house wine and get a separate check without a glare from the bartender or waitress. Yes, your birthday comes but once a year, but the Visa bill comes monthly and includes interest, and your friends will be even gladder you were born if they don't celebrate your next birthday by finally paying off celebrating your previous one.

When somebody's conversation makes your ears want to talk your arms and legs into a suicide pact

In keeping with the subject of this section—those who ramble on—we'll take the scenic route to the answer, starting with a visit to your head.

The brain likes cognitive shortcuts. They save time and energy. So, like those little plastic-wrapped cheese and cracker snackpacks some companies sell, your brain keeps pre-packed thinking sets on its shelves to help speed you through life. These thinking sets, called heuristics, are made up of knowledge and experience you've acquired. For example, there's the *what to do when you come to a door* thinkpack. This thinkpack allows you to react automatically when you come to a door; you don't have to wonder what a doorknob is and figure out how to use it every time.

But sometimes these pre-packed cognitive shortcuts can end up being a mismatch with the situation we're in, and you can use that to your advantage when you've had your attention commandeered by a blabbermouth. There's a famous bit of research by social psychologist Ellen Langer that suggests we have a cognitive shortcut that makes us likely to comply with a request if it comes with a reason—even if the reason is ridiculous. Langer asked people waiting to use the copier in a library whether she could cut in front of them. When she asked without giving a reason for taking cuts—"Excuse me. I have five pages. May I use the Xerox machine?"—60 percent of those waiting let her go ahead of them. However, when she asked "May I use the Xerox machine because I'm in a rush?" *94 percent* let her go ahead. But even a ridiculous reason—"Excuse me. I have five pages. May I use the Xerox machine *because I have to make some copies?*"—had 93 percent of the people agreeing to let her go first.

So, at a party or event, when you find yourself trapped in some person's conversational tentacles, our tendency to let down our guard in the face of a request with a reason attached can help you escape while preserving the windy person's feelings and dignity. To get away, just give them a reason—almost any reason—even "Excuse me. Sorry to interrupt, but I need to go over there for a second." Of course, it's kinder if you can give your reason a little more meat, like "Excuse me, but there's something funny about my drink" or "I'm sorry to interrupt, but I need to hit the bathroom," and kinder still if you can actually be seen heading in the direction of the bar or bathroom afterward. (If you are waylaid on the way, well, at least you seemed to be bartender- or toilet-bound before it happened.)

The Human Stain: When you leave your mark on another guest or the host's furnishings.

As I noted in the "Communicating" chapter, you should avoid repeated and rambling apologies. Apologize big the first time, showing that you are horrified and embarrassed and get that it's a big deal that you spilled red wine all over their beige carpet or shattered their Qing dynasty ashtray. Don't keep chirping that you're sorry every few seconds or minutes like a cuckoo on crack. This only extends the incident and forces the spillee into the position of saying something minimizing to shut you up, like "It really isn't a big deal," when they, in fact, very likely think it is.

You should take steps to clean up your mess immediately after you make it—if you know a little something about, say, stain removal or restoration of one-of-a-kind antique crockery. Otherwise, ask the host for direction, lest you simply help make whatever you've done even worse.

When the breakage or spillage or other debacle seems to be your fault, you should offer to pay to make things whole (or beige) again. In worst-case scenarios (like when dry cleaning doesn't remove a stain), this may mean buying somebody a new pair of pants or financing the reupholstery of the host's couch. Sometimes, the item won't be replaceable. In this case, send flowers and a note or try to buy something comparable to make up for whatever you stained or broke.

If you are only partially at fault, you can offer to share in the cost of the replacement. If the contents of your bank account won't allow for immediate payment of your share, you can offer to pay over time. And, finally, if you are sincere in your offer to pay, you may need to be a bit pushy. If it isn't feasible to bring them cash, perhaps send a check and call and insist the host cash it. Don't use a host's embarrassment at taking money from you as a sneaky way out.

The trade-off in not offering to shell out is a stain on your character—in others' minds and your own (assuming you don't have all the conscience of shrubbery). In the long run, doing the right thing—making good on your clumsiness in dollars—will probably cost you far less in social opprobrium and personal self-loathing.

The senseless death of the thank-you note

Somebody spends hours cleaning their house and even more shopping, cooking, and laying out the spread for a party, all of which probably cost them a bunch of money, and your response is . . . calling out "Bye!" and maybe adding a "Hey, thanks!" as you go out the door? E-mailing a thank you the next day is the minimum you should do—and is fine if somebody simply put out beer, chips, veggies, and dip. When somebody has you to dinner, a little more effort seems in order. This isn't to say that you need to pluck a goose, sharpen a quill into a pen, and write a 1,000-word letter waxing on about the stuffed mushrooms in a spidery longhand. I like to send antique postcards I buy in bulk on eBay (150 for $34 last time I bought 'em). Best of all, there's just enough room to scrawl some thanks for the fab grub and maybe an amusing aside. But what the antique postcard lacks in space for verbosity it makes up for in groovy-osity. As the late crime writer Elmore Leonard admiringly put it after he got my postcard thanking him for having me at his Christmas party, "looked like it got lost in the mail for 75 years."

A FEW WORDS ON THE INVISIBLE MAN

One thing I loved about my late friend Cathy Seipp was that you didn't need to be socially acceptable to be included in her circle or invited to her parties; you just needed to be interesting and unlikely to set furniture on fire. Cathy understood that the "losers" and oddballs of the world don't actually have "cooties" or anything else that's catching. They maybe have Asperger's syndrome or some undiagnosed lack of social graces—along with some compelling things to say, if only you'll give them the chance.

If you're having an intimate dinner party and you want just the right mix of people to keep the conversation flowing and mostly fascinating, it's understandable that you'd be somewhat particular about whom you invite. And sometimes when you're at a party, a particular conversation just won't lend itself to bringing in a total newcomer. But if you're throwing a big bash or if you're at an event and spot somebody all alone—shifting on their heels and looking uncomfortable—consider whether you have enough social and psychological capital to be a little more inclusive. Maybe think back to a time when you were the excluded one or the new person walking through the door, not knowing anybody, and how that felt.

I've been there. A lot. As the odd kid nobody liked growing up, I was pretty much picked last even for being picked last. The good thing is, that seems to have given me a sort of radar for the excluded and uncomfortably adrift. I say hello, invite them into the conversation, introduce them, see that they aren't all alone. Doing this for other people also encourages me to do it for myself. Whenever I don't know anybody at a party or event, I don't dwell on it; I don't give in to fear; I change it—as soon as possible—with a smile and a three-word sentence: "Hi, I'm Amy." Works every time.

— 10 —

FRIENDS WITH SERIOUS ILLNESSES

What to do when a friend is really, really sick and could maybe even die

"I just want to let everyone know that having cancer hasn't made me a better person."
—Cathy Seipp, 1957–2007

As somebody for whom being mature means resisting the temptation to give the finger in traffic, I'm at a loss for what I should say to you upon learning that you have inoperable cancer or some other terminal or otherwise-horrible illness. Sure, there's the generic "I'm really sorry"—which seems seriously inadequate, since it's what I'd say if you had a flat tire.

Take cancer. There are really, really wrong things to say upon hearing somebody's cancer diagnosis, and lots of people say them. Attempting to relate, they scan their brain for stuff filed under "cancer," and up pop the chemo horror stories: "Wow, cancer. My friend had cancer and had chemo, and not only did her hair fall out but her head fell off, too!"

Some manage to see the upside in being ravaged by a disease: "I'd give anything to be that thin!" Others root around for something comforting in the spiritual-sayings bin: "You know, they say everything happens for a reason." Great. Their cancer-stricken friend can't help but think, "What, God looked at me and thought, 'You suck, so I'm going to rub you out'?"

Of course, some people are just assholes no matter what the situation. Cancer survivor Rosanne Kalick blogged about a colon cancer patient who had a casual acquaintance ask him about his colostomy bags, "Paper or plastic?"

So, what *should* you say when a friend tells you they have cancer or some other horrible disease?

"I know you can do this," meaning, "I know you, and I know that whatever comes, you will deal with it." Don't say "you'll be fine," since you don't know that they will be.

—Cancer patient Jeanne Sather, assertivecancerpatient.com

"I'm so sorry this is happening. It could happen to any of us. Life is so unfair sometimes." This helps remove the blame or shame that people with cancer sometimes feel.

—Cancer survivor Lori Hope, author of *Help Me Live: 20 Things People with Cancer Want You to Know*

"You're very strong. I can't believe cancer would be dumb enough to try to go after you."

What I wish I'd said to my late friend Cathy Seipp.

What should you say as your friend's battling their disease?

Some people will want to talk about it; some won't. Some will want advice; some won't. Take your direction from your friend by letting them talk and just listening, by asking what works for them, or by thinking about the kind of person they are.

Mystifyingly, when Cathy was fighting lung cancer, people who knew her well and should have known better would ask me to forward her their suggestions that she eat Tibetan mushrooms or stand on her head and snort dried deer antlers. They meant well, but they weren't thinking too hard. Cathy was highly rational and a vocal believer in evidence-based Western medicine—the kind dispensed by her Cedars-Sinai cancer specialists, as opposed to the kind dispensed in an Internet forward from somebody who believes that the government faked the moon landing.

On the flip side are patients with some form of cancer that's been shown to be very curable with chemotherapy, only they're forgoing it for the recommendations of the girl from the drum circle who works part-time at the health food store. Are you supposed to honor your friend's belief in tofu enemas as a cancer cure? The answer is, there isn't one correct answer. It really depends upon the person and the situation. Sometimes it's an act of friendship to be an asshole and refuse to let somebody die unnecessarily, but it will be a pointless act if they'll most likely keep doing whatever they were doing but lose you as a friend when they need you most.

What if you say or do the wrong thing?

You're human. You're going to say or do something stupid. Just accept that. The worst thing you can do is be so afraid of saying or doing the wrong thing that you do nothing at all. Of course, the most hurtful thing you can do is vanish.

For some, another person's cancer is the ultimate form of cooties, making them feel suddenly and uncomfortably mortal. Don't be ashamed if you feel this way. But, admit it to yourself, talk to friends about it, do whatever it takes to resist the urge to make like Jimmy Hoffa and disappear. If you just buck up and go visit the person, you'll probably find that they want to talk not about cancer but about whatever dumb crap you always talked about before. Ultimately, what you say is a lot less important than what you do. As the old saying about success goes, a lot of being successful in comforting somebody seriously ill is just showing the hell up.

HOW TO BE A FRIEND TO SOMEBODY SERIOUSLY ILL

Avoid nebulous offers to help, like "If there's anything I can do . . ."

This is about as helpful as calling them up and *baaah*-ing like a sheep. Instead, be specific: "I'm going to the grocery store. How 'bout I pick you up a roast chicken and some sautéed green beans?"

(Find out whether they prefer to be called, texted, or e-mailed with your request to help.) Ask for their grocery list and about other errands you could run. If they're too tired to tell you what they need, make your best guess or ask other friends or their family members.

Other things you can do:

- Pick things up for them at the pharmacy, the pet store, their pot dealer.
- Drive their day of the car pool.
- Take them to doctor's appointments or chemo, both so they have a ride and so they won't be alone.
- Clean their house or, if you can afford it, hire a cleaning person.
- When you visit, look around for stuff that needs doing. Wash dishes, do laundry, clean their toilet. (If they're a control freak, ask first.)
- Do what you can to offer support to their family and close caregivers. (This could mean dropping by with a bunch of pizzas or taking their kids on an afternoon outing.)
- Give them bed-appropriate entertainment: magazines, a book of sudoku, an iPad plus a movie subscription. (Maybe get a bunch of friends to go in on these.)
- Bring home-cooked meals—ideally in containers they can throw away so they don't have to wash dishes. (Avoid "creative" casseroles. Stick to recognizable foods.)
- Bring food they like to eat (taking into account any doctor's orders). This is no time to finally convert that carnivore to vegetarianism.
- E-mail other friends of theirs to suggest these and other substantive ways they can help.

Help a fiercely independent person feel okay about being helped.
It's hard for some people to be open to outreach from others. Let

them know that you understand that they feel that way, but suggest that part of being a friend is letting friends be a friend to you.

The nuances of cards, e-mail, and hugs: When you care enough to think twice before you send the very best.

Blogger Omnibus Driver's mother had terminal brain cancer. Well-meaning friends would send her cheerful "get well" cards (which is kind of like writing to a paraplegic, "Hope you're up and running soon!"). "She wasn't freaking going to *get well*, damn it," Omnibus wrote. "If people have to send a card, they should send a 'thinking of you' card instead."

Though you might want to hug a friend upon hearing about their diagnosis, timing is everything. My journalist friend Lynda Gorov, who had breast cancer, wrote, "Don't get me started on germ-laden hugs from strangers when your cell count is zero from chemo." The *impulse* to hug them will surely be appreciated, but if you aren't sure whether it's okay, ask first.

Your friend with the disease will probably appreciate everyone's expressions of concern, but it's hard to fight for your life and return hundreds of e-mails. Don't hold seriously ill people to the same social standards you would other friends. Consider using CaringBridge.org to build your friend a free, password-protected website complete with a patient-care journal to update family and friends and a guestbook for messages of love and support. Friends can leave a string of comments on an entry, and the sick person can respond with a single "Thank you all so much." If your sick friend is a multitasking overachiever who might feel guilty about only responding in brief, it might be helpful let them know it's okay to take a sabbatical from always putting the "to do" in today.

Think before you "think pink."

A lot of people take for granted that they're supporting a friend with breast cancer by wearing a pink ribbon or buying Yoplait with a pink lid. Sure, companies that "go pink" give some portion of the sale of each pinked-up product to help stop breast cancer. But a number of breast cancer patients see this as "pinksploitation": using cancer to sell products. They would rather you give a more sizable donation (or even $10 or $25) to a cancer research center instead of thinking you're buying a yogurt and making a difference. Or as Boing Boing blogger Xeni Jardin, who's tweeted her breast cancer diagnosis and treatments, tweeted during the breast cancer marketing month of "Pinktober":

> One of the most beautiful things you can do for a woman w/breast cancer is accompany her to treatment. Just bear witness. Don't wear pink.

Reply Retweet Favorite More

Help make cancer feel less like identity theft.

Cancer (or any big, serious disease) can overtake a person's identity, along with their body. The person who's ill can start to feel like they've transformed from, for example, "Cathy, who happens to have cancer," into "CANCER (with Cathy)." It doesn't help that friends and loved ones often decide that the proper way to behave is to go around speaking in hushed tones and trying to eke out profound thoughts, which most of us don't do well even when cancer or another awful disease isn't on the menu. These friends mean well, but what some seriously ill people seem to appreciate—even cherish—is *the mundane*: anything that helps their day-to-day life feel like it did before the disease took over. Cathy, for example, like many other cancer patients people told me about, didn't want to discuss life and death or her lung pump; she wanted me to hang out and gossip with her and watch *Everybody Loves Raymond*.

Funerals are no fun, least of all for the dead person.

Why not celebrate your friend while they're alive to enjoy it? Just take care to do it not in the way *you'd* want to be celebrated but in the way they would. A bunch of us put on a roast for Cathy because for her, what would be almost as awful as having cancer would be having people's pity. So, like her other close friends, I showed her how much I cared by standing up at the Figueroa Hotel and reading a bunch of really insulting remarks about her:

> Ideologically, although Cathy identifies as Republican, her politics are really as follows: She's right, everyone else is wrong, and unless they agree with her, they're also stupid. But, no, you're thinking, surely it goes deeper than that. And, to be fair, well . . . not really.

She loved it.

Start your own "Team Cathy."

In the year before she died, Cathy, who was divorced and had a daughter who'd just gone off to college, told me she was afraid to be alone. I might've found it hard to say the right thing about cancer, but I immediately thought, *Okay, we can do "You won't be alone"*; I just wasn't quite sure how. I called my friend and Cathy's, French journalist Emmanuelle Richard, who thought for a moment and then said in her cute, accented English: "I weel make a Google calendar."

There were already a bunch of us—about fifteen of Cathy's good friends—seeing to Cathy's various needs. No sooner did Emmanuelle e-mail out the link and the password than we became "Team Cathy." We'd log in to the Google calendar and sign up for days or nights to be with her, and those who could only take a few hours out of their workday would sign up to run errands or take Cathy to doctor's appointments.

We also created a Team Cathy e-mail list. It came in handy one afternoon when her microwave microed and waved its last. I blasted out an e-mail to the list: "Cathy needs a new microwave by 4 p.m., when I need to heat her next pain pack." TV writer Rob Long e-mailed: "I'm in San Jose, but I can order one on Amazon to arrive tomorrow morning." About five others in closer proximity offered to go out and get one, but Cathy's dad ended up picking one up at Home Depot on his way over that afternoon.

The whole Team Cathy thing was pretty amazing. I think that for Cathy, it was a daily demonstration of how much she was loved. It showed all of us that family isn't just blood relatives and people you marry but people who treat you like family. It also dispelled the ugly notion that being divorced or single means you'll "die alone." If anything, Cathy died crowded, with nurses scolding all of her friends for violating the fire codes.

— 11 —

THE APOLOGY

There are a lot of ways to say "Screw you, you stupids. I meant every word," but Kansas state representative Virgil Peck opted for "My statements yesterday were regrettable. Please accept my apology."

Peck had voiced his creative suggestion for how Kansas might thin its illegal immigrant population: Just do like they do with feral hogs—go up in helicopters and shoot the fuckers.

Not surprisingly, Peck, a Republican, had the Kansas House Democratic Caucus calling for his resignation. Equally unsurprisingly, the Republican Party leadership (perhaps noticing that one in six U.S. citizens in the 2010 census were Hispanic) prodded Peck to say he was sorry.

Yeah, right. Slip of the tongue and all that. Except that in tongue-slip terms, this was a tongue that not only slipped but was possessed by demons who rode it like a pony.

In the annals of bullshittery, Peck's apology edged ahead of one of my perennial favorites—the recorded message "Your call is very important to us . . ." which you hear while you're on endless hold with, say, the cable company. We know what they're really telling us:

> Your call doesn't mean shit to us. We know you have a choice of cable carriers . . . or would, if you took a huge loss selling your house and moved.

Finally, a human comes on the line. They tell you how *deeply* sorry they are about your cable outage—the exact same words they've read off a printed sheet to every other customer they've ever spoken to. That awful monotone they read in—the drone of a person with dead eyes[52]—tells you exactly what they're really thinking:

> Oh, *boohoo,* your cable's out. I'm not sorry. I don't care. I made some crappy choices in life and ended up working the night shift at the fucking cable company.

Sure, it's the clueless numpties running these companies who make the rep stick to the scripted bootlicking instead of talking like a person, but the lip-service apology still makes me seethe. After the first "I'm very sorry you were inconvenienced . . ." I tell the rep, "I know you're supposed to say that, but please, please . . . don't apologize. Can you just help me with my problem?"

I never really processed why I get so steamed by a few insincere words from a call center worker until I started answering a question I received for my advice column about a husband who refused to apologize. It turns out that the deep need we feel for an apology after we're wronged emerged out of the evolution of human cooperation, which makes it possible for us to live together in groups. As I wrote in that column:

> Humans seem to have an evolutionary adaptation to help us guard against being chumped, a sort of inner

[52] To be fair, there are many helpful employees who work answering company phone lines. It's just that when you need the most help, you seem to end up with the other kind.

police dog to see that we aren't all give and give to people who are all take and take. When our sense of fairness is violated, we need a sign from the violator that we aren't idiots to trust them in the future. An apology can't undo a wrong that's been done, but it's an offering that suggests that their future actions will be more partnerlike than selfishjerklike.

I went on to lay out the elements of a sincere apology:

- Admitting you were wrong.
- Expressing remorse.
- Pledging it won't happen again.
- Making amends.

I then realized why these call center employees' apologies made me so mad. They're completely meaningless. The person on the phone is saying the apology words to me, but there are several reasons they actually aren't "qualified" to apologize to me:

- They don't know me, and they didn't personally wrong me.
- There's no point in convincing me that I can trust them in the future, since it's wildly unlikely I'll ever get the same tech support person on the phone twice.
- They might feel some sympathy that my favorite show cut out three minutes before the end—*again!*—but unless they snuck into my backyard with big wire cutters, it would be crazy if they personally felt remorseful.

Ultimately, we both know their apology has very little to do with me or the fact that my cable sucks big green goat balls and everything to do with being in a job where continuing to feed your children means always having to say you're sorry.

HOW TO BAKE AND EAT YOUR VERY OWN CROW PIE

The apology: A reconciliation in four parts

Let's not have any illusions about our own greatness. As Albert Ellis, the late co-founder of cognitive therapy, put it, to be human is to be "fallible, fucked up, and full of frailty." And that's probably on a good day.

Accept that you're going to screw up. You'll snap at somebody who doesn't deserve it, drop the bowling ball on somebody's toe, or leave their gate open, let their dog get out, and then run him over when you're driving around trying to find him. In short, you're human and you suck. But, starting from that premise is your best bet for sucking less. It frees you up to admit your shortcomings and apologize for your failures—which gives you some chance at repairing your relationship with your friend with the now very flat dog.

APOLOGIZING, PART I: ADMITTING YOU WERE WRONG

An apology is basically Metamucil for the Soul—a remarkably speedy evacuator of backed-up guilt. Unfortunately, many people seem to favor Chickenshit for the Soul—refusing to apologize because they see an admission of wrongdoing on their part as a sign of weakness.

It actually takes a big person to admit to having been small and piggy. Humans are prone to self-justification—the ego-protecting tendency to insist we're right and to shove away any evidence to the contrary. You need self-respect and strength of character to cough up the admission "I was wrong." Socking yourself in the ego by doing this red-flags your bad behavior in your mind so you can avoid making a habit of it, and it's a peace offering you give to the person you've wronged, telling them that you're willing to invest in making things right.

Apology expert and psychiatrist Aaron Lazare explained in

Psychology Today that "the exchange of shame and power between the offender and the offended" is what makes an apology work. By slighting somebody, you've kicked them in their self-concept, but by admitting you've wronged them, you're reversing the shame they feel and putting it on yourself. "In acknowledging your shame," wrote Lazare, "you give the offended the power to forgive."

Getting the forgiveness of the person you've hurt and repairing your relationship with them starts with coming clean about what you've done.

The nuances of coming clean:

- *Details matter.*
  Before you apologize, do a full jerktopsy—a postmortem dissection of your moment of jerkhood. Ask yourself:

  - *Why* what you did was wrong.
  - *What* it must mean to the person you wronged.
  - *How* things could and should have been different.

  Expressing all of this in appropriate detail to the injured person tells them that you "get it" about what you've done—which helps keep them from suspecting that "So sorry for going all 'Bennnd over!' on you" really means "Won't be long till it's 'Bennnd over!' all over again!"

- *Don't dally.*
  Don't make somebody wait for an apology like it's a bus that may never come. The sooner you apologize the better. It will be a psychological relief for you, as well as a way to avoid having your victim's bad feelings fester and grow.

  The exception to this speed rule would be when somebody you've hurt is too upset to face you, in which case you should wait or send a note—preferably the sort delivered by a postal worker. A snail-mailed apology takes more effort than an e-mail, suggesting that you care enough not to take the easiest way out. As a bonus, a postal mailbox doesn't have a spam folder or the delete function.

- *No excuses.*

  Excuses are statements tacked onto an apology that start with "but" (". . . but you left your lunch right there in the break-room refrigerator, where anyone could eat it!"). The "but" can be either expressed or implied. It's an attempt to water down responsibility by sticking blame on somebody or something else—very often on the injured party. Here, in italics, is a statement with an implied "but" from basketball's one-man show Kobe Bryant, who, most charmingly, called a referee "a faggot":

> What I said last night should not be taken literally. *My actions were out of frustration during the heat of the game, period.* The words expressed do NOT reflect my feelings towards the gay and lesbian communities and were NOT meant to offend anyone.

In other words:

> Memo to all you faggots out there: I only gay-bash when I'm really frustrated.

Excuses are different from *explanations*, in which you offer background information on why you did what you did—without shirking responsibility. Your goal in offering an explanation should be helping the injured party feel better by giving them additional details that make them feel less disrespected, overlooked, or screwed over.

- *No hedgy-wedgy language.*
  "I'm sorry you feel that way" and "I'm sorry you feel hurt by that" aren't apologies but apology-flavored attempts to duck responsibility, making it sound like things would have been different if only the other person weren't so damn sensitive. Granted, this approach can sometimes be an intentional tactic when somebody's been unfair—a protest dressed up in a little apology suit.

  Another no-go is speaking in passive voice—saying you're sorry such and such "happened," as if it were a news story you heard about. Wrong. It wasn't a bank robber or giant cartoon squirrel that left your friend sitting alone in the restaurant. It was you. You flaked. Again. There's no linguistic dance move you can do to change that.

APOLOGIZING, PART II: EXPRESSING REMORSE

For an apology to be meaningful, you actually have to feel bad about what you did, not just feel bad that you got caught.

Assuming you aren't a sociopath, if you're diligent about digging into the Why, What, and How of some wrong you've done, that queasy little feeling called guilt should come up. Guilt is the human moral alarm clock. When you recognize that you've shortshrifted somebody—on time, effort, niceness, 50 bucks you owe them—that icky, pit-of-the-stomach feeling you get should help keep you from snaking them again.

You add weight to your apology if, in addition to feeling guilt and remorse for what you've done, you feel shame for acting in a way that's out of character with the person you want to be. By communicating exactly how crappy you feel, you help the person you've hurt believe you'll behave more fairly in the future, which helps them forgive you and move on. Conversely, if you don't feel bad about what you've done, why would you feel bad about doing it again?

APOLOGIZING, PART III: PLEDGING IT WON'T HAPPEN AGAIN (IF THAT'S ACTUALLY THE CASE)

Although your remorse doubles as an unspoken pledge that you won't go all inconsiderate buttwad on somebody again, they may need more convincing that you won't reoffend. If so, be prepared to offer supporting points and exhibits. And do keep in mind that your promise that you won't repeat your behavior carries more weight if you actually don't.

There was this large businessman behind me in line at the airport with a huge, sharp-edged wheeled suitcase that he kept smashing into the backs of my ankles. This hurt, plus my ankles happened to be ensconced in a brand-new pair of boots.

The first time he hit me, he said he was sorry. The line moved, and he slammed his bag into me again. "Sorry!"

A third time. "Sorry!"

I turned and glared. "Please be more careful."

Unbelievably, there was a fourth time. And there it was, like a Swiss cuckoo clock: "Sorry!"

I whirled around and death-stared him. "You're not sorry," I fumed. "If you were sorry, you'd take care not to hit me again. And again. And again. But, you clearly couldn't care less that you're hitting me and hurting me, although it must be kind of a drag to have me turning around and calling you on it."

As satisfying as I found it to lay into him, there's a good chance the effect on him was like that in the Gary Larson cartoon where the man is scolding his dog and the dog hears only "*Blah, blah,* Ginger, *blah, blah, blah* . . ." The reality is, by the time somebody's 250 pounds of narcissistic, inconsiderate adult, sometimes the best you can do in response to their rudeness is to take a shot at publicly humiliating them. There's no reforming the hard-core narcissist, but making him want to avoid the angrywoman afterglow might inspire him to take a little more care with the next person's ankle meat.

Good intentions, poor follow-through

While it's best not to say "I'm sorry" while showing "Couldn't give a squashed crap," what matters a great deal is where your apology is coming from: whether you're sincerely sorry or you're just looking to minimize the post-offense hassle. The truth is, in our imperfect world, there are those who have every intention of rising to the occasion—especially for those they care about—but have a tendency to rise too little and too late or to sleep in entirely. In other words, as my boyfriend likes to joke, I should write a companion book to Stephen Hawking's *A Brief History of Time* called Amy Alkon's *An Even Briefer History of Being On Time.*

I love my boyfriend and feel guilty about that stressed look he gets when we have to be somewhere at a certain time and I come to the door in some state of semi-clad unmade-up-ness. But, I am a congenital multitasker, am rather vain, and have always been overly optimistic about the elasticity of an hour.

When I make us late, I of course apologize—but I sure don't pledge that it'll never happen again. Because it will. What makes my boyfriend feel better are two things: seeing that I'm really trying and seeing improvement in the wake of my reading a book on time management. I still sometimes fail, sometimes just by a few minutes and sometimes by more. When I do, I tell my boyfriend how bad I feel for making him wait (for the eleventy bajillionth time) and scold myself for not estimating that I'd need that extra twenty minutes to answer all my existential questions about my earrings. I put up a mental Post-it note to do that the next time around and will actually follow through—only to notice just as we're walking out the door that the scarf I'm wearing is just *tragically wrong.*

APOLOGIZING, PART IV: MAKING AMENDS

When you do harm to somebody, the toddler in the china shop rule applies: "You break it; you pay for it." Sometimes, a verbal apology alone is restitution enough. Other times, when an offense is greater, it takes time, energy, and cold hard cash. As for what, specifically, you should do to make amends, don't be asking the person you hurt. Hey, Lazy, *you* wronged *them*; you do the work to figure it out. Just ask yourself, *How would I feel if somebody did that to me, and what would make things okay again?*

It isn't always possible to replace exactly what you took from somebody. You can't unhurt a person's feelings. You can speak the words "I'm sorry" and then say it again with flowers. Think of this as the baker's dozen of reparations—giving the injured person what you owe them, plus a little extra on the top. (Kind of like a goodwill surcharge.) Say you are careless with your Coke and spill it all over somebody's white jacket. Figure out what dry cleaning will cost the person (maybe $12), and then flip them a $20. You should also flip them your phone number in case the stain doesn't come out and you (*sigh!*) need to buy them a replacement. If it seems clear to both of you that what happened is only partly your fault, offer to kick in for part of the cost.

Fine yourself when it's impossible to make amends.

Sometimes when you put some feel-bad into the world, there's no way to make amends to the exact person you did it to, like if it happened in traffic and that person is long gone. But if you can't make good to them specifically, why not make good in general? Buy a homeless guy a sandwich; wash the elderly neighbor's car; donate $10 to a good cause.

You get the forgiveness you seem willing to pay for.

A number of studies show that a costly apology is a more meaningful apology, that you're more likely to be forgiven if your apology involves some sort of payout or is accompanied by a gift. But very often, in making amends, it really is the thought that counts. Being honest about what you've done and forthcoming about what you owe shows that you don't take whatever you did lightly. You're demonstrating that you value the person you wronged enough to invest in rebalancing your relationship. That's why following up an apology with a sincere offer to make good, financially or in some other substantial way, may be all it takes for the person you've wronged to feel vindicated and forgive you—maybe after telling you there's no need for you to go through with your plan to pay up.

Amazingly, many people who are apologizing end up being penny-wise and apology-foolish. They clench their little fists at their sides, keeping the dollars it would take to fix their mistake huddled in their wallet, and tell themselves they got away with something. They do get to go home with their $12 or $20 or whatever—as well as the knowledge that they're an ethically-squat cheap bastard. They also reveal a lack of empathy—not exactly the stuff repeat business, solid reputations, and lifelong friendships are made of.

Though saying you're sorry can cost you emotionally, a sincere apology has such power that it can end up saving the person who makes it thousands or even millions of dollars. Seen any medical malpractice awards lately? If you win one, you and your lawyer may be in line to buy the Canary Islands from Spain. Because an apology can be seen in court as an admission of guilt, malpractice attorneys often advise doctors who mess up in caring for a patient to refrain from apologizing to the patient or their family. Yet, research suggests that doctors who apologize are less likely to be sued.

In fact, it turns out that money isn't always the motivator behind suits against doctors or healthcare facilities. In 1999, a medical malpractice attorney told health policy professor Albert Wu, MD, that in his experience, a great deal of patient ire at medical errors comes out of physician attitude and denial rather than the negligence itself.[53] He believes that about half of the malpractice cases

---

[53] *Annals of Internal Medicine*, 131.12 (1999): 970–72.

he's been involved in could have been avoided. "What the majority of patients really wanted was simply an honest explanation of what happened and, if appropriate, an apology," the attorney said. When neither was offered, "they felt doubly wronged and then sought legal counsel."

When financial settlements are made, they're typically more moderate if they come in the wake of an apology. The Lexington, Kentucky, VA Medical Center lost two big malpractice suits in 1987, paying out over $1.5 million. After implementing a policy for doctors to disclose errors and apologize to patients, they paid an average of $15,622 per claim (from 1990 to 1996), reported Steve S. Kraman, MD, the doctor managing their disclosure program.[54]

By diminishing patients' anger and desire for revenge, the medical center also avoids prolonged and expensive court battles, which cost the government approximately $250,000 per case to defend. They now resolve more cases in across-the-table settlement meetings with just an attorney, a paralegal, and a few other hospital employees present.

Back in my world, a woman who hit and damaged my parked car also managed to stay out of court—unlike the nasty old man who'd previously sideswiped my parked car and thought he'd gotten away with it. (After I went Nancy Drew on his ass, tracked him down, and petitioned the city attorney to prosecute him, he not only had to pay to fix my car but also did a day of jail time.)

Upon seeing the damage the woman did to my car, I would have been my usual relentless self: putting up fliers on phone poles, walking the neighborhood to seek witnesses, requesting video footage from neighbors with surveillance cameras. Except . . . she left this note on my windshield: "I scraped your car while backing out. Very sorry. Here's my number. Please call and I will pay to fix."

I meant to call. And I kept meaning to call. But, there's nothing

[54] *Annals of Internal Medicine*, 131.12 (1999): 963–67

like a satisfying apology—full accountability followed by an offer to make good with cash—to keep a girl off her broom. Without any need to *make* her pay, even picking up the phone to *ask* her to pay kept sinking lower and lower down my to-do list . . . until it finally just slipped off.

TO BE HUMAN IS SOMETIMES TO BE AN ANGRY ASSHOLE

Sometimes, your anger at something somebody's said or done will just get the best of you. Even if that somebody is only landing verbal punches, the message that you're being attacked gets dispatched to the brain, jumps on the amygdala's anger train—bypassing reason—and launches you into that adrenaline-driven "fight" part of the fight-or-flight reaction.

Reminding yourself of the process before you get into a conflict could possibly help you pull back when some interaction starts to get heated. You disengage by pausing and switching gears entirely: saying something like "I'm sorry. I'm behaving badly. Can we start over?" Remember also that you can sometimes help the other person mitigate how you've been behaving by offering an explanation (such as your already being upset over a flat tire or bad news) to support your contention that you don't think they deserve to be barked at; you just let your bad mood push you in a direction it shouldn't have.

At the time, they might be too far gone on the anger train to say anything other than "Fuck you!" but there's a good chance that upon cooling down, they'll reflect on your attempt to pull back and recognize the goodwill behind it, as well as how counterproductive it is to remain in a small-scale state of war. To further encourage such pacifying thoughts, you could make another goodwill gesture in a few hours or days. Say the ugliness was between you and a neighbor. You might leave a bottle of wine or a vase of flowers from your garden and an apology note on their porch. If more discussion is needed, you could ask them to meet you for coffee and a friendlier chat to work out a solution that works for both of you.

Don't treat grudges like beloved pets.

When somebody's remorseless about injuring you, it's wise to be mindful of the need to keep your distance while also accepting that what's done is done. However, when somebody who's wronged you shows you that they are genuinely sorry and gives you reason to believe they mean it and won't repeat their behavior, it's time to scrub their name from the no-fly list in your brain and shoo away your bad feelings about them.

Clinging to being wounded is like dragging around a giant bag of dirty laundry on one of those big iron chains from a ship. In other words, it probably does "hurt you as much as it hurts them." To release a grudge, you simply resolve to go forward and inform the person you're doing it by saying or writing, "Apology accepted. I'm going to forget this happened, and we can move on from here."

Help other people make good.

Sometimes, somebody wrongs you because they're a mean-spirited turdblossom who lives to induce pain. But sometimes, a person just gets sloppy; they are stressed and tired and didn't give enough thought to how they were treating you.

When this could be the case, you might give the person a chance to make good by gently informing them that they hurt you and possibly by adding what you think would have been a kinder approach. As I've said elsewhere in this book, it's usually best to do this in writing rather than in person, as it helps the person save face, minimizes defensiveness, and gives them time to consider what you're saying. And even if you get no response or an unsatisfying response, your taking positive action—telling the person they've wronged you—is how you yank yourself out of the victim's seat and keep from dragging a grudge around.

About a year and a half ago, one of the elders of behavioral science hurt my feelings. I have long had great respect for his work and even admired him as a human being. We'd communicated a number of times over the years, with my e-mailing him letters of appreciation about his work a couple of those times, and I had also written about his research and frequently recommend his books to readers who write me for advice.

This time, I had e-mailed him to invite him on my science-based radio show to discuss his most recent book. I would have accepted it just fine if he'd turned me down, giving me any remotely plausible excuse. But the way he did respond—just "Sorry, I cannot"—made me feel bad for over a year, so I finally e-mailed him. I told him that I had always thought very highly of him and hated that whenever I saw one of his books on my shelf, I'd flash on his curt reply and my disappointment that he, of all people, had been unkind to me. I went on to write:

> Maybe you weren't feeling well or thought my show probably wasn't worth the time. I accept that you may have thought that. But I just wanted to suggest, respectfully, that responding so curtly is what conflict resolution specialist Dr. Donna Hicks explains as a dignity violation—treating someone as if they have no value.
>
> I often have to turn down people who ask me things I don't have time for, but even if I think they're crackpots, I pretend otherwise when I write them. It takes just a few extra moments to preserve somebody's dignity, to say, "I'm so sorry, I wish I could, but I'm extremely busy with research, etc." Whether that's true is immaterial. It's kind. It allows the person to believe "it's not me; it's just that there isn't time . . ."
>
> I have great respect for you and great gratitude for all the work you've done and the foundation it's laid for all who carry on with the research. I just needed to stop thinking of that curt reply from you every time you and your work come to mind and I thought this might help me change the channel.
>
> All the best,
> Amy Alkon

His reply was all it took to release me from bad-feelings jail:

You are right, of course, and I apologize.
>

He continued that he gets about five such invites a day from journalists and only does about one interview every six months. He added:

. . . and I am a one finger typist.
>
> But I will try to take your advice, even though it means quite a few
> extra hours typing per month.
>
> Thanks for bringing me up short on this.
>
> all the best

I hated to think of him wasting science time on typing. I wrote back, suggesting a macro program so he could type a single code word and hit RETURN to drop already-created statements into e-mail, which he could personalize with just a "Dear So-and-So."

His reply:

very helpful, I'll try this out.

Very helpful indeed. Now, instead of hurt feelings, I again have warm feelings about him and sometimes a little laugh at the thought of him pecking away, one-fingered, at his keyboard.

— 12 —

TRICKLE-DOWN HUMANITY

The pursuit of happiness is the wrong way to go about getting it. Of course, that's not what we're led to believe. America is all about pursuing happiness. It's written right into our Declaration of Independence as something we have an "unalienable" right to do. But positive psychologist Sonja Lyubomirsky and other happiness researchers find that what many of us think will boost our happiness—getting a raise or a clean bill of health, buying a new car or a new set of boobs—can make us happier, but *not much happier* and not for very long. As the novelty of the bigger boobs wears off or we get used to the idea that we aren't sick after all, we go right back to being however happy or unhappy we were before.

Even big, important life events don't come with the happiness boost we're led to believe they will. Psychologist Richard Lucas did a massive study that found that getting married leads to only a two-year bliss-bump, on average, before spouses slide back to their pre-engagement level of happiness or unhappiness. Yes, it seems that even "happily ever after" comes with an expiration date.

The good news is, "*meaningfully* ever after" seems to have legs. In 1945, upon being liberated from a Nazi concentration camp, Viennese psychiatrist and neurologist Viktor Frankl wrote *Man's Search for Meaning*, originally published in German as *Saying Yes to Life in Spite of Everything: A Psychologist Experiences the Concentration Camp.* Frankl wrote about the horrors and inhumanities of the camps, but the book centers around his observations on how essential finding meaning seems to be, in living a satisfying life and even in having the will to go on.

Frankl recalled that two of his fellow prisoners who'd expressed their intention to kill themselves "both used the typical argument—they had nothing more to expect from life." Getting them to change their minds took getting them to realize that they still had something meaningful to live for. For one, it was his child who was waiting for him in a foreign country. The other was a scientist whose series of books still needed to be finished. "His work," Frankl wrote, "could not be done by anyone else, any more than another person could ever take the place of the father in his child's affections."

To understand how meaning relates to happiness, it's important to understand that being happy doesn't necessarily mean getting into a cheery mood. Sure, feeling cheery is a kind of happiness, but a deeper, more sustaining happiness is an overall sense of well-being and satisfaction with your life. In Frankl's words, this sort of happiness "cannot be pursued; it must ensue." He went on to explain that "it only does so as the unintended side effect of one's dedication to a cause greater than oneself or as the byproduct of one's surrender to a person other than oneself."

It's kind of amazing that we, as self-interested beings, would be so outwardly directed in what gives us the will to go on. But Frankl's thinking[55] has been supported by research in recent years by Lyubomirsky, social psychologists Roy Baumeister and Kathleen Vohs, and many others. These studies repeatedly confirm that the way to personal fulfillment is through our relationship with and positive effect on others.

---

[55] Aristotle, the eighteenth-century economist Adam Smith, and the Dalai Lama are other members of Frankl's choir.

Don't mistake this as an argument for asceticism. I'm not suggesting that you give away everything you have and shuffle the streets in cardboard sandals, and I don't think you're a bad person if you want a Ferrari and a thirty-room mansion with a moat. But if you also want to be successful at being happy, the bumper sticker on the back of your Ferrari should probably be something like:

He who dies ~~with~~ AFTER SHARING the most toys wins.

HOW TO LIVE MEANINGFULLY

Living meaningfully means being bigger than just yourself. It means making the world a better place because you were here. It is possible to do this through your job, especially if your work involves helping others but even if it does not.

In *Practical Wisdom*, psychologist Barry Schwartz writes movingly of Luke, a janitor at a teaching hospital who cleaned the room of a man's comatose son twice in short order. The patient's father, who had been keeping a vigil by his son's bedside for months, had been out on a smoke break when Luke first cleaned the room. On his way back, he passed Luke in the hall and, in Luke's words, "just freaked out," accusing him of not cleaning the room.

"At first I got on the defensive, and I was going to argue with him," Luke said. But he caught himself. He'd heard that the son had been in a fight, had gotten paralyzed, and would never come out of his coma. Instead of snapping back, Luke simply said, "I'm sorry. I'll go clean the room." And then he went in and cleaned it again so the father could see him doing it.

Because Luke's job description only includes janitorial-type activities, Schwartz notes that "it would have been reasonable to have simply explained to the father that he'd already cleaned the room, and perhaps to have brought in his supervisor to mediate if the father remained angry." But Luke felt that he had a job beyond his custodial work, in alignment with the mission of the hospital—relieving suffering—which is what he accomplished for that father, and without an iota of medical training.

Empathy as a sort of moral cruise director

Luke's split-second decision to tamp down his natural human defensiveness and show kindness to the grieving father took empathy—but empathy that went beyond mere feelings. A feeling alone doesn't mean much, which is why I love psychologist Bruce D. Perry and journalist Maia Szalavitz's expanded definition of empathy in *Born for Love*.

> The essence of empathy is the ability to stand in another's shoes, to feel what it's like there and *to care about making it better if it hurts*. [The italics are mine.]

Their definition tag-teams empathy—standing in another's shoes, feeling what they feel—with compassion: caring about making it better. This is empathy as more than a rush of feeling; it's empathy as the start of an action plan.

Where I think Perry and Szalavitz are too limited is in how they modify "to care about making it better" with "if it hurts." We can "make it better" whether people appear to be hurting or not. We all have daily issues, and when we're having a shitburger of a day, having somebody go out of their way for us makes us feel better; it makes us feel like we matter, which is huge.

How to stop living in a strangerhood without calling a moving van

It's especially important that we start treating strangers like they matter.

As I explained earlier in the book, the increase in rudeness we're experiencing traces back to how we're living so antithetically to millions of years of our evolved psychology, in societies too big for our brains—vast strangeropolises where some of us can go an entire day without seeing any (or many) people we know.

Going about life in a sea of strangers not only enables the rude but also causes us stress and anxiety—as well as hindering feelings of well-being, and maybe not just because of the surge in rudeness. Psychiatrist Randolph Nesse, also an evolutionary psychologist, believes that our emotions, both positive and negative, are a signaling system for us, messaging us to give us a thumbs-up or thumbs-down about our participation in activities that, in the course of human evolution, would have conferred either an advantage or a detriment in mating or survival.

The fact that doing good for others has such a positive impact on our well-being suggests that we may be doing ourselves both social and psychological harm by living in strangerhoods instead of communities. In fact, Nesse contends that depression and other forms of psychological suffering may, in part, result from how we are now living in a vast, stranger-filled environment that runs so contrary to our nature, where we're lacking in both social support and opportunities to be socially supportive.[56]

I'm not suggesting a massive change of address, some mandated restructuring of our spread-out society into countless gated five-street townlets. But it seems to make sense to change our thinking and behavior so we can once again get both the social and psychological benefits of living in a community. This takes recognizing that it isn't natural for us to reach out to strangers—and then making a habit of doing it anyway.

[56] Online communities do help in some ways, but there, too, we're often in a sea of "friends."

Compassion is the opiate of the masses. (This is a good thing.)

When Karl Marx wrote "Religion . . . is the opiate of the masses," he was putting down religion for providing bogus comfort, but he managed to acknowledge that religion, like opiates, can be soothing.[57]

Compassion also provides soothing, both on a personal level and, if enough people practice it, on a societal one. Remarkably, social psychologist David DeSteno has found that compassion has spillover—that feeling compassion for one person makes us far more likely to take action on behalf of another. Even more remarkably, although we don't naturally concern ourselves with the welfare of strangers, it seems we can summon compassion for a stranger simply by rethinking whom we consider an outsider. Sometimes, we even do this rethinking unconsciously.

DeSteno and fellow social psychologist Piercarlo Valdesolo did a study looking at how "synchronous movement" in people, such as doing the same march or dance steps at the same time, affects compassion. Referencing prior research, they explain that moving in sync with others seems to lead to an "increased sense of joint identity, or of being on the 'same team.' " In their experiment, subjects were seated across a table from each other and told to tap their fingers to beats they heard in headphones they wore. For some tablemates, the same beats played simultaneously, causing them to tap at the same time. Other tablemates heard sequences that led each to tap at different times.

In the next part of the study, subjects then witnessed their tapping partner getting cheated on in a computer game and, as a result, unfairly being assigned a pile of tedious word problems to solve before he could go home. The subjects were told that they could help him if they wanted.

---

[57] I prefer the Madalyn Murray O'Hair version: "Marx was wrong—religion is not the opiate of the masses, baseball is."

Synchrony, it turns out, made a big difference in who offered to help. Fifty percent of those subjects who tapped in synchrony asked to pitch in, whereas less than 20 percent of those tapping asynchronously did. On a questionnaire, the synchronous tappers reported feeling greater similarity with their partners and having greater compassion for them than the asynchronous tappers did for theirs.

This doesn't mean we need to start mimicking finger-drumming strangers. In fact, DeSteno, in a videotaped talk for PopTech[58], noted that we shouldn't assume there's anything "magic" about finger tapping, per se. They'd gotten similar results with subjects wearing various colored wristbands who'd rated another subject's behavior as more ethical when that person had the same color band they did. What's important is the upshot. DeSteno explained in *The New York Times* that these findings suggest that "the compassion we feel for others is not solely a function of what befalls them: if our minds draw an association between a victim and ourselves—even a relatively trivial one—the compassion we feel for his or her suffering is amplified greatly."

How to transform a stranger into a fellow human

DeSteno suggests drawing a compassion-increasing association between yourself and, say, some guy who lives down your block by thinking of that guy as a fan of the same local restaurant instead of a member of a different ethnicity. The problem is, when we encounter strangers, we're often lacking in any sort of shared context that would allow us to quickly imagine a connection. This is why I think we need to look at all people, including strangers, as *co-humans*, related to us in how they surely love their dog, hate Microsoft Word, feel pain when they get cut, and prefer chocolate to broccoli.

---

[58] PopTech is a terrific science- and innovation-fostering nonprofit whose videos, including DeSteno's eighteen-minute talk on his compassion research, can be seen at PopTech.org.

All it takes to get in the habit of treating people as co-humans is *making it a habit*—daily or, better yet, throughout the day. This means not only resolving to make things better for people but actively looking for those to do that for—both strangers and people you know—and spreading warmth and goodwill. This might just mean noticing a guy who comes into a place looking lost and flashing him a friendly smile or complimenting a woman on her pretty hair. (Her hair doesn't have to be gorgeous; it just needs to look attractive enough that she'd believe you if you said something nice about it.)

To take this up a notch, when you're about to get in your car and you see that your meter still has twenty minutes on it, scan the street for a driver who appears to be searching for a space and wave him over. You're not only making his day easier but also transforming yourself and him from two strangers into two humans acting connected to each other. And, very likely, by positively changing how he feels about his day and, in some small way, about people in general, you motivate him to pay it forward—and so on and so on—transforming the strangerhood into more of a neighborhood.

Taking this a step further, some kindness that would be a minor and unremarkable gesture when done for a friend can have an enormously powerful effect when done for a stranger. An LA-dwelling friend, originally from Boulder, Colorado, was visiting there with her girlfriend, when they came upon an older woman, probably in her early seventies, on a street-side bench, fanning herself from the heat, looking very not-from-Boulder. In a hardcore New York accent, she asked them where she could get a Diet Coke. My friend gave her detailed directions, and she and her girlfriend continued on their way. They had only gone a few steps when her girlfriend blurted out, "I'm going to go buy her one."

Dumbstruck, my friend said, "You don't have to do that."

"She's old, and she seems tired," her girlfriend said, and they walked to the nearest place with drinks—a bar—got a can of Diet

Coke (which the bartender gave them, free, though they didn't reveal their mission), and brought it back.

"Here you go," her girlfriend said, handing it to the woman.

"OH, MY GOD!" the woman said, nearly screaming. "You're kidding me! Good God!"

For a second, my friend thought she was angry.

"GOD BLESS YOU! I can't believe you did that!" The woman went on and on.

My friend later told me, "I try to be a nice person, but I gave the woman just what she'd asked for, and my girlfriend thought, 'That woman looks hot, and she's old, and she clearly isn't from Boulder. How could I make her day easier?' "

"I'm honestly too shy to naturally do what she did," my friend added, "but I think I should get over that. It was such a small thing—it took literally five minutes—and I've actually never seen a woman more happy in a moment. It totally turned her world around."

WAYS YOU CAN MAKE THE WORLD A BETTER PLACE FOR YOUR CO-HUMANS (AND, IN TURN, FOR YOURSELF)

Do random acts of judicious kindness.

Sometimes, we engage in knee-jerk goodness—goodness that ultimately isn't so good. An act that, on the surface, seems kind, generous, and helpful may actually be none of these.

For years, I sneered at the term "putting your dog to sleep" as a nefarious euphemism that helped people feel better about killing a dog that had become inconvenient for them. If you value life and love your dog, keeping him or her on the planet as long as possible seems like the right thing to do. It did to me—until the vet told me that my darling fifteen-year-old Yorkie, Lucy, was in kidney failure.

We weren't at the end yet, he reassured me. He gave me meds and instructions on caring for her, but I came home in tears and called my friend Debbie. She started to cry, too, and then told me what she'd learned in putting her beloved elderly bichon, Marley, to sleep a few months before. It took her three times going to the shelter to go through with it. That third and final time, when she saw what a peaceful process it actually turned out to be, how they really do just fall into a deep sleep as they're going out, she realized that she'd been wrong to hang on to Marley for as long as she did and that she'd done it for her benefit and not Marley's. By telling me this, she helped me understand that being *judiciously good* means recognizing that keeping your dog alive when he or she no longer has a very good quality of life is prolonging suffering, not prolonging life.

About a month later, one awful morning when I saw that Lucy was struggling to keep her furry little butt up, this meant that I was prepared to do the right thing, right away. A few hours later, when the vet opened, I rushed her there, and as I held her, petted her, and cooed to her, he gave her an injection, and she closed her eyes and floated away. I still miss her terribly and completely, down to her tiny little musty wet doggy smell, which now only faintly lingers in some of her sweaters, but I take solace in realizing that I gave her both a good life—the best I possibly could—and a "good death."

Engineering professor Barbara Oakley studies the area of psychology that this sad situation with Lucy could have fallen into, altruism gone wrong: attempts intended to help that instead result in unanticipated harm—for the recipient, for the helper, or sometimes for both.

For instance, we may tell ourselves that we're doing good when saying yes to someone's request for help feels better at that moment than saying no. Oakley, in a paper on "pathological altruism" for the *Proceedings of the National Academy of Sciences*, gives the example of a brother trying to overcome an addiction to painkillers. "When he goes through withdrawal, you get more painkillers to help him feel better, and you cover for him when his work supervisor calls. You genuinely want to help your brother, but the reality is that you are enabling his addiction." Paradoxically, being *judi-*

ciously kind would mean letting him suffer for days, allowing him to hate you for it, and being there to hold his hand and mop his brow.

We don't give much thought to the potential negative effects of helping upon the person offering the help, but we sometimes do kind deeds at too great an expense to ourselves. Unhealthy giving is even painted as a virtue—"Give till it hurts!"—but bailing somebody out should be considered a bust if you're going beyond your means in time or money or jeopardizing your job, your health, or your continued ownership of your house.

Oakley notes that we are especially blind to the ill effects of overgiving when whatever we're doing allows us to feel particularly good, virtuous, and benevolent. To keep from harming ourselves or others when we're supposed to be helping, Oakley emphasizes the importance of checking our motives when we believe we're doing good. "People don't realize how narcissistic a lot of 'helping' can be," she told me. "It's all too easy for empathy and good deeds to really be about our self-image or making *ourselves* happy or comfortable."

Stand up for yourself and what you believe in.

As I mentioned in the "Communicating" chapter, I'm often afraid to go talk to people, but that doesn't seem a good enough reason to avoid doing it. The same goes for standing up for yourself, your beliefs, or others you see getting stomped on, but the reality is, not everyone belongs on or is well-suited for the front lines of activism. If you can't be out front, maybe you can bring up the rear, supporting the frontliners with an e-mail thanking them or with a donation, by publicizing what they're doing, or just by bringing them a plate of cookies.

Engage in "kindsourcing."

"Crowdsourcing" involves reaching out to a large group of people, usually online, to get ideas or help. "Kindsourcing" is my term for a somewhat more indirect way to inspire a bunch of people to take action. It involves reaching out to others, online and off, with stories of impressively kind and generous altruistic acts that many will be inspired to pass on.

Research by social psychologists Sara Algoe and Jonathan Haidt finds that observing or even just hearing about others' kind deeds motivates people to want to follow suit. It seems that powerful positive feelings rise up in us upon witnessing moral beauty: feelings of warmth, awe, and "elevation"—a term Thomas Jefferson came up with for what he described as a swelling of the chest and a longing to emulate compassionate acts we've observed.

In the words of one of Algoe and Haidt's research participants:

> Watching my grandmother aid this helpless, suffering woman near the days of her death caused me to feel a sense of responsibility to those around me. I began to feel more appreciative for my well-being and the fact that I was healthy. I felt the desire to be like my grandma and have the same goodwill and huge heart. I wanted to help!

Give yourself regular performance reviews.

I don't have perfect manners. What I do have is a habit of looking at my behavioral failures, assessing how I screwed up, promising myself I'll do better, and doing my best to follow through.

Express appreciation.

We feel a deep need to matter.

Because our lives have meaning through the positive effect we have on others, it means a lot to us to hear that we've made a difference. There also seem to be substantial benefits for the person doing the appreciating and radiating benefits for society. Gratitude researcher Robert Emmons observed in a 2003 paper that getting people to focus on the benefits they've gotten from others leads them to feel "loved and cared for" and makes them more likely to help others. Positive psychologist Lyubomirsky notes in *The Myths of Happiness* that numerous studies from her lab and her colleagues' labs show that "people who regularly practice appreciation or gratitude . . . become reliably happier and healthier, and remain happier for as long as six months after the experiment is over."

Getting in the habit of expressing gratitude takes regularly considering what you have to be grateful for—both big and little acts people do for you and the qualities you admire about them. In relationships, for example, we too often only express appreciation for the obvious—the stuff that comes in a little velvet box or has four tires and a big bow on top. You can also tell your partner how much you respect him for the way he handled some tough situation or how sweet and loving you think it was that he took a long detour on his way home to pick up your favorite dessert.

It really doesn't take much to let somebody know they matter:

- Spread good gossip. Sometimes a person who appreciates another person will tell everyone but them. When someone says something nice about somebody and you know they wouldn't mind your passing it on, do that.
- Express appreciation for people whose good qualities tend to go unremarked, like the lady who manages the coffeehouse and makes everyone who comes in feel welcomed.
- When you're dealing with a company, especially if you're a complainer when things are bad, be a complimenter when they're good. Obviously, you can send an appreciative letter or e-mail when an employee goes above and beyond for you. But maybe lesser good works are worthy of mention, too, like when the lady in the call center isn't some checked-out drone reading off a sheet but is friendly, is patient, knows her stuff, and does her best to be helpful. Maybe show her a little love by saying how much you appreciate that at the end of the call.
- Write a letter thanking a person who's made a difference in your life. It doesn't have to be a person you know. In 2009, it

came out in the press that Apple co-founder Steve Jobs, who had pancreatic cancer, wasn't doing too well. I mailed him a letter[59] telling him that "there's nothing in my life that's changed and improved it as much as Apple computers" and that, in 2003, I'd even gotten my boyfriend at the Apple computer store.[60]

Make people laugh.

I joked in a column that if laughter were really the best medicine, hospitals would forgo the morphine drip and hang a chimp in overalls from that pole by a patient's bed. The truth is, research finds that laughter is pretty great medicine, both physically and psychologically, which means you can heal the world a little by going around in a Halloween costume on May 21. (I keep meaning to have little cat ears made, the same color as my hair, and then wear them out and about.)

You can also put out humor in unexpected places. I love Smart cars. "Love" them as in once, while on a walk with my boyfriend, I ran over and hugged one. My 2004 Honda Insight, at 1,900 pounds, is only barely a car and only a little bigger than a Smart Fortwo. One Sunday afternoon, I noticed a white Smart car parked directly across the street from my car. I typed up a note, printed it on hot-pink typing paper in big letters, and stuck it under the Smart's windshield wiper. I wish I'd saved a copy of it or could remember more than the first line: "My Honda Insight wants to date your Smart car . . ."

I thought I'd give the car's owner and a few dog walkers a laugh and that would be that. To my delight, the owner played along. I found this note on my windshield:

---

[59] I sent the letter via snail mail because I'd heard he sometimes responded to e-mail and I wasn't looking to have a cancer patient go to the effort to reply.

[60] Gregg likes to credit our relationship to "Steve Jobs's retail strategy."

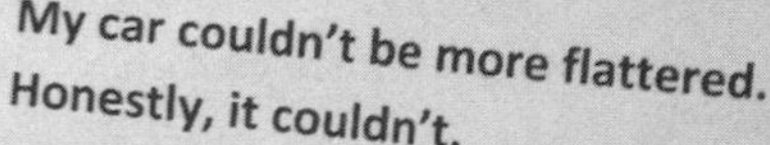

My car couldn't be more flattered. Honestly, it couldn't.

But, with nearly fifty thousand miles of life already passed, it knows that bald tires are just around the corner. The grove is gone. Estate plans are more likely than date plans.

Just for a moment though, recalling his youth is France, my Smart Car thought "it will soon be spring, and maybe that counts for something". The thought quickly passed and he headed home to the cats.

I left my response on my car:

Teach your kids empathy and social skills.

Raise a kinder, more generous next generation by modeling kindness and generosity for them, by asking them to imagine how others must feel, and by encouraging them to do kind acts to show them how great it feels to do something nice for somebody in need.

Ask your kids who the underdogs are—the kids other kids are mean to—and to think about how difficult it must be for them. If your kids have enough social capital that it won't hurt them, suggest that they could help the underdog kids stop feeling so sad and alone if they reached out and included them, and then ask them ways they might do that.

When another kid is disruptive in class or is causing problems for yours, ask your child, "Why do you think they do that?" My neighbors' daughter Lilly had a problem in first grade with a boy kicking her under the table. Her mother, after making sure she was okay and had told the teacher, explained that the boy might have a hard time controlling his impulses or sitting still. She asked whether that seemed like the case. Lilly told her that he would get up and jump on desks sometimes and that he got in trouble a lot for not sitting down when he was supposed to in class. "Do you think it's hard to be that way?" her mother asked her, and they discussed how it must feel for him.

We tend to assume that kids will just pick up social skills as they go on in life, but Carlin Flora, my former editor at *Psychology Today* and the author of *Friendfluence*, suggests a more proactive approach: Bring up hypothetical scenarios to them like "What should you do if you want to join a game that kids are already playing at recess?" and play out the outcomes with questions like "What should you say to them, and what should you say if they say no?"

"Don't judge their answers," Flora adds. "Just listen and then perhaps share your own ideas and values."

Treat everyone with dignity but "the little people" with more dignity.

We pretty much automatically treat people on the upper rungs of the socioeconomic ladder with respect, but I think it's especially important to treat busboys, supermarket bag boys, lawn workers, and the homeless with as much—or *more*—respect than the "important" people. (Everybody sucks up to bigwigs; in fact, many could probably use a vacation from it.)

You respect the dignity of the often-disrespected by taking notice of them (instead of treating them like they're invisible, as many do) and talking to them like they're your equal, which they are, as a co-human. Respecting the dignity of homeless cohumans also means being mindful that the big boot of life has come down on them in harsh ways and doing things to ease their struggle. Even small gestures, like putting your recyclables out in a bag next to the trash bin so a person doesn't have to root through your garbage, make a difference. No, it's not the same as giving them "three hots and a cot," but just because you aren't prepared to save the world in big ways every day doesn't mean you should give up on trying to relieve people's suffering in the small, manageable ways you can.

Mentor people—officially or unofficially.

There are formal mentoring situations in workplaces, but you can also spend a few hours mentoring some recent grad you sit next to on a plane or, when you see something in some kid you meet, take them under your wing. Advertising copywriter Len Gelstein, now a photographer, did that for me when I first got to New York, becoming my friend and guide when I was in my early twenties and at my most lost. He was everything I think a mentor should be: the old hand showing the newbie how it's done, passing along good values and habits, and encouraging embracing failure as an expected and essential part of the process of figuring out the right path. I talked to him recently and joked that I have a mind like a steel sieve but can still quote some of the things he told me, like "Worry that somebody's going to steal your idea if you only have one idea."

Most people think of mentoring as an activity limited to the professional sphere, but you can even mentor an eight-year-old. There's a great little girl who lives behind me. Her mom's attention has recently been commandeered by her intrepid toddler, a kid who pretty much spends his days looking for an electrical outlet to stick a fork into so he can see what happens. When her weary mom lamented to me that the little girl wasn't getting as much attention from her, I started going over for a few minutes every day to take a look at her drawings or watch and comment on her progress on her cartwheels. I come up with things to ask, show, and tell her that could be helpful to her. Reflecting on this, I think the findings from research on generosity seem to be right on. As much as I'm intending to help *her*, when I'm going out my back door and she runs up and gives me a hug or when, while washing a mug, I look across at the crayoned "I love love you love" card on my kitchen windowsill, I can't help but feel I'm getting the better end of the deal.

Ask yourself, How can I be somebody's good fairy or secret Santa today?

As my friend observed when her girlfriend brought a Diet Coke to the older lady on the bench in Boulder, small kindnesses that would be no big deal if you did them for someone you know can be earth-shifting when performed for someone you don't.

To get yourself in the habit of reaching out to others, you might try a Generosity Week: commit to do at least one kind act a day for a different person every day for seven days straight. Don't just repeat the same act of kindness; do whatever you think would best serve a particular person in a particular moment, like maybe bringing out a bottle of lemonade on a hot day to the guy your landlord hires to take care of the lawn or crossing the warehouse-store parking lot to help a woman with an almost-escaping shopping cart who has her hands full loading stuff into her car. Assuming you aren't struggling financially, when you see a family at the diner getting out of a car that looks like it's held together with chewing gum and hope, you could give the cashier money to pay for their lunch. So they don't think you did it out of pity, tell them—or tell the cashier to tell them if you're gone when their already-paid check comes—that you just thought they looked like a really nice family and that you wanted to do something nice for them.

You can sometimes do something nice for a whole bunch of people, like by noticing that everyone in a restaurant seems to be shivering and being the one to ask the manager to turn down the AC. In the wake of a one-penny increase in the cost of mailing a letter, the founder of the field of positive psychology, Martin Seligman, went to the post office to buy a sheet of 100 1-cent stamps. He wrote in *Flourish* that he stood fuming in an "enormous, meandering line" for forty-five minutes along with numerous fuming others. When he finally made it to the front, instead of getting just one sheet of 100 stamps, he asked for ten sheets, which cost him all of $10. He then turned to the people in line behind him, held out the sheets, and shouted, "Who needs one-penny stamps? They're free!" People burst into applause and clustered around him as he handed out the sheets. "Within two minutes," he says, "everyone was gone, along with most of my stamps. It was one of the most satisfying moments of my life."

HOW TO LIVE FOREVER

People are drawn to stories about heaven and reincarnation, though there's no actual proof of either—no co-worker who went to heaven but decided not to stay and came back on Monday with a snow globe from Saint Peter. Yet, there is one surefire way to ensure we live on, and it's through making a difference in others' lives. Take psychiatrist Mark Goulston, whom I wrote about in the "Communicating" chapter. He may end up in an urn on one of his children's end tables, but through the suicidal woman he helped—the one[61] who went on to get her life together, get married, have children, and become a therapist herself—his life has meaning far into the future.

Any one of us can live on through the good things we do—even much smaller things than saving a life. Every time you extend yourself for another person, you change our world for the better by putting them in the mood to pay it forward. You're also engaging in a form of flash-mentoring—very briefly acting as their guide for what our world can be, as opposed to what we've been allowing it to be: a society of glowering strangers putting their heads down as they pass one another, stopping only to shout into their cell phones.

There will be new manners issues that arise in the future: "What if you're reading somebody's thoughts and they get offended?" "Hey, your robot's blocking the aisle!" or "Your driverless spaceship just cut off my driverless spaceship!" But until we start moving into 150-person space colonies, our overriding problem—living in societies too big for our brains—will remain.

So, changing the way we all relate to one another isn't just something we should do; it's something we *must* do. Wc have incredible freedoms in modern Western society, and with those come responsibility. This includes the responsibility to fill in what's missing in the vast strangerhoods we're now living in by turning toward other people, especially strangers, and effectively saying, "Hi, I'm your fellow human. How can I reduce your pain and suffering today?"

Doing this requires our living by choice instead of by behav-

---

[61] Chapter 3, "Communicating," page 17.

ioral default: Choosing to live connected instead of alienated. Choosing to be a neighbor instead of a bystander. And ultimately, choosing to live *meaningfully ever after*, by choosing, every day, to "leave the campground better than we found it," one co-human we do a little something nice for at a time.

INDEX